PRACTICING HSK GRAMMAR

HSK

语法精讲精练

编著/张　婧

翻译/吕东莲　徐　娟

华语教学出版社
SINOLINGUA

First Edition 2008

Second Printing 2010

ISBN 978-7-80200-451-1

Copyright 2008 by Sinolingua

Published by Sinolingua

24 Baiwanzhuang Road, Beijing 100037, China

Tel: (86) 10-68320585

Fax: (86) 10-68326333

http:// www.sinolingua.com.cn

E-mail: hyjx@sinolingua.com.cn

Printed by Beijing Foreign Languages Printing House

Distributed by China International Book Trading Corporation

35 Chegongzhuang Xilu, P.O. Box 399

Beijing 100044, China

Printed in the People's Pepublic of China

前　言

　　汉语水平考试(HSK)越来越受到留学生的重视,参加汉语水平考试(HSK)的留学生在逐年增多。语法学习是语言学习的基础,能否熟练掌握汉语语法并正确加以运用是提高汉语水平和汉语水平考试(HSK)成绩的关键。

　　我校每年都根据学生的需求,在历次汉语水平考试(HSK)来临之前,开设汉语水平考试(HSK)辅导班,以帮助不同汉语水平的学生在汉语水平考试(HSK)中取得理想成绩。本书就是在历次讲稿的基础上,参考、查阅了大量相关书籍,几经修改补充而成的。

　　全书集中讲解了量词、副词、介词、连词、助词、能愿动词、重叠、常见句式、补语、关联词语与复句、语序等语法项目。编者试图用通俗易懂的语言,通过简明的公式和例句,解释留学生在学习中遇到的疑点、难点。针对不同的语法项目,本书设计了大量相关练习,便于留学生实际操练;同时对全部练习的答案给予了较为详细的解析说明,使留学生不仅"知其然",而且"知其所以然",以期达到事半功倍的效果。

　　本书不仅适用于具有初中级汉语水平的留学生备考前使用,也可作为日常学习和自学时的参考用书。

　　作为本书的编者,同时作为一名长期从事对外汉语教学的老师,衷心地希望本书能够帮助留学生朋友们逐渐熟练地掌握和运用常用语法项目,使自己的汉语水平得到提高。本书的讲解、答疑部分配有英文翻译,感谢我校吕东莲、徐娟二位老师为此付出的辛勤劳动。

　　本书在编写、出版的过程中,得到了华语教学出版社翟淑蓉编辑的具体指导和大力帮助,在此由衷地表示感谢。

张　婧

2008 年 3 月于中国传媒大学

Preface

Hanyu Shuiping Kaoshi (HSK) gets more and more attention from foreign students and the number of student taking this exam is increasing on a yearly basis. Grammar is the basis of language learning, whether Chinese grammar can be mastered and used appropriately is taken as a key to improving Chinese language proficiency and HSK scores.

Taking foreign students' requirements into consideration, every year our University arranges tutoring classes on the coming of each HSK to help students of different levels achieve satisfactory scores in the exam. This book is based on teaching materials of these tutoring classes, and many relevant books are referred to as well.

The book explains such grammatical items as Quantifier, Adverb, Preposition, Conjunction, Auxiliary Word, Optative Verb, Reduplication, Common Sentence Structures, Complement, Connective, Complex Sentence and Word Order. Simple language, concise formulas and sample sentences are used to explain the confusing and difficult points encountered by foreign students during their study. As for the different grammatical items, there are plenty of related exercises for the students to practice. There are also very detailed answers to the exercises, which enable the students to not only "know the hows", but also "know the whys", thus considerably improve their learning efficiency.

This book can be used not only by foreign students who have elementary or intermediate level of Chinese in preparation for the exam, but also as a reference book for daily learning and self-study.

As the compiler of this book and a teacher having taught the Chinese language to foreigners for many years, I sincerely hope that it can help foreign students in gradually mastering and using the common grammatical items and improving their proficiency of Chinese. There is English translation for parts such as Examination Points, Answers and Explanations. My thanks go to Ms. Lü Donglian and Ms. Xu Juan for their translation work.

My thanks also go to Ms. Zhai Shurong, editor of Sinolingua, who has offered kind guidance and help during the writing and publishing of this book.

Zhang Jing
Communication University of China
March 2008

目 录
Contents

1. 量词
   Quantifier 1

2. 副词
   Adverb 31

3. 介词
   Preposition 67

4. 连词
   Conjunction 95

5. 助词
   Particle 121

6. 能愿动词
   Optative Verb 141

7. 重叠
   Reduplication 152

8. 常见句式
   Common Sentence Patterns 160

9. 补语
   Complement 186

10. 关联词语与复句
    Relative Phrases and Complex Sentences 208

11. 语序
    Word Order 241

附录　HSK 真题　语法结构 (30 题, 20 分钟) 249

主要参考文献 252

1 量词 Quantifier

考点精讲 Examination Points

一、量词的分类与格式 Classification and format of quantifier

分类 Classification	格式 Format	举例 Examples	说明 Explanation
名量词 Noun quantifier	数词＋量词＋名词 Numeral + quantifier + noun	一本书 一伙罪犯	表示人或事物的数量 Indicating the number of people or article
动量词 Verb quantifier	动词＋数词＋量词 Verb + numeral + quantifier	看一遍 去一次	表示动作的数量 Indicating the number of action

二、量词的语法特征 Grammatical features of quantifier

1. 有些名词可以用做量词。

   Some nouns can be used as quantifiers.

名词	量词
一个抽屉	一抽屉书
一辆车	一车人
一把刀	切了一刀
一只脚	踢了一脚

2. 在口语表达中，如果数词是"一"，而且仅为"一"时，数词可省略。

   In spoken Chinese, when the numeral is "one", it is usually omitted.

   例：借我本书，好吗?

   　　我去看个朋友。

   　　你去趟他家吧。

Quantifier

三、附录 Appendix

常用搭配表 Common matching words for quantifiers

名量词 Noun quantifier	搭配词 Matching nouns
把	尺子 勺子 扇子 剪子 梳子 椅子 斧子 刀 锁 伞 钥匙 牙刷 梳子 扫帚 剑 鼻涕 土 沙子
杯	水 茶 酒 牛奶 咖啡 饮料
本	书 杂志 画报 小说 字典 词典
笔	钱 账 生意 财富 收入 花销 开销
部	电影 影片 电视剧 著作 电话 手机
场	雨 雪 病 灾难 战争 风波 梦 误会 官司 演出 比赛 辩论
册	书
层	楼 台阶 土 灰 奶油
打 (dá)	铅笔 袜子
滴	水 油 汗 血 眼泪 墨水
顶	帽子 轿子
堆	东西 草 粮食 土 煤 垃圾
队	战士 警察 大雁
对	夫妻 恋人 双胞胎 鸳鸯 翅膀 花瓶 耳环 枕头 沙发
朵	花 云
番	工夫 事业 话 心意
封	信 电报 邮件
副	棋 牌 手套 眼镜 对联 耳机 面孔 样子 手铐
幅	画 字 地图 画像 肖像 布
根	针 绳子 棍子 扁担 腰带 木头 柱子 灯管 竹子 葱 草 香蕉 骨头 神经 筋 肠子 头发 香肠 冰棍 琴弦
股	山泉 力量 劲儿 风气 暖流 味道
行 (háng)	树 字 诗 眼泪 脚印 大雁
户	人家 农民 居民
架	机器 飞机 机关枪
间	房子 屋子 卧室 教室 办公室 书房 厨房 病房
件	衣服 上衣 衬衫 毛衣 大衣 外衣 内衣 行李 事情 案子 乐器 武器 凶器 礼物

届	运动会 年会 学生 毕业生 领导
颗	星星 心 宝石 钻石 牙齿 种子 子弹 炸弹
棵	树 草 菜 葱 苗
块	钱 糖 面包 蛋糕 手表 香皂 黑板 玻璃 砖
粒	米 药 种子 粮食 瓜子 葡萄 珍珠 子弹 沙子
列	火车 车厢
辆	车 汽车 出租车 公共汽车 自行车 摩托车 坦克
面	墙 镜子 旗帜 鼓
门	功课 课程 知识 学科 科学 技术 亲戚 心思 大炮
幕	歌剧 话剧 戏剧 舞剧
批	货物 产品 军火 学生 旅客 志愿者
匹	马 骆驼 骡子 布 绸缎
篇	文章 论文 课文 日记 小说 散文 随笔 报道
片	药 肉 面包 树叶 海 树林 草地 庄稼 心意 瓦 心意
群	人 鸡 羊 鸭子 蜜蜂
扇	门 窗户
首	诗 词 歌 乐曲
双	手套 鞋 袜子 筷子 手 脚 儿女
所	医院 学校 幼儿园
套	家具 图书 衣服 房子 办法 唱片 餐具 邮票
条	狗 鱼 蛇 黄瓜 毛巾 床单 船 路 裙子 裤子 腿 命 信息
头	牛 猪 骆驼 大象 驴 蒜
项	工作 工程 政策 制度 任务 计划 建议 运动
页	纸 书
盏	灯 茶
张	纸 报 画 票 照片 卡片 唱片 文凭 床 桌子 脸 嘴 饼
支	笔 枪 歌 烟 箭 曲子 队伍
枝	花
只	手 脚 眼睛 耳朵 鸟 猫 狗 羊 鞋 手镯 箱子 船 军舰
幢	房子 别墅
座	钟 山 桥 庙 楼 塔 宫殿 城市 雕塑 纪念碑

Quantifier

动量词 Verb quantifier	简单说明 Brief explanation	搭配词 Matching verbs
次	动作的次数 to indicate the number of times of an action	来 去 看 听 唱 买 吃 喝 学习 参观 讨论 商量 模仿
回	动作的次数,多用于口语 to indicate the number of times of an action, usually used in spoken Chinese	来 去 唱 吃 参观
趟	与有"行走"意义的动词搭配,表示来回 to match with verbs indicating "walk" to show a round trip	来 去 跑 走
遍	从头到尾的全过程 to indicate the whole process of an action	看 说 读 念 听 跳 唱 写 复习
番	表示用时较多、用力较大及过程较长,数词只能用"一" to indicate an action which is time or energy consuming or lasts for a long time. The matching numeral can only be "one".	表扬 打量 调查 解释 思 考 教育 嘱咐 整顿
顿	用于餐饮、批评、打骂等 be used along with verbs related to meals, criticism or abuse	吃 饿 喝 骂 打 揍 批评 教训
下儿	动作的次数,可表示"动作快、时距短"或轻松随便的语气 to indicate the number of times of an action, in a casual tone or showing the action is fast and short	打 磕 敲 摸 捏 洗 砸

强化练习 Exercises

■ 每个句子中有一个或两个空,请在 ABCD 四个答案中选择唯一恰当的一个。

Please choose the correct answer for each blank from the four choices of A, B, C, and D.

1. 妈妈慢慢睁开眼,看了我一_____,又闭上了。
   A. 面　B. 眼　C. 遍　D. 趟

2. 她的这_____手又细又长。
   A. 二　B. 副　C. 两　D. 双

3. 我家有_____小孩儿自行车。
   A. 两辆　B. 二辆　C. 两轮　D. 二个

4. 操场上,一_____学生在打篮球。

A. 伙　B. 群　C. 批　D. 层

5. 我出国旅游,给妈妈买回一 _____ 具有外国风情的衣服。
A. 件　B. 张　C. 把　D. 支

6. 她真聪明,这首歌她只听了一 _____ 就会唱了。
A. 下　B. 阵　C. 遍　D. 声

7. 这件事大家有不同的看法,你一言我一语,展开了一 _____ 大讨论。
A. 通　B. 篇　C. 场　D. 章

8. 这 _____ 鞋是我新买的,我穿着有点儿瘦,给你吧!
A. 二　B. 两　C. 俩　D. 双

9. 颐和园真美,我去过一 _____ 了,可还想再去。
A. 遍　B. 个　C. 次　D. 下

10. 我就是在这 _____ 学校上学。
A. 间　B. 所　C. 顶　D. 座

11. 小孟酷爱看报,每次都买七八 _____ 报纸。
A. 本　B. 片　C. 份　D. 册

12. 小刘雄心勃勃,总想干出一 _____ 轰轰烈烈的大事业。
A. 番　B. 个　C. 项　D. 件

13. 小李会用三种语言唱这 _____ 歌。
A. 个　B. 首　C. 张　D. 段

14. 这 _____ 照片是我在张家界拍的。
A. 片　B. 张　C. 幅　D. 册

15. 大多数人的生活就像一 _____ 平淡的诗,没有太大的起伏。
A. 支　B. 首　C. 曲　D. 张

16. 这 _____ 珍贵的邮票共八枚,遗憾的是我只有六枚。
A. 张　B. 套　C. 册　D. 本

17. 这套图片共40 _____ ,精选了周恩来一生各个重要时期的历史照片。
A. 套　B. 枚　C. 个　D. 张

18. 中国乒乓球队一举夺得了男单、女单、男双、女双、混合等五 _____ 冠军。
A. 项　B. 个　C. 类　D. 种

19. 这条马路真宽,可以同时并行十 _____ 汽车。
A. 辆　B. 列　C. 次　D. 架

20. 《家有儿女》这 _____ 电视剧拍得真好,老少皆宜。

A．部　B．件　C．项　D．份

21．黛安娜因车祸突然去世了,这 _____ 消息震惊了世界。
A．张　B．篇　C．则　D．页

22．这 _____ 银杏树已经二百多岁了。
A．棵　B．颗　C．条　D．粒

23．我们打扑克,每次都是两 _____ 牌合在一起玩儿。
A．部　B．局　C．副　D．盘

24．天气热了,我给孩子买了一 _____ 纯棉的毛巾被。
A．片　B．条　C．张　D．面

25．这 _____ 台灯的造型真新颖。
A．架　B．盏　C．台　D．部

26．我真看不惯他那 _____ 傲慢的嘴脸。
A．副　B．派　C．张　D．幅

27．小雨语文考试不及格,爸爸知道了打了他一 _____。
A．趟　B．顿　C．手　D．脚

28．妈妈一 _____ 推心置腹的话,让我心服口服。
A．个　B．群　C．番　D．块

29．我家四世同堂,爷爷、父母、老公和我,再加上孩子总共六 _____ 人。
A．位　B．口　C．头　D．户

30．爷爷伤心极了,眼里流出两 _____ 混浊的泪水。
A．颗　B．条　C．行　D．股

31．这 _____ 衣服你穿着真好看。
A．个　B．只　C．套　D．张

32．孩子刚学走路,还走不稳,你要扶她一 _____。
A．次　B．把　C．回　D．趟

33．这 _____ 衬衫上的花,是她母亲手绣的。
A．套　B．件　C．条　D．个

34．逛了半天书店,我才买了一 _____ 书。
A．页　B．本　C．张　D．件

35．这部电影太精彩了,我还想再看一 _____。
A．本　B．趟　C．遍　D．个

36. 天气虽热,可广场上还有一_____孩子在踢足球。
    A. 群 B. 批 C. 团 D. 队

37. 跟他合伙做了几_____生意,才知道他是个爱财不重情意的人。
    A. 笔 B. 把 C. 份 D. 批

38. 弟弟买了一_____新球袜。
    A. 幅 B. 副 C. 双 D. 件

39. 妈妈六十大寿,女儿给她买了一_____翡翠手镯。
    A. 把 B. 根 C. 件 D. 只

40. 任务完成得非常出色,老总请大家吃了_____庆功饭。
    A. 趟 B. 顿 C. 回 D. 次

41. 刘老师的教学经验非常丰富,决不是几_____纸能概括得了的。
    A. 本 B. 张 C. 种 D. 袋

42. 这_____别墅真漂亮。
    A. 间 B. 幢 C. 个 D. 点

43. 大队人马被前面的这_____高山挡住了去路。
    A. 顶 B. 个 C. 座 D. 辆

44. 你的脸型很适合戴这_____鸭舌帽。
    A. 条 B. 顶 C. 支 D. 件

45. 他写的报告一共才两_____纸。
    A. 副 B. 页 C. 块 D. 份

46. 我把这_____法国香水送给你,请收下。
    A. 支 B. 台 C. 瓶 D. 双

47. 白雪公主太累了,她把七_____小床拼在一起睡下了。
    A. 张 B. 座 C. 块 D. 条

48. 总经理限会计三天查清这_____帐。
    A. 部 B. 份 C. 笔 D. 把

49. 刘老师出的这_____数学题,难住了全班的同学。
    A. 首 B. 道 C. 本 D. 段

50. 这个城市刚刚受过一_____严重的台风侵袭。
    A. 丝 B. 次 C. 片 D. 份

51. 小姑娘好像莲叶托着的一_____小荷花。
    A. 束 B. 朵 C. 些 D. 个

52. 一_____水也能反映出太阳的光辉。
    A. 粒　B. 碗　C. 滴　D. 湖

53. 他的文章以口语化、自然、亲切、感人而取胜,通篇没有一_____华丽的词藻。
    A. 条　B. 片　C. 句　D. 个

54. 小麻雀躺在地上飞不起来了,它的几_____长翎拧在了一起。
    A. 节　B. 段　C. 块　D. 根

55. 我朝路旁望去,见有一_____嘴部嫩黄、头生柔毛的小麻雀。
    A. 头　B. 口　C. 只　D. 支

56. 我跳过石头,顺着一_____小路走去,不多远,就进了山。
    A. 条　B. 个　C. 丝　D. 片

57. 雨过天晴,湛蓝的天空挂起一_____艳丽的彩虹,把天空装点得分外美丽。
    A. 条　B. 道　C. 片　D. 面

58. 他是一_____学习好、身体好、有理想的好青年。
    A. 群　B. 批　C. 些　D. 名

59. 眼前的一切像是精工巧匠精心镶嵌的一_____华美的贝雕画。
    A. 幅　B. 副　C. 个　D. 片

60. 售货员同志,请把那_____皮手套拿给我。
    A. 幅　B. 副　C. 只　D. 件

61. 四周一片黑暗,而灯火明亮的戏台,好像镶嵌在黑色幕布上的一_____璀璨的明珠。
    A. 颗　B. 棵　C. 些　D. 片

62. 他正从一捆书里掏出一_____书匆匆往怀里塞。
    A. 册　B. 页　C. 本　D. 根

63. 他看到一_____慌张中带着倔强,倔强中带着粗野的眼睛。
    A. 双　B. 个　C. 幅　D. 名

64. 每一_____盛开的花都像是张满了的帆。
    A. 只　B. 朵　C. 棵　D. 片

65. 在辞别的时候,拿破仑向该校校长送上了一_____价值三个路易的玫瑰花。
    A. 把　B. 袋　C. 束　D. 捆

66. 母亲一_____酷爱文学,并在这方面有较高的修养。
    A. 生　B. 声　C. 时　D. 辈

67. 妈妈气急了,打了弟弟一_____。
    A. 下　B. 场　C. 番　D. 份

68. 这是一 _____ 令人高兴而又振奋的事情。
   A. 项 B. 件 C. 个 D. 段

69. 小李从新疆买回几 _____ 库尔勒香梨。
   A. 斤 B. 尺 C. 点 D. 滴

70. 新开垦的十 _____ 地全部种上了水稻。
   A. 片 B. 亩 C. 件 D. 双

71. 天空飞过两 _____ 飞机。
   A. 辆 B. 行 C. 架 D. 群

72. 他是武打演员,在拍片时,后背挨了一 _____ 。
   A. 次 B. 刀 C. 回 D. 阵

73. 那 _____ 万吨巨轮是我国自己设计、自己制造的。
   A. 辆 B. 架 C. 艘 D. 匹

74. 我上学校来了好几 _____ ,今天总算找到你了。
   A. 回 B. 会 C. 阵 D. 顿

75. 跑了三 _____ ,也没买到我要的工具书。
   A. 下 B. 趟 C. 阵 D. 番

76. 她不图报答与歌颂,只是一心一意帮助他人,让人与人之间多了一 _____ 真诚与爱心。
   A. 次 B. 份 C. 个 D. 回

77. 我们的学校就设在山上的一 _____ 古庙里。
   A. 所 B. 座 C. 幢 D. 排

78. 主人把一大 _____ 冒着热气的红薯、芋头放到我们面前。
   A. 杯 B. 盆 C. 捆 D. 瓶

79. 一天晚上,没有一 _____ 风,树叶死了似的,动都不动。
   A. 丝 B. 块 C. 条 D. 片

80. 小姑娘用一 _____ 小竹棍挑着小灯笼,在院里走来走去。
   A. 只 B. 根 C. 把 D. 段

81. 冰心老人的作品总具有一 _____ 自然、亲切、温和、清新的阴柔之美。
   A. 块 B. 片 C. 种 D. 个

82. 他的烟瘾真大,一上午就抽了三 _____ 香烟。
   A. 把 B. 包 C. 部 D. 个

83. 你们赶紧把这 _____ 武器运到前线去。
   A. 匹 B. 面 C. 批 D. 片

84. 他拉着几＿＿＿＿＿马走着。
   A. 批 B. 匹 C. 个 D. 扇

85. 小弟弟真淘气,整天爬上又爬下,全＿＿＿＿＿上下都是土。
   A. 面 B. 部 C. 身 D. 首

86. 北大医院是一＿＿＿＿＿非常有名的医院,那里的医生医术高,态度好。
   A. 把 B. 件 C. 节 D. 家

87. 别把那＿＿＿＿＿电池随手扔掉,应该放到回收箱里。
   A. 副 B. 件 C. 节 D. 棵

88. 昨天的那＿＿＿＿＿雨真大,雨刷都不管用了,汽车只好停在路边。
   A. 部 B. 场 C. 滴 D. 粒

89. 她们是一＿＿＿＿＿双胞胎,可是长得一点都不像。
   A. 个 B. 块 C. 只 D. 对

90. 风中的那＿＿＿＿＿纱窗,摇摇晃晃,快要掉下来了。
   A. 扇 B. 面 C. 片 D. 条

91. 今年这＿＿＿＿＿初中毕业生,比去年少了两万人。
   A. 节 B. 届 C. 对 D. 股

92. 小王新买了一＿＿＿＿＿三室两厅两卫的房子。
   A. 间 B. 件 C. 节 D. 套

93. 战争打响了,十几＿＿＿＿＿大炮一起开火。
   A. 个 B. 双 C. 门 D. 支

94. 大家就喜欢他那＿＿＿＿＿不服输的劲儿。
   A. 把 B. 副 C. 番 D. 股

95. 第一＿＿＿＿＿赴西藏的医务工作者是北京各大医院派出的。
   A. 匹 B. 批 C. 对 D. 场

96. 我刚学滑冰,站都站不稳,滑倒好几回,弄了一＿＿＿＿＿泥。
   A. 杯 B. 身 C. 筐 D. 盆

97. 这列火车共有十二＿＿＿＿＿车厢。
   A. 段 B. 节 C. 间 D. 条

98. 《红楼梦》我看了好几＿＿＿＿＿了,越看越爱看。
   A. 下 B. 趟 C. 遍 D. 阵

99. 一 _____ 风刮过，把乌云刮跑了，太阳露了出来。
   A. 回 B. 次 C. 顿 D. 阵

100. 这 _____ 散文的文字特别优美。
   A. 张 B. 篇 C. 页 D. 份

答疑解惑 Answers and Explanations

1. 选择 B。"眼"在这道题中是名词借用为动量词，表示"看"的次数，强调时间很短，符合题意。名词"面"借用为动量词，表示人们会见的次数：见一面、会晤过一面。"遍"是动量词，指一个完整的动作，强调动作从头到尾的全部过程。"趟"也是动量词，强调人们来回走动的次数，来回一次叫"一趟"。

The answer is B. The noun "yǎn" here is used as a verb quantifier, indicating the number of times of "kàn", emphasizing the duration of the action is short; the noun "miàn" can also be used as a verb quantifier, indicating the number of times of people meeting each other; "biàn" is a verb quantifier indicating a complete action, and it stresses the whole process of the action from the beginning to the end; "tàng" is also a verb quantifier, indicating the number of times of a round trip, and "yí tàng" refers to a round trip.

2. 选择 D。"双"多指成对的事物或肢体：一双手、两双鞋、三双筷子等，符合题意。"副"表示配成套的东西：一幅眼镜、一副棋等。"二"和"两"都是数词，不是量词。

The answer is D. "Shuāng" often modifies things with matching left and right parts, such as body parts or organs, or things that are used in pair, e.g.: yì shuāng shǒu, liǎng shuāng xié and sān shuāng kuàizi, etc., thus it is the correct answer. "Fù" is often used to modify things in sets, e.g.: yí fù yǎnjìng, yí fù qí and etc. "Èr" and "liǎng" are numerals, not quantifiers.

3. 选择 A。"车"较常用的量词就是"辆"。"两"和"二"都表示"2"，但在与量词搭配使用时，要用"两"，而不用"二"：两个人、两本书等。

The answer is A. The quantifier for car is "liàng". Although "liǎng" and "èr" both indicate "two", when used together with quantifiers, "liǎng" should be used instead of "èr", e.g.: liǎng gè rén, liǎng běn shū.

4. 选择 B。"伙"、"群"和"批"都是集合量词，但是"伙"常用于贬义词：一伙流氓、一伙强盗等。"批"用于同时行动的人们、同时出现或消失的物件或事物，它强调时间性：一批物资、一批志愿者。"群"指聚集在一起的人或物，强调聚集性：一群牛、一群年轻人。另外"群"还可以计量岛屿、群山和楼群等。"层"用于表示重叠、积累的东西：一层楼、双层玻璃。

The answer is B. "Huǒ", "qún" and "pī" are all group quantifiers, but "huǒ" is often derogatory, e.g.: yì huǒ liúmáng, yì huǒ qiángdào. "Pī" is used to modify people who take actions together or things appearing or disappearing at the same time, with the emphasis on the time, e.g.: yì pī wùzī, yì pī zhìyuànzhě. "Qún" is used to modify people or things that gather together, with the emphasis on the gathering, e.g.: yì qún niú, yì qún niánqīng rén. Besides, "qún" can also be quantifier for islands, mountains and buildings. "Céng" modifies things that are tiered, e.g.: yì céng lóu, shuāng céng bōli.

5. 选择 A。"衣服"的常用量词是"件","件"泛指或特指上衣,符合题意。"张"做量词时,用法有三:①用于可以卷起或展开的纸张、皮子:一张纸、两张地图;②用于人或动物的脸和有平面的东西:一张脸、一张床;③用于张开、闭拢的东西:一张弓、一张网。"把"做量词时,用法有四:①用于有把手的器具:一把刀、一把伞;②表示一手抓起的数量:一把土、一把瓜子;③用于表示某些抽象的事物:一把年纪、一把好手;④和表示"用手进行的动作"的动词搭配使用:拉一把、洗一把脸。"支"的用法有三:①用于队伍:一支军队;②用于歌曲、乐曲:一支歌、一支曲子;③用于杆状的东西:一支枪、二十支蜡烛。

The answer is A. The quantifier for "yīfu" is "jiàn", which generally or specifically refers to and modifies coats. There are three usages for "zhāng" as a quantifier: ① to modify things such as paper, leather that can be rolled up or spread, e.g.: yì zhāng zhǐ, liǎng zhāng dìtú; ② to modify the face of people or animals and things with a surface, e.g.: yì zhāng liǎn, yì zhāng chuáng; ③ to modify things that can be opened and closed, e.g.: yì zhāng gōng, yì zhāng wǎng. There are four usages for "bǎ" as a quantifier: ① to modify instruments with a handle, e.g.: yì bǎ dāo, yì bǎ sǎn; ② to modify a handful of things, e.g.: yì bǎ tǔ, yì bǎ guāzǐ; ③ to modify some abstract things, e.g.: yì bǎ niánji, yì bǎ hǎoshǒu; ④ to match with verbs which require the use of hand, e.g.: lā yì bǎ, xǐ bǎ liǎn. "Zhī" as a quantifier can be used in three ways: ① to modify the troop, e.g.: yì zhī jūnduì; ② to modify songs, melody, e.g.: yì zhī gē, yì zhī qǔzi; ③ to modify a long and thin cylindrical object, e.g.: yì zhī qiāng, èrshí zhī làzhú.

6. 选择 C。"遍"是动量词,指一个完整的动作,强调动作从头到尾的全部过程。"下"做量词时,用法有四:①用于动作的次数:打一下、敲三下;②用在动词后表示尝试,时间很短,前面的数词只能用"一":看一下、研究一下;③表示快速,可带"子":突然停电了,屋里一下子漆黑一片;④表示本领、技能,前面的数词用"两"或"几",后可带"子"或"儿":有两下子、他就会那几下儿。"阵"做量词时,用法有二:①表示突然发生的事情或动作:一阵风、一阵掌声;②表示事情或动作持续了一段时间:忙一阵、高兴一阵。"声"表示发出声音的次数:一声叹息。

The answer is C. "biàn" is a verb quantifier indicating a complete action, and it stresses the whole process of the action from the beginning to the end. There are four usages for "xià" as a quantifier: ① to indicate the number of times of an action, e.g.: dǎ yí xià, qiāo sān xià; ② to indicate a small try and the matching numeral can only be "one/a", e.g.: kàn yí xià, yánjiū yí xià; ③ to indicate a sudden action, usually followed by "zǐ", e.g.: tūrán tíngdiàn le, wū li yí xiàzi qīhēi yí piàn; ④ to indicate certain skill or ability, with the matching number being "liǎng" or "jǐ", and can be followed by "zǐ" or "ér", e.g.: yǒu liǎngxiàzi; tā jiù huì nà jǐ xiàr. "Zhèn" as a quantifier can be used as follows: ① to indicate a sudden action, e.g.: yí zhèn fēng, yí zhèn zhǎngshēng; ② to indicate a matter or an action that lasts for some time, e.g.: máng yí zhèn, gāoxìng yí zhèn. "Shēng" indicates the number of times of a sound being given, e.g.: yì shēng tànxī.

7. 选择 C。"场"做量词时,表示事情的经过,着重于事物发生的时间长。事情经过一次叫一场:一场战争、一场暴风雪。"通 (tòng)"做动量词时,与其搭配使用的多为有消极意义的动词:一通批评。"篇"用于完整的文章、小说等:一篇课文、三篇随笔。"章"表示歌曲、诗文的段落:第一乐章、本书一共十章。

The answer is C. "Cháng" as a quantifier indicates the process of a thing, with the emphasis on the long duration of time, and "yì cháng" means something happened once, e.g.: yì cháng zhànzhēng, yì cháng bàofēngxuě. When "tòng" is used as a verb quantifier, it often matches with verbs which have negative meanings, e.g.: yí tòng pīpíng. "Piān" as a quantifier modifies indicating a whole piece of writing such as essay or novel, e.g.: yì piān kèwén, sān piān suíbǐ. "Zhāng" indicates the paragraph or chapter of songs or poems, e.g.: dì-yī yuèzhāng, běn shū yí gòng shí zhāng.

8. 选择 D。"鞋"的量词是"双"或"只"—一双鞋、两只鞋。"二"和"两"都是数词,不是量词。"俩"本身就是数量词,后面不再接其他量词。

The answer is D. The quantifier of shoes is "shuāng" or "zhī", e.g.: yì shuāng xié or liǎng zhī xié. "Èr" and "liǎng" are numerals, not quantifiers. "Liǎ" itself can be a numeral–quantifier and can not be followed by other quantifiers.

9. 选择 C。"次"表示可以重复出现的动作次数,符合题意。"遍"是动量词,指一个完整的动作,强调动作从头到尾的全部过程。"个"是最常用的个体量词:一个同学、一个星期、一个动作。

The answer is C. "Cì" indicates the number of times of an action that can appear repeatedly, which matches the topic, while "biàn" is a verb quantifier indicating a complete action, and it stresses the whole process of the action from the beginning to the end. "Gè" is one of the most commonly used individual quantifiers, e.g.: yí gè tóngxué, yí gè xīngqī, yí gè dòngzuò.

10. 选择 B。"所"做量词时,用于房屋(只指建筑物)、学校、医院等单位(包括建筑物、企事业机构):一所房子、一所大学。"间"是计量房间数量的最小单位:一间教室、一间办公室等。"顶"用于某些有顶的东西,如帽子、帐篷等。"座"用于大型房屋、桥、碑、塔、山等大型天然风景和人工建筑：一座立交桥、一座大楼。

The answer is B. "Suǒ" as a quantifier modifies nouns such as houses (buildings only), schools or hospitals (buildings and institutions), e.g.: yì suǒ fángzi, yì suǒ dàxué. "Jiān" indicates the minimal unit of rooms, e.g.: yì jiān jiàoshì, yì jiān bàngōngshì, etc. "Dǐng" modifies things with a top, such as caps or tents. "Zuò" modifies large natural scenes and man-made architecture such as houses, bridges, monuments, towers and mountains, e.g.: yí zuò lìjiāoqiáo, yí zuò dàlóu.

11. 选择C。"份"做量词时，用法有四：①表示整体分成的部分：把蛋糕分成四份；②由不同部分组成的整体：一份快餐；③指报刊、文件等：一份《北京晚报》、一份报告，符合题意；④指思想感情等抽象的事物：一份欣喜等。"本"用于书本簿册，如：一本书、一本集邮册等。"片"做量词时，用法有三：①表示平而且薄的东西：一片面包；②用于较大面积的平面：一片蓝天；③用于景色、气象、情感等抽象事物：一片欢呼、一片柔情。"册"表示装订好的本子，一本就叫做一册。

The answer is C. There are four usages for "fèn" as a quantifier: ① to indicate the parts divided from the whole, e.g.: bǎ dàngāo fēnchéng sì fèn; ② to indicate the whole formed by different parts, e.g.: yí fèn kuàicān; ③ to modify quantities of periodicals or papers, e.g.: yí fèn běijīng wǎnbào, yí fèn bàogào; ④ to modify something abstract such as thoughts or feelings, e.g.: yí fèn xīnxǐ. "Běn" is used to modify books or pamphlets, e.g.: yì běn shū, yì běn jíyóucè. "Piàn" as a quantifier can be used in three ways: ① to modify things that are flat and thin, e.g.: yí piàn miànbāo; ② to modify things with a large and wide surface, e.g.: yí piàn lántiān; ③ to modify abstract things, e.g.: yí piàn huānhū, yí piàn róuqíng. "Cè" is used to modify bound books, each one is called "yí cè".

12. 选择A。"番"既可以做名量词，又可以做动量词。做名量词时，用法有二：①修饰言语、心思等，数词只能用"一"：一番好意；②用于景象、气象等：好一番良辰美景、一番太平景象等。做动量词时，用法有二：①计量动作的次数，多用于费时费力的动作：动一番脑筋、三番五次；②表示倍数：翻一番。"个"是一个最常用的个体量词，口语中，常与"事情"搭配使用，但不与"事业"搭配。"项"用于分项目的事物，如：一项开支、一项比赛等。"件"做量词时，用法有四：①泛指或特指上衣：一件衬衫等；②用于事情、文件、案件等：一件快件、一件凶杀案件、一件往事等；③用于个体事物，多为类名：一件行李、一件礼物。

The answer is A. "Fān" can be used both as a noun quantifier and as a verb quantifier. When used as a noun quantifier, it is used in two ways: ① to modify words and thoughts, and the matching numeral can only be "one", e.g.: yì fān hǎoyì; ② to indicate a scene and climate, e.g.: hǎo yì fān liángchén-měijǐng, yì fān tàipíng jǐngxiàng. When used as a verb quantifier, it is used in two ways: ① to indicate the number of times of actions, especially actions that are time and energy consuming, e.g.: dòng yì fān nǎojīn, sānfān-wǔcì; ② to indicate a multiple, e.g.: fān yì fān. "Gè" is one of the most commonly used individual quantifier, it can be used in spoken language with "shìqing", but not with "shìyè". "Xiàng" is used to modify things that have subentries, e.g.: yí xiàng kāizhī, yí xiàng bǐsài. There are four usages for "jiàn" as a quantifier: ① to generally or specifically refer to coats, shirts or jackets, e.g.: yí jiàn chènshān; ② to modify things, documents and papers, e.g.: yí jiàn kuàijiàn, yí jiàn xiōngshā ànjiàn; ③ to modify some individual things, e.g.: yí jiàn xíngli, yí jiàn lǐwù.

13. 选择 B。"首"用于计量诗词、歌曲等：一首古诗、一首儿歌，符合题意。
The answer is B. "Shǒu" is used to modify poems or songs, e.g.: yì shǒu gǔshī, yì shǒu érgē.

14. 选择 B。"张"用于可卷起或展开的纸张。"幅"一般指面积比较大、带有较强艺术性的东西，如布、旗类、美术作品等。
The answer is B. "Zhāng" as a quantifier modifies things that can be rolled up or spread such as paper or leather. "Fú" usually modifies an object of large size or artistic works, such as cloth, flags and artworks.

15. 选择 B。"首"用于计量诗词、歌曲等：一首古诗、一首儿歌，符合题意。
The answer is B. "Shǒu" is used to modify poems or songs, e.g.: yì shǒu gǔshī, yì shǒu érgē, so it is the best answer.

16. 选择 B。"套"做量词时，用法有二：①用于成组的事物：一套西装；②指本领或手段：一套拳等。"张"可指单张邮票，但不可指成套的邮票。
The answer is B. "Tào" as a quantifier can be used in two ways: ① to indicate things in a set, e.g.: yí tào xīzhuāng; ② to indicate an ability or a skill, e.g.: yí tào quán. "Zhāng" can be used to indicate a single stamp, but not a set of stamps.

17. 选择 D。量词"张"的用法①用于可以卷起或展开的纸张、皮子等：一张纸、两张地图，符合题意。"枚"用于较小的硬币、徽章、邮票等：一枚奖章、一枚邮票等。
The answer is D. The first usage of "zhāng" as a quantifier is to modify things that can be rolled up or spread, e.g.: yì zhāng zhǐ, liǎng zhāng dìtú. "Méi" is used to modify small coins, medals or stamps, e.g.: yì méi jiǎngzhāng, yì méi yóupiào, etc.

18. 选择 A。"项"用于分项目的事物，如：一项开支、一项比赛等，符合题意。"种"的用法有二：①表示种类，用于人或东西，强调事物的区别性：两种人、多种水果、每一种语言；②用于不同的心情或感觉，或别的抽象事物，强调事物的特殊性：一种爱、一种现象、一种心情等。
The answer is A. "Xiàng" is used to modify things that have subentries, e.g.: yí xiàng kāizhī, yí xiàng bǐsài, and matches the topic. "Zhǒng" as a quantifier can be used in two ways: ① to indicate kinds of people or things, emphasizing their difference, e.g.: liǎng zhǒng rén, duō zhǒng shuǐguǒ, měi yì zhǒng yǔyán; ② to indicate different moods or

feelings or other abstract things, emphasizing their specialty, e.g.: yì zhǒng ài, yì zhǒng xiànxiàng, yì zhǒng xīnqíng.

19. 选择A。"车"较常用的量词是"辆"。"列"用于火车或成排的人或物:一列火车、一列人马。"次"表示动作的次数:看一次、问一次。"架"用于有支架或有机械装置的东西:一架飞机、一架钢琴。

The answer is A. The commonly used quantifier for "chē" is "liàng". "Liè" as a quantifier modifies a train or people or things in a line, e.g.: yí liè huǒchē, yí liè rénmǎ. "Cì" indicates the number of times of action, e.g.: kàn yí cì, wèn yí cì. "Jià" as a quantifier modifies things with a stand or mechanical device, e.g.: yí jià fēijī, yí jià gāngqín.

20. 选择A。"部"做量词时,用法有二:①用于书籍、电影等:一部专著、一部电影,符合题意;②用于机器或车辆:一部手机、一部轿车。

The answer is A. "Bù" as a quantifier can be used in two ways: ① to modify books or movies, e.g.: yí bù zhuānzhù, yí bù diànyǐng; ② to modify machines or vehicles, e.g.: yí bù shǒujī, yí bù jiàochē.

21. 选择C。"则"做量词时,表示故事、消息的计量,如:一则笑话、一则新闻,符合题意。"页"多用于指书本中一张纸的一面,如:第一页。

The answer is C. "Zé" as a quantifier modifies stories or information, e.g.: yì zé xiàohua, yì zé xīnwén. "Yè" as a quantifier indicates a page in a book, e.g.: dì-yī yè.

22. 选择A。"棵"用于植物的计量,如:一棵小草、一棵红高粱等。"颗"用于圆形或块状较小的东西:一颗宝石、一颗牙等。"条"做量词时,用法有四:①用于细长形状的东西:一条小溪、一条马路;②用于组合成长条的东西:一条裙子、一条领带;③用于和身体有关的叙述:一条人命;④用于某些长形的动物、植物:一条鱼、一条丝瓜等。"粒"用于小碎块状的东西,如:一粒米、一粒葡萄等。

The answer is A. "Kē (棵)" indicates the number of plant, e.g.: yì kē xiǎocǎo, yì kē hóng gāoliáng. "Kē (颗)" is used to modify round or small things, e.g.: yì kē bǎoshí, yì kē yá. There are four usages for "tiáo" as a quantifier: ① to indicate things that are long and thin, e.g.: yì tiáo xiǎoxī, yì tiáo mǎlù; ② to indicate things that are long and compound, e.g.: yì tiáo qúnzi, yì tiáo lǐngdài; ③ to indicate something related to human body, e.g.: yì tiáo rénmìng; ④ to indicate animals or plants with a long shape, e.g.: yì tiáo yú, yì tiáo sīguā. "Lì" modifies things that are tiny, e.g.: yí lì mǐ, yí lì pútao.

23. 选择C。"副"做量词时,用法有四:①表示配成套的东西:一副手套、一副象棋,符合题意;②用于楹联:一副春联;③用于指人的相貌或表情:一副愁眉苦脸的样子;④用于中药的计量:一副汤药。"部"做量词时,用法有二:①用于比较厚重的书籍、电影等:一部专著、一部电影;②用于机器或车辆:一部手机、一部轿车。"局"表示棋类或球类比赛活动,活动一次叫一局。"盘"

做量词时,用法有三:①用于用盘子装的东西:一盘菜、一盘水果;②用于盘绕起来的圆形物:一盘录像带、一盘蚊香;③用于棋牌类运动:一盘棋、一盘比赛。

The answer is C. "Fù" as a quantifier can be used in four ways: ① to indicate things in a whole set, e.g.: yí fù shǒutào, yí fù xiàngqí; ② to modify couplets, e.g.: yí fù chūnlián; ③ to modify appearance or expressions, e.g.: yí fù chóuméi–kǔliǎn de yàngzi; ④ to indicate the amount of Chinese traditional medicine, e.g.: yí fù tāngyào. "Bù" as a quantifier can be used in two ways: ① to modify relatively thick books or long movies, e.g.: yí bù zhuānzhù, yí bù diànyǐng; ② to modify machines or vehicles, e.g.: yí bù shǒujī, yí bù jiàochē. "Jú" modifies board games or ball matches, with one game as "yì jú". "Pán" as a quantifier can be used in three ways: ① to indicate things held in a plate, e.g.: yì pán cài, yì pán shuǐguǒ; ② to indicate round things twisted together, e.g.: yì pán lùxiàngdài, yì pán wénxiāng; ③ to indicate board or card games, e.g.: yì pán qí, yì pán bǐsài.

24. 选择 B。"条"可以用于指组合成长条的东西:一条裙子、一条领带,符合题意。"面"做量词时,用法有三:①用于扁平或能展开的东西:一面墙、一面镜子;②用于见面次数:见过几面;③用于纸张、书页以及立方体的一个平面。

The answer is B. "Tiáo" as a quantifier can indicate things that are made long, e.g.: a skirt, a tie, and matches the topic. "Miàn" as a quantifier can be used in three ways: ① to indicate things that are flat or can be spread, e.g.: yí miàn qiáng, yí miàn jìngzi; ② to indicate the number of times of meeting, e.g.: jiànguò jǐ miàn; ③ to indicate one side of paper, a page or a cube.

25. 选择 B。"盏"用于灯,如:一盏路灯,符合题意。"架"用于有支架或有机械装置的东西。"台"做量词时,用法有二:①用于机器设备:一台电脑;②用于一次完整的演出:一台演出、一台京剧。

The answer is B. "Zhǎn" as a quantifier is used to modify lamp, e.g.: yì zhǎn lùdēng, and matches the topic. "Jià" as a quantifier modifies things with a stand or mechanical device. "Tái" as a quantifier can be used in two ways: ① to indicate machines or equipment, e.g.: yì tái diànnǎo; ② to modify an entire performance, e.g.: yì tái yǎnchū, yì tái jīngjù.

26. 选择 A。量词"副"用于指人的相貌或表情:一副愁眉苦脸的样子。符合题意。"幅"一般指面积比较大、带有较强艺术性的东西,如布、旗类、美术作品等。"派"做量词时,用法有二:①用于不同意见或观点的人群:两派意见;②用于抽象的景色、气势、表现等,不表示表情,数词只能用"一":一派北国风光等。

The answer is A. "Fù" is a quantifier to modify appearance or expressions, e.g. yí fù chóuméi–kǔliǎn de yàngzi. "Fú" usually modifies an object of large size or artistic works, such as cloth, flags and artworks. "Pài" as a quantifier can be used in two ways: ① to indicate people with different opinions: liǎng pài yìjiàn; ② to modify abstract view, style or behavior, and the matching number can only be "one", e.g.: yí pài běiguó fēngguāng. It cannot indicate appearance or expressions.

27. 选择 B。"顿"做量词时,用法有二:①用于饮食的次数:三顿饭;②用于打骂、劝说、批评的次数:骂一顿、说了一顿。"趟"是动量词,表示来回走动的次数,来回一次叫"一趟"。名词"手"借用为量词时,用于指有一定水平的技术:妈妈会烧一手好菜。名词"脚"借用为量词时,用于指用脚完成的动作的次数:踢了一脚。

The answer is B. "Dùn" as a quantifier can be used in two ways: ① to indicate the number of times of meals, e.g.: sān dùn fàn; ② to indicate the number of times of abuse, persuasion or criticism, e.g.: mà yí dùn, shuōle yí dùn. "Tàng" is also a verb quantifier, indicating the number of times of a round trip, and "yí tàng" refers to one round trip. When the noun "shǒu" is used as a quantifier, it indicates certain skills or techniques, e.g.: Māma huì shāo yì shǒu hǎocài. When the noun "jiǎo" is used as a quantifier, it indicates the number of times of action done by foot, e.g.: tīle yì jiǎo.

28. 选择 C。量词"番"表示言语、心思,数词只能用"一",符合题意。"块"做量词时,用法有二:①用于人民币,相当于"元";②用于块状或片状的东西:一块香皂、一块蛋糕等。

The answer is C. The quantifier "fān" is to indicate talks and thoughts, and the matching number can only be "one". "Kuài" as a quantifier can be used in two ways: ① to indicate RMB, meaning "yuán"; ② to modify things with the shape of a block or sheet, e.g.: yí kuài xiāngzào, yí kuài dàngāo.

29. 选择 B。名词"口"借用为量词时,用法有六:①用于计算家庭、城市、村镇的人数:六口人;②用于计算猪:一口大肥猪;③用于有口或有刃的东西:一口井、一口宝剑;④计量与口腔有关的东西:一口牙、一口气;⑤用于吃喝的计量:喝一口、咬一口;⑥表示语音,数词只能用"一":一口京腔。"位"用法有二:①用于人,并表示尊敬之意:一位教授;②用于计算数位:两位数。名词"头"做量词时,用法有二:①用于计量较大的牲畜:一头牛、一头驴;②计量蒜头:一百头大蒜。"户"用于人家的计量:一户居民等。

The answer is B. There are six usages for the noun "kǒu" used as a quantifier: ① to indicate the number of persons in a family, city or town, e.g.: liù kǒu rén; ② to indicate the number of pigs, e.g.: yì kǒu dà féi zhū; ③ to modify things with an opening or a blade, e.g.: yì kǒu jǐng, yì kǒu bǎojiàn; ④ to measure things related to mouth, e.g.: yì kǒu yá, yì kǒu qì; ⑤ to measure the amount of things eaten or drunk, e.g.: hē yì kǒu, yǎo yì kǒu; ⑥ to indicate accent, and the matching number can only be "one", e.g.: yì kǒu jīngqiāng. "Wèi" as a quantifier can be used in two ways: ① to modify people, showing respect, e.g.: yí wèi jiàoshòu; ② to count digits, e.g.: liǎng wèi shù. When the noun "tóu" is used as a quantifier, it can be used in two ways: ① to modify large livestock, e.g.: yì tóu niú, yì tóu lǘ; ② to modify a head of garlic, e.g.: yìbǎi tóu dàsuàn. "Hù" as a quantifier indicates the number of household, e.g.: yí hù jūmín.

30. 选择 C。"行 (háng)"用法有四：①用于成行的人：一行士兵；②用于成行的动物或植物：一行大雁、一行树；③用于成行的其他事物：两行眼泪、一行诗。④计量工种、行业：干一行爱一行。"股"用法有三：①用于成条的东西：一股泉水、一股毛线；②用于气体、气味、力气等：一股花香、一股干劲；③用于成批的人，多含有贬义：一股敌人。"股"在计量水流时，强调的是线条粗、量大，而且还重在说明水流向外涌出的样子。

The answer is C. "Háng" as a quantifier can be used in four ways: ① to indicate people in a line, e.g.: yì háng shìbīng; ② to indicate animals or plants in a line, e.g.: yì háng dàyàn, yì háng shù; ③ to indicate other things in a line, e.g.: liǎng háng yǎnlèi, yì háng shī; ④ to indicate the types of work or trade, e.g.: gàn yì háng, ài yì háng. There are three usages for "gǔ" as a quantifier: ① to indicate things in stream, e.g.: yì gǔ quánshuǐ, yì gǔ máoxiàn; ② to modify gas, smell, strength, e.g.: yì gǔ huāxiāng, yì gǔ gànjìn; ③ to indicate people in group, usually in a derogatory sense, e.g.: yì gǔ dírén. When "gǔ" is used to modify water, it emphasizes the large stream and amount of water as well as the out-flowing of water.

31. 选择 C。量词"套"可表示配套成组的事物：一套西装、一套课本。
The answer is C. "Tào" as a quantifier can be used to indicate things in a set, e.g.: yí tào xīzhuāng, yí tào kèběn.

32. 选择 B。量词"把"可以与表示"用手进行动作"的动词搭配使用，"把"用在动词后，数词限用"一"或"两"：拉一把、洗一把脸，符合题意。动量词"次"表示动作的次数：练习一次。动量词"回"表示动作的次数，强调动作发生的时间和次数，多用于口语：参观一回。"趟"修饰人们来回走动的次数。
The answer is B. "Bǎ" as a quantifier matches verbs with the meaning of doing with hand, e.g.: lā yì bǎ, xǐ yì bǎ liǎn. "Bǎ" is used after the verb, and the matching number can only be "yī" for one, or "liǎng" for two. "Cì" indicates the number of times of an action, e.g.: liànxí yí cì. Verb quantifier "huí" indicates the number of times of an action in spoken language, with the emphasis on the time and the number of the action, e.g.: cānguān yì huí. "Tàng" modifies the number of times of a round trip.

33. 选择 B。量词"件"泛指或特指上衣。
The answer is B. "Jiàn" as a quantifier generally or specifically refers to coats, jackets or shirts.

34. 选择 B。"本"用于书本簿册：一本书、一本集邮册。
The answer is B. "Běn" is used to modify books or pamphlets with sheets, e.g.: yì běn shū, yì běn jíyóucè.

35. 选择 C。动量词"遍"强调动作从头到尾的全部过程。

The answer is C. "Biàn" is a verb quantifier, and it stresses the whole process of an action from the beginning to the end.

36. 选择 A。"群"、"批"、和"队"都是集合量词。"群"指聚集在一起的人或物,强调聚集性。如：一群牛、一群年轻人等。"批"用于同时行动的人们、同时出现或消失的物件或事物,它强调时间性：一批物资、一批志愿者等。"队"用于成行列的人,如：一队人马。"团"做量词时,用法有二：① 用于一些圆形或球形的东西：一团纱布；② 用于抽象事物：一团和气等。

The answer is A. "Qún", "pī" and "duì" are all group quantifiers. "Qún" is used to modify people or things that are gathering together, with the emphasis on the gathering, e.g.: yì qún niú, yì qún niánqīngrén. "Pī" is used to modify things that appear or disappear at the same time or people who take actions together, with the emphasis on the time of action, e.g.: yì pī wùzī, yì pī zhìyuànzhě. "Duì" modifies people in a line, e.g.: yí duì rénmǎ. "Tuán" as a quantifier can be used in two ways: ① to indicate things that are round or in the shape of a ball, e.g.: yì tuán shābù; ② to modify abstract things, e.g.: yì tuán héqì.

37. 选择 A。名词"笔"借用为量词时,常与有关钱款的名词连用：一笔钱、一笔买卖,符合题意,其他量词均无此用法。

The answer is A. When noun "bǐ" is used as a quantifier, it often matches nouns related to money, e.g.: yì bǐ qián, yì bǐ mǎimài. Other quantifiers are not used in such a way.

38. 选择 C。"双"常表示左右对称、成双使用、穿戴在肢体上的东西,符合题意。

The answer is C. "Shuāng" is usually used to indicate a pair of things or things that are used in pair or things worn on the body.

39. 选择 D。"只"用法有四：① 用于某些成对东西中的一个：一只袜子、两只鞋,符合题意；② 用于动物：一只鸭子、一只老虎；③ 用于某些器具：一只手表；④ 用于船只：一只小船。"根"做量词时,用法有三：① 用于带根的较细的菜类：一根胡萝卜；② 用于毛发类的东西：一根头发；③ 用于细长的东西：一根火柴。

The answer is D. There are four usages for "zhī" as a quantifier: ① to indicate one thing in a pair, e.g.: yì zhī wàzi, liǎng zhī xié, which is the best choice for the topic; ② to modify animals, e.g.: yì zhī yāzi, yì zhī lǎohǔ; ③ to modify some objects, e.g.: yì zhī shǒubiǎo; ④ to modify ships and boats, e.g.: yì zhī xiǎochuán. When "gēn" is used as a quantifier, it can be used in three ways: ① to indicate thin vegetables with roots, e.g.: yì gēn húluóbo; ② to indicate things like hair, e.g.: yì gēn tóufa; ③ to modify long and thin things, e.g.: yì gēn huǒchái.

40. 选择B。动量词"顿"多用于饮食的次数:三顿饭,符合题意。动量词"趟"表示来回走动的次数,来回一次叫"一趟"。动量词"回"表示动作的次数,强调动作发生的时间和次数,多用于口语。

The answer is B. "Dùn" as a quantifier can be often used to indicate the number of times of meals, e.g.: sān dùn fàn. "Tàng" is a verb quantifier, indicating the number of times of an action, and "yí tàng" refers to a round trip. Verb quantifier "huí" indicates the number of times of an action in spoken language, with the emphasis on the time and the number of the action.

41. 选择B。量词"张"可以计量卷起或展开的纸张、皮子等。

The answer is B. "Zhāng" as a quantifier can modify things that can be rolled up or spread such as paper or leather.

42. 选择B。"幢"用于大型楼房,多用于书面语:一幢高楼,符合题意。"间"是房间的最小计量单位:一间办公室。"点"做量词时,用法有三:①表示少量(可以儿化):一点时间;②用于事项:几点看法;③用于时间:八点钟。

The answer is B. "Zhuàng" modifies large buildings, often in written language, e.g.: yí zhuàng gāolóu. "Jiān" indicates the minimal unit of rooms, e.g.: yì jiān bàngōngshì. "Diǎn" as a quantifier can be used in three ways: ① to indicate a little (usually pronounced with "ér"), e.g.: yì diǎn shíjiān; ② to indicate things, e.g.: jǐ diǎn kànfǎ; ③ to indicate time, e.g.: bā diǎn zhōng.

43. 选择C。"座"用于房屋、桥、碑、塔、山等大型天然风景和人工建筑:一座高山、一座大楼等。"顶"用于某些有顶的东西。"辆"用于车辆计数。

The answer is C. "Zuò" modifies large natural scenes and man-made buildings such as houses, bridges, monuments, towers or mountains, e.g.: yí zuò gāoshān, yí zuò dàlóu. "Dǐng" modifies things with a top. "Liàng" is a quantifier for vehicles.

44. 选择B。"顶"用于某些有顶的东西,如帽子、帐篷等,符合题意。

The answer is B. "Dǐng" modifies things with a top, such as caps or tents.

45. 选择B。"页"用于指书本中一张纸的一面:第一页,符合题意。

The answer is B. "Yè" as a quantifier indicates a page in a book, e.g.: dì-yī yè.

46. 选择C。名词"瓶"借用为量词时,表示用瓶装的东西:一瓶酒、一瓶酱油。

The answer is C. When the noun "píng" is used as a quantifier, it indicates things packed in a bottle, e.g.: yì píng jiǔ, yì píng jiàngyóu.

47. 选择 A。量词"张"用于计量有平面的东西：一张茶几、一张床，符合题意。

The answer is A. "Zhāng" as a quantifier can be used to modify things with a surface, e.g.: yì zhāng chájī, yì zhāng chuáng.

48. 选择 C。"笔"做量词时，可以用于计量款项或与钱款有关的事物，"笔"前可加形容词如"大"和"小"：一笔钱、一大笔买卖。

The answer is C. When "bǐ" is used as a quantifier, it can be used to indicate things related to money, and can be preceded by the adjective "dà" and "xiǎo", e.g.: yì bǐ qián, yí dà bǐ mǎimài.

49. 选择 B。"道"做量词时，用法有四：①用于江河等长条形的东西：一道沟、一道皱纹；②用于门墙等：一道难关、一道门；③用于命令、题目等：四道题、一道命令，符合题意；④次：一道程序等。

The answer is B. "Dào" as a quantifier can be used in four ways: ① to indicate things in a long shape such as rivers, e.g.: yí dào gōu, yí dào zhòuwén; ② to modify doors or walls, e.g.: yí dào nánguān, yí dào mén; ③ to modify an order or a question, e.g.: sì dào tí, yí dào mìnglìng; ④ to indicate the number of times, e.g.: yí dào chéngxù.

50. 选择 B。动量词"次"表示动作的次数或反复出现的事情：练习一次，符合题意。"丝"做量词时，用法有二：①用于极细的东西极小的量：一丝春雨；②用于微小的行为、表情或想法：一丝微笑、一丝希望等。

The answer is B. "Cì" indicates the number of times of an action or something that happens repeatedly, e.g.: liànxí yí cì. When "sī" is used as a quantifier, it can be used in two ways: ① to indicate a very thin thing or a very tiny amount, e.g.: yì sī chūn yǔ; ② to indicate trivial actions, expressions or thoughts, e.g.: yì sī wēixiào, yī sī xīwàng.

51. 选择 B。"朵"用于花朵和云彩或与它们相像的东西：一朵棉花、一朵水花。

The answer is B. "Duǒ" modifies flowers or clouds or similar things, e.g.: yì duǒ miánhuā, yì duǒ shuǐhuā.

52. 选择 C。"滴"用于滴下的液体的数量：几滴汗、两滴眼泪等。"粒"用于小碎块状的东西：一粒米、一粒葡萄等。名词"碗"借用为量词时，表示用碗装的东西：一碗饭、一碗粥等。名词"湖"借用为量词时，表示湖容纳的东西：一湖碧波。

The answer is C. "Dī" is used to indicate the number of liquid drops, e.g.: jǐ dī hàn, liǎng dī yǎnlèi. "Lì" modifies things that are tiny, e.g.: yí lì mǐ, yí lì pútáo. When noun "wǎn" is used as a quantifier, it indicates things held in a bowl, e.g.: yì wǎn fàn, yì wǎn zhōu. When noun "hú" is used as a quantifier, it indicates things contained in a lake, e.g.: yì hú bìbō.

53. 选择 D。"个"是一个最常用的个体量词,可以计量语素的量:一个词、两个短语、三个句子、几个句群、一个语段等。"句"用于语言、句子:一句话。

The answer is D. "Gè" is one of the most commonly used individual quantifiers, which measures the number of morphemes, e.g.: yí gè cí, liǎng gè duǎnyǔ, sān gè jùzi, jǐ gè jùqún, yí gè yǔduàn, etc. "Jù" is used for sentences, e.g.: yí jù huà.

54. 选择 D。"根"做量词时,可用于毛发类的东西:一根头发、一根羽毛,符合题意。"节"用法有二:①表示自然成节的东西:一节藕、一节电池;②用于文章的段落、音乐的节拍:第一小节等。

The answer is D. When "gēn" is used as a quantifier, it can be used to indicate things like hair, e.g.: yì gēn tóufa, yì gēn yǔmáo. "Jié" can be used in two ways: ① to indicate things with nodes, e.g.: yì jié ǒu, yì jié diànchí; ② to indicate the paragraph of essays or music, e.g.: dì-yī xiǎojié.

55. 选择 C。"只"、"头"、"口"都是可用做表示动物的量词,但有一些差别。"只"多指飞禽、走兽:一只鸭子、一只老虎,符合题意。"头"用于计量较大的牲畜:一头牛、一头驴。"口"用于某些家畜如猪。

The answer is C. "Zhī", "tóu", "kǒu" are quantifiers to indicate animals, but have different usages. "Zhī"often modifies birds and beasts, e.g.: yì zhī yāzi, yì zhī lǎohǔ, which matches the topic. "Tóu" can modify large livestock, e.g.: yì tóu niú, yì tóu lú. "Kǒu" is used to modify some livestock such as pigs.

56. 选择 A。量词"条"可以用于计量细长的东西。

The answer is A. The quantifier "tiáo" can be used to indicate things that are long and thin.

57. 选择 B。量词"道"可以用于计量江河以及长条形的东西:一道沟、一道皱纹。

The answer is B. "Dào" as a quantifier can be used to indicate things in long shape such as rivers, e.g.: yí dào gōu, yí dào zhòuwén.

58. 选择 D。"名"用法有二:①用于人数:三名战士;②用于名次:第一名。"群"和"批"都是集合量词。

The answer is D. "Míng" as a quantifier can be used in two ways: ① to indicate the number of people, e.g.: sān míng zhànshì; ② to indicate the standing in competition, e.g.: dì-yī míng. "Qún" and "pī" are both group quantifiers.

59. 选择 A。量词"幅"可以用于计量较大的字画、摄影作品:一幅水墨画、一幅书法作品。

The answer is A. "Fú" as a quantifier can be used to modify relatively large pieces of calligraphy and paintings or photographs, e.g.: yì fú shuǐmòhuà, yì fú shūfǎ zuòpǐn.

60. 选择 B。"副"可以计量能分合、配合使用的东西：一副手套、一副象棋。

The answer is B. "Fù" as a quantifier can be used to indicate things that are used together but in separate form, e.g.: yí fù shǒutào, yí fù xiàngqí.

61. 选择 A。"颗"用于圆形或块状较小的东西：一颗宝石、一颗牙等，符合题意。"棵"用于植物的计量。"些"表示不定量的人或事物的数量：一些人、那些书等。"片"表示平而且薄的东西。

The answer is A. "Kē (颗)" is used to modify round or small things, e.g.: yì kē bǎoshí, yì kē yá. "Kē (棵)" indicates the number of plant. "Xiē" indicates the uncertain number of people or things, e.g.: yìxiē rén, nàxiē shū. "Piàn" can be used to modify things that are flat and thin.

62. 选择 C。"本"用于书本簿册：一本书、一本集邮册。"册"表示装订好的本子，一本就叫做一册：本套丛书一共十二册。"页"用于指书本中一张纸的一面：第一页。量词"根"不表示与书本有关的东西。

The answer is C. "Běn" is used to modify books or pamphlets, e.g.: yì běn shū, yì běn jíyóucè. "Cè" is used to modify bound books, each one is called "yí cè", e.g.: Běn tào cóngshū yígòng shí'èr cè. "Yè" as a quantifier indicates a page in a book, e.g.: dì-yī yè. "Gēn" cannot be used to indicate things that have connection with books or pamphlets.

63. 选择 A。"双"常表示人或动物左右对称的肢体或器官：一双手、一双眼睛。

The answer is A. "Shuāng" is usually used to modify body parts or organs in pair of humans or animals, e.g.: yì shuāng shǒu, yì shuāng yǎnjīng.

64. 选择 B。"朵"用于花朵和云彩或与它们相像的东西：一朵棉花、一朵水花。

The answer is B. "Duǒ" modifies flowers or clouds or things similar to them, e.g.: yì duǒ miánhuā, yì duǒ shuǐhuā.

65. 选择 C。"束"的用法有二：①用于捆扎在一起的丝条状的、或小片状的东西：一束花；也可用"一把花"，但量词"把"并不强调捆扎，而是指一手抓起的数量，随意性较大。②用于细长的光线等：一束灯光。"袋"用于袋装的东西。"捆"用于随意捆绑在一起的细条状的东西：一捆青菜、一捆书等。

The answer is C. "Shù" as a quantifier can be used in two ways: ① to modify strips or small pieces of things that are bundled together, e.g.: yí shù huā. "Yì bǎ huā" is also correct, but the quantifier "bǎ" does not stress the state of being bundled together, but a random quantity or a handful of something; ② to modify lights, e.g.: yí shù dēngguāng. "Dài" modifies things packed in bags. "Kǔn" as a quantifier indicates thin strips of things randomly bundled together, e.g.: yì kǔn qīngcài, yì kǔn shū.

66. 选择 A。"一生"就是"一辈子"。
The answer is A. "Yìshēng" means throughout one's life.

67. 选择 A。量词"下"用于动作的次数:打一下、敲三下,符合题意。
The answer is A. The usage for "xià" as a quantifier is to indicate the number of times of an action, e.g.: dǎ yí xià, qiāo sān xiù.

68. 选择 B。量词"件"可用于修饰事情、案件、公文等:一件往事,符合题意。"项"用于分项目的事物。"段"用于长条东西分成的若干部分。
The answer is B. "Jiàn" as a quantifier is used to modify things, cases or documents, e.g.: yí jiàn wǎngshì. "Xiàng" is used to modify things that have subentries. "Duàn" indicates parts of longish things being divided.

69. 选择 A。"斤"是重量单位:两斤苹果,符合题意。"尺"是长度单位:一尺布。"点"做量词时,用法有三:①表示少量(可以儿化):一点时间;②用于事项:几点看法;③用于时间:八点钟。"滴"用于滴下的液体的数量。
The answer is A. "Jīn" is a unit of weight, e.g.: liǎngjīn píngguǒ. "Chǐ" is a unit of length, e.g.: yì chǐ bù. "Diǎn" as a quantifier can be used in three ways: ① to indicate a little amount (usually with the suffix 'ér' in spoken language), e.g.: yì diǎn shíjiān; ② to indicate things, e.g.: jǐ diǎn kànfǎ; ③ to indicate time, e.g.: bā diǎn zhōng. "Dī" is used to indicate the number of liquid drops.

70. 选择 B。"亩"是地积单位:三亩地。"片"用于地面和水面时,不表示准确的面积。"件""双"无此用法。
The answer is B. "Mǔ" is a unit of area, e.g.: sān mǔ dì. When "piàn" is used to modify ground and water surface, it does not indicate the exact area. "Jiàn" or "shuāng" does not have this kind of usage.

71. 选择 C。"架"用于有支架或有机械装置的东西:一架飞机、一架钢琴等。"辆"用于车辆计数。
The answer is C. "Jià" as a quantifier modifies things with a stand or mechanical device, e.g.: yí jià fēijī, yí jià gāngqín. "Liàng" is a quantifier for vehicles.

72. 选择 B。名词"刀"借用为量词时,强调用刀进行动作的次数:切一刀。动量词"次"表示动作的次数,如:练习一次。动量词"回"表示动作的次数,多用于口语:参观一回。"阵"做量词时,用法有二:①表示突然发生的事情或动作:一阵风、一阵掌声;②表示事情或动作持续了一段时间:忙一阵、高兴一阵。

The answer is B. When noun "dāo" is used as a quantifier, it emphasizes the number of times of action done by a knife, e.g.: qiē yì dāo. Verb quantifier "cì" indicates the number of times of an action, e.g.: liànxí yí cì. Verb quantifier "huí" indicates the number of times of an action in spoken language, e.g.: cānguān yì huí. "Zhèn" as a quantifier can be used as follows: ① to indicate a sudden action, e.g.: yí zhèn fēng, yí zhèn zhǎngshēng; ② to indicate a matter or an action that lasts for some time, e.g.: máng yí zhèn, gāoxìng yí zhèn.

73. 选择 C。"艘"用于较大的船只:一艘军舰。"辆"用于车辆计数,"架"用于有支架或有机械装置的东西:一架飞机、一架钢琴等。"匹"用法有二:①用于马、驴、骡子等体型较大的动物:一匹马;②用于成卷的布:两匹绸缎。

The answer is C. "Sōu" modifies large ship, e.g.: yì sōu jūnjiàn. "Liàng" is a quantifier for vehicles, "jià" as a quantifier modifies things with a stand or mechanical device, e.g.: yí jià fēijī, yí jià gāngqín. "Pǐ" can be used in two ways: ① to modify large animals such as horses, donkeys or mules and so on, e.g.: yì pǐ mǎ; ② to indicate cloth rolls, e.g.: liǎng pǐ chóuduàn.

74. 选择 A。动量词"回"表示动作的次数,强调动作发生的时间和次数,多用于口语,如:参观一回。"会"和数词"一"搭配使用,可以儿化,表示很短的时间:休息一会儿。"阵""顿"无此用法。

The answer is A. Verb quantifier "huí" indicates the number of times of an action in spoken language, with the emphasis on the time and number of the action, e.g.: cānguān yì huí. When "huì" matches the numeral "one" (usually with the suffix 'ér' in spoken language), it indicates a short time, e.g.: xiūxi yíhuìr. "Zhèn", "dùn" can not be used in such a way.

75. 选择 B。"趟"是动量词,修饰人们来回走动的次数。

The answer is B. "Tàng" is a verb quantifier, indicating the number of times of a round trip.

76. 选择 B。量词"份"可以用于计量思想感情等抽象的事物:一份欣喜。

The answer is B. The quantifier "fèn" can be used to modify something abstract such as thoughts or feelings, e.g.: yí fèn xīnxǐ.

77. 选择 B。"座"用于房屋、桥、山等大型天然风景和人工建筑:一座立交桥、一座大楼等。"所"用于房屋、学校、医院等单位(包括建筑物,企事业机构):一所房子、一所幼儿园。"幢"用于大型楼房,多用于书面语:一幢高楼。"排"用于横排的人和物:一排士兵、一排洁白的牙齿等。

The answer is B. "Zuò" modifies large natural scenes and man-made architectures such as houses, bridges or mountains, e.g.: yí zuò lìjiāoqiáo, yí zuò dàlóu. "Suǒ" as a quantifier modifies nouns such as houses, schools or hospitals (including the buildings or the institutions), e.g.: yì suǒ fángzi, yì suǒ yòu'éryuán. "Zhuàng" modifies large buildings, often in written language, e.g.: yí zhuàng gāolóu. "Pái" indicates people or things in a row, e.g.: yì pái shìbīng, yì pái jiébái de yáchǐ.

78. 选择 B。名词"盆"借用为量词时,表示用盆装的东西:一盆衣服、一盆花。名词"杯"借用为量词时,表示用杯子盛的东西:一杯茶、一杯酒。"捆"用于捆绑在一起的东西:一捆青菜、一捆书等。名词"瓶"借用为量词时,表示用瓶子装的东西:一瓶药、一瓶水等。

The answer is B. When the noun "pén" is used as a quantifier, it indicates things held in a basin, e.g.: yì pén yīfu, yì pén huā. When the noun "bēi" is used as a quantifier, it indicates something held in a cup, e.g.: yì bēi chá, yì bēi jiǔ. "Kǔn" as a quantifier indicates things bundled together, e.g.: yì kǔn qīngcài, yì kǔn shū. When the noun "píng" is used as a quantifier, it indicates objects held in a bottle, e.g.: yí píng yào, yí píng shuǐ.

79. 选择 A。名词"丝"借用为量词时,用于形容极细微的东西,含有夸张之意,表示数量极少。如:一丝春雨,符合题意。

The answer is A. When noun "sī" is used as a quantifier, it can be used to indicate things very thin and tiny, with a sense of exaggeration of an extremely small amount, e.g.: yī sī chūn yǔ.

80. 选择 B。"根"做量词时,用于计量细长的东西,符合题意。

The answer is B. When "gēn" is used as a quantifier, it can be used to modify long and thin things.

81. 选择 C。量词"种"用于表示不同的心情或感觉,或别的抽象事情:一种现象、一种心情等。

The answer is C. "Zhǒng" as a quantifier can be used to modify different moods or feelings or other abstract things, e.g.: yì zhǒng xiànxiàng, yì zhǒng xīnqíng.

82. 选择 B。"包"用于成包的东西:一包饼干、一包糖,符合题意。

The answer is B. "Bāo" indicates things in packets, e.g.: yì bāo bǐnggān, yì bāo táng.

83. 选择 C。集合量词"批",用于大量同时出现或消失的物件或事物:一批物资。"匹"可以用于成卷的布和动物。"面""片"无此用法。

The answer is C. "Pī" is used to modify a large amount of goods that appear or disappear at the same time, e.g.: yì pī wùzī. "Pī" can be used to indicate cloth rolls or animals. "Miàn" and "piàn" cannot be used in such a way.

84. 选择 B。"匹"用于马、驴、骡子等体型较大的动物。"扇"用于门、窗或可以开合的东西：一扇天窗、一扇大门等。"批""个"无此用法。

The answer is B. "Pǐ" can be used to modify large animals such as horses, donkeys or mules and so on. "Shàn" modifies doors, windows or things that can be opened and closed, e.g.: yí shàn tiānchuāng, yí shàn dà mén. "Pǐ" and "gè" cannot be used in such a way.

85. 选择 C。"身"做量词时,用法有三:①指全身衣服:一身西服;②指全身被覆盖,数词只能用"一":一身水;③用于抽象事物,形容数量大:一身债。

The answer is C. "Shēn" as a quantifier can be used in three ways: ① to indicate a dress, yì shēn xīfú; ② to indicate the whole body is covered, and the matching numeral can only be "one", e.g.: yì shēn shuǐ; ③ to indicate abstract things large in amount, e.g.: yì shēn zhài.

86. 选择 D。"家"做量词时,用法有二:①用于计算人家:一百家住户;②用于企事业单位:一家出版社、两家银行,符合题意。

The answer is D. When "jiā" is used as a quantifier, it can be used in two ways: ① to measure the households, e.g.: yìbǎi jiā zhùhù; ② to indicate companies or institutions, e.g.: yì jiā chūbǎn shè, liǎng jiā yínháng.

87. 选择 C。"节"可以表示自然成节的东西:一节藕、一节电池,符合题意。

The answer is C. "Jié" can be used to indicate things with nodes or sections, e.g.: yì jié ǒu, yì jié diànchí.

88. 选择 B。"场"做量词时,可以表示风霜雨雪等自然现象:一场大风、一场暴风雪,符合题意。

The answer is B. "Cháng" as a quantifier can indicate natural phenomena such as wind, rain or snow, e.g.: yì cháng dàfēng, yì cháng bàofēngxuě.

89. 选择 D。"对"是名量词,用于修饰性别、正反、左右等配合成双数的人、动物或事物:一对夫妻、一对耳环等。

The answer is D. "Duì" is a noun quantifier, indicating people, animals or things that are formed in pair because of different gender, different sides, left and right, e.g.: yí duì fūqī, yí duì ěrhuán.

90. 选择 A。"扇"专用于门、窗或可以开合的东西:一扇天窗、一扇大门等。

The answer is A. "Shàn" modifies doors, windows or things that can be opened and closed, e.g.: yí shàn tiānchuāng, yí shàn dàmén.

91. 选择 B。"届"用于定期召开的会议或毕业的班级等:96 届毕业生、下届奥运会。

The answer is B. "Jiè" indicates an scheduled meeting or a graduated class, e.g.: 96 jiè bìyèshēng, xià jiè Àoyùnhuì.

92. 选择 D。量词"套"用于成组的事物,符合题意。"间"用于单间房屋的计数:一间办公室。"件"用于某些较小的个体事物。"节"表示自然成节的东西。

The answer is D. "Tào" as a quantifier can be used to indicate things in a series, e.g.: yì jiān bàngōngshì. "Jiān" indicates the number of rooms. "Jiàn" can be used to modify some individual things. "Jié" can be used to indicate things with nodes or sections.

93. 选择 C。"门"做量词时,用法有三:①用于技术、课程、科学的种类:三门课、一门外语;②指亲属或婚事:一门亲事、一门亲戚;③用于重型武器:一门大炮,符合题意。

The answer is C. When "mén" is used as a quantifier, it can be used in three ways: ① to indicate the types of technology, course or science, e.g.: sān mén kè, yì mén wàiyǔ; ② to indicate the kinship or marriage, e.g.: yì mén qīnshì, yì mén qīnqi; ③ to indicate heavy weapons, e.g.: yì mén dàpào.

94. 选择 D。量词"股"可以用于气体、气味、力气等:一股花香、一股干劲,符合题意。"把"用于表示某些抽象的事物:一把年纪、一把好手。"副"用于指人的相貌或表情:一副愁眉苦脸的样子。"番"表示经历、意义,数词只能用"一":一番好意。

The answer is D. "Gǔ" as a quantifier can be used to modify gas, smell and strength, e.g.: yì gǔ huāxiāng, yì gǔ gànjìn. "Bǎ" can modify some abstract things, e.g.: yì bǎ niánji, yì bǎ hǎoshǒu. "Fù" can be used to modify appearance or expressions, e.g.: yí fù chóuméi—kǔliǎn de yàngzi. "Fān" indicates experience or meaning and the matching numeral can only be "one", e.g.: yì fān hǎoyì.

95. 选择 B。"批"是集合量词,可以用于同时行动、有同一目标的人:一批宇航员、一批志愿者,符合题意。

The answer is B. "Pī" as a classifier can be used to modify people taking actions together or with the same goal, e.g.: yì pī yǔhángyuán, yì pī zhìyuànzhě. It matches the topic.

96. 选择 B。量词"身"指全身被覆盖,但前面的数词只能用"一":一身水。名词"杯"、"筐"、"盆"表示用杯子、筐或盆盛的东西。

The answer is B. "Shēn" as a quantifier can be used to indicate the whole body is covered, and the matching numeral can only be "one", e.g.: yì shēn shuǐ. When the nouns "bēi", "kuāng" and "pén" are used as quantifiers, they indicate things held in a cup, a basket or a basin.

97. 选择 B。"节"表示自然成节的东西：一节藕、一节电池，符合题意。

The answer is B.   "Jié" can be used to indicate things with nodes or sections, e.g.: yì jié ǒu, yì jié diànchí.

98. 选择 C。"遍"强调动作从头到尾的全部过程：听一遍、写一遍。

The answer is C. "Biàn" stresses the whole process of an action from the beginning to the end, e.g.: tīng yí biàn, xiě yí biàn.

99. 选择 D。"阵"表示突然发生的事情或动作：一阵风、一阵掌声，符合题意。"回"表示动作的次数，多用于口语：参观一回。"次"表示动作的次数：练习一次。"顿"用于打骂、劝说、批评的次数。

The answer is D.   "Zhèn" as a quantifier can be used to indicate a sudden action, e.g.: yí zhèn fēng, yí zhèn zhǎngshēng. "Huí" indicates the number of times of an action in spoken language, e.g.: cānguān yì huí. "Cì" indicate the number of times of an action, e.g.: liànxí yí cì. "Dùn" can be used to indicate the number of times of abuse, persuasion and scolding.

100. 选择 B。"篇"专用于小说、文章等：一篇散文、三篇课文。

The answer is B.   "Piān" as a quantifier modifies essays, articles, or novels, e.g.: yì piān sǎnwén, sān piān kèwén.

② 副词 Adverb

● 副词最主要的特点是用在动词或形容词性成分的前面做状语。从语义上看,副词可以分别表示时间、范围、程度、情态方式、语气、频度和否定。
● 学习的时候,要特别注意对意思相近的副词进行辨析,把握它们在意义和用法上的差别。

The most important usage of adverbs is to serve as an adverbial modifier before verbs or adjective components. From semantic perspective, adverbs can indicate time, scope, degree, manner, tone, frequency and negation.

Learners should pay special attention to the adverbs similar in meaning, and grasp their differences in meaning and usage.

考点精讲 Examination Points

1. 本来、原来

本来 běnlái	原来 yuánlái	例句 Examples
形容词,表示原有的。前后情况发生变化,修饰抽象名词,不能构成"的"字结构。 Adjective, indicating something original is changed. It's used to modify abstract nouns, and cannot form the "de" pattern.	形容词,表示原有的。前后情况未发生变化,可修饰抽象名词和具象名词,能构成"的"字结构。 Adjective, indicating something original is not changed. It can be used to modify both abstract and concrete nouns, and can form the "de" pattern.	1. 洗得次数多了,这件衣服已经看不出本来 / 原来的颜色了。 2. 我还住在原来的地方。 3. 我本来 / 原来的专业是医学。 4. 原来的工作人员已经被辞退了。 5. 那份计划是原来的,这是修改过的。
副词,表示原先、先前,既可用于动词或形容词前,又可用于主语前。 Adverb, indicating originally, before. It can be used before verbs, adjectives or the subjects.	副词,表示原先、先前,既可用于动词或形容词前,又可用于主语前。 Adverb, indicating originally, before. It can be used before verbs, adjectives or the subjects.	1. 我本来 / 原来打算暑假回国的。 2. 她本来 / 原来又年轻又漂亮。
表示理所当然。 Indicating something should have been done.	无此用法。 It cannot be used in this way.	今天的事情本来就应该今天做完。

表示赞同别人的观点，用于主语前,后有停顿。 Indicating agreement, used before the subjects and followed by a pause.	无此用法。 It cannot be used in this way.	A：这部电影真有意思! B：本来嘛,这可是一部获奖的片子。
无此用法。 It cannot be used in this way.	表示发现了以前不知道的情况，含有恍然大悟的意思,可用于主语前或后。 Indicating the discovery of something in a sudden that is unknown before, used before or after the subjects.	1. 你原来就是小王。 2. 原来你就是小王。

2. 不、没有

不 bù	没有 méiyǒu	例句 Examples
否定主观意愿。 Indicating the negation of a subjective will.	否定客观叙述。 Indicating the negation of an objective statement.	1. 老王怕热,他不去武汉。（主观意愿) 2. 老王没有去过武汉。（客观陈述)
可以否定过去、现在和未来。 Indicating the negation of the past, present and future.	只否定过去。 Only indicating the negation of the past.	1. 他明天不去开会。（未来) 2. 他昨天没有去开会。（过去)
否定所有的能愿动词。 "Bù" can be used to negate all the modal verbs.	只否定"能(够)""要""敢"等少数能愿动词。 "Méiyǒu" can only be used to negate a few modal verbs like "néng (gòu)", "yào", "gǎn".	1. 你不可以离开这里。 2. 他没有能离开这里。
用在动词前,否定动作本身。 When it is used before verbs, it negates the action itself.	用在动词前,是对已经发生的动作或状态否定。 When it is used before verbs, it negates that an action or a state has happened.	1. 我不看电视。（否定"看") 2. 我没有看电视。（否定"看了")
用在形容词前,对性质的否定。 When it is used before adjectives, it negates the nature of the adjectives.	用在形容词前,是对性质变化的否定。 When it is used before adjectives, it negates the change of the nature of the adjectives.	1. 他身体不好。（否定"好") 2. 她身体没有好。（否定"好了")
否定经常性、习惯性的动作。 It negates regular and habitual actions.	不能否定经常性、习惯性的动作。 It cannot negate regular and habitual actions.	他经常不吃早饭。（经常性动作)

3. 不必、未必、何必

不必 búbì	未必 wèibì	何必 hébì	例句 Examples
表示不需要、用不着，相当于"不用"，但语气较强。 Indicating "need not, not have to", similar to "bú yòng", but is stronger in tone.	表示否定，相当于"不一定、不见得"，语气委婉。 Indicating negation, similar to "bùyídìng, bújiànde", but is more indirect in meaning.	表示"不必"，是反问语气，语气比"不必"重。 Indicating "need not", with the rhetorical tone, and stronger than "búbì".	1. 你打电话告诉他们吧，不必亲自去了。(不用亲自去) 2. 他未必知道这件事情。(不一定知道) 3. 你打电话告诉他们吧，何必亲自去呢？(没必要亲自去，语气重)

4. 不免、难免

不免 bùmiǎn	难免 nánmiǎn	例句 Examples
副词，意思是避免不了。表示某种情况顺理成章地发生 (这种情况不一定是不好的)。 Adverb, meaning unavoidable. It indicates that something happens naturally (which is not necessarily a bad thing).	形容词，意思是很难避免 (不好事情的发生和不好情况的出现)。 Adjective, meaning hard to avoid. (Usually it refers to bad things.)	1. 他第一次出国，难免/不免有点儿想家。 2. 想到这里他不免感到庆幸。
词后不可跟否定句。 It cannot be followed by a negative sentence.	词后可跟否定句。 It can be followed by a negative sentence.	你这么说，他难免不太高兴。
不可用在"是……的"格式中。 It cannot be used in the pattern "shì...de".	可用在"是……的"格式中。 It can be used in the pattern "shì...de".	留学生写错字是难免的。
不可以做谓语。 It cannot serve as the predicate.	可以做谓语。 It can serve as the predicate.	年轻人遇到失恋这件事很难免。
不可以做定语。 It cannot serve as the attribute.	可以做定语。 It can serve as the attribute.	开车上路，发生碰撞是难免的事。

5. 毕竟、到底、究竟

毕竟 bìjìng	到底 dàodǐ	究竟 jiūjìng	例句 Examples
表示对某种原因的强调,用于动词前或"N 毕竟是 N(N 是同一名词)"结构中。 It indicates the emphasis on a certain reason, used before a verb or in the pattern "N bìjìng shì N (N stands for the same noun)".	语义、用法同"毕竟"。 It has the same meaning and usage with "bìjìng".	语义、用法同"毕竟"。 It has the same meaning and usage with "bìjìng".	他毕竟/到底/究竟是你的父亲,你应该尊敬他。
表示终于、最后,多用于转折关系的复句中。 It indicates eventually, finally, often used in transitional complex sentences.	表示经过某种过程以后最终出现的结果,有"终于"的意思。句中多有"了"或其他表示完成的词语。 It indicates the result that finally comes out after some process, meaning "finally". In this case, there are always words like "le" indicating something is finished.	无此用法。 It cannot be used in this way.	1. 虽然我们失败过很多次,但我们毕竟成功了。 2. 经过几年的努力,我们到底成功了。
无此用法。 It cannot be used in this way.	用于疑问句中,要求明确的答复。 When used in a question, it demands a definite answer.	语义、用法同"到底"。 It has the same meaning and usage with "dàodǐ".	你到底/究竟是哪国人?
无此用法。 It cannot be used in this way.	用于有疑问词的非疑问句中。 It can be used in a non-interrogative sentence with interrogative words.	语义、用法同"到底"。 It has the same meaning and usage with "dàodǐ".	谁也不知道他到底/究竟来不来。
无此用法。 It cannot be used in this way.	短语,表示到最后的意思。 When it is used as a phrase, it indicates till the end.	无此用法。 It cannot be used in this way.	无论遇到什么困难,我们都会坚持到底。
无此用法。 It cannot be used in this way.	无此用法。 It cannot be used in this way.	名词,表示事情的原因、经过和结果。 When it is used as a noun, it indicates the reason, course and result of a matter.	发生什么事情啦?大家都想知道个究竟。

6. 才、就

才 cái	就 jiù	例句 Examples
数量短语 + 才 +……，表示时间晚、时间长、数量大或年龄大。 "Numeral phrase + cái + ..." indicates being late or long in time, large number or old age.	就 + 数量短语 +……，表示时间晚、时间长、数量大或年龄大。"就"轻读，名词前常加"光""仅"等副词。 "Jiù + numeral phrase + ..." indicates being late or long in time, large number or old age. In this case "jiù" is unstressed in pronunciation, and adverbs like "guāng" or "jǐn" are often used before the noun.	1. 妹妹七岁才上小学。(说话人认为妹妹上小学的时间晚) 2. 她光裙子就几十条。(说话人认为她的裙子多)
才（+ 动词）+ 数量短语 +……，表示时间早、时间短、数量少或年龄小。 "Cái (+ verb) + numeral phrase + ..." indicates being early or short in time, small number or young age.	数量短语 + 就 +（动词）……，表示时间早、时间短、数量少或年龄小。"就"重读，前有时加"一共"。 "Numeral phrase + jiù + (verb)" indicates being early or short in time, small number or young age. In this case "jiù" is stressed in pronunciation, and sometimes follows "yígòng".	1. 他才有十几本书。(说话人认为他的书少) 2. 妹妹五岁就上学了。(说话人认为妹妹上小学的年龄小)
表示强调，多用于感叹句。 When it indicates an emphasis, it is often used in the exclamatory sentence.	表示强调、肯定的语气。 It indicates an emphasziing and affirmative mood.	1. 他才是好人呢！ 2. 他就是你要找的人。
动 $_1$……+ 才 + 动 $_2$，表示两个动作间隔时间长。 "Verb$_1$ ... + cái + verb$_2$" indicates the long period between two actions.	动 $_1$……+ 就 + 动 $_2$，表示两个动作间隔时间短。 "Verb$_1$... + jiù + Verb$_2$" indicates the short period between two actions.	1. 他看了半天，才明白。 2. 他看了一眼，就明白了。
只有 /（正）因为 / 由于 / 为了……，才…… Zhǐyǒu / (zhèng) yīnwèi / yóuyú/wèile..., cái...	只要 / 如果 / 既然……，就…… Zhǐyào/rúguǒ/jìrán..., jiù...	1. 正因为他每天坚持锻炼身体，他的身体才这样好。 2. 既然能买到今天的火车票，我今天就走。

7. 差点儿、几乎

差点儿 chàdiǎnr	几乎 jīhū	例句 Examples
表示希望实现的事情将要实现但最终没有实现，有惋惜的语气。只用于动词的肯定形式前。 It means something hoped for is about to come true but finally fails. In this case, it can only be used before the positive form of verbs, with a sense of pity.	语义、用法同"差点儿"，多用于书面语。 It has the same meaning and usage with "chàdiǎnr", but often used in written form.	只晚了几分钟，我们差点儿 / 几乎就赶上那辆车了。(没赶上)

表示希望实现的事情将要不能实现但最终还是实现了, 有庆幸的语气。只用于动词的否定形式前。 It means something hoped for may fail but finally come true. In this case, it can only be used before the negative form of verbs, with a tone of feeling lucky.	语义、用法同"差点儿", 多用于书面语。 It has the same meaning and usage with "chàdiǎnr", but often used in written form.	多亏你提醒, 我们差点儿/几乎没赶上那辆车。(赶上了)
表示不希望实现的事情将要实现但最终没有实现, 有庆幸的语气。用于动词前, 肯定形式和否定形式语义相同。 It means something unwanted is going to come true but finally fails. In this case, it can be used both before the negative or positive form of verbs, with a tone of feeling lucky.	语义、用法同"差点儿", 多用于书面语。 It has the same meaning and usage with "chàdiǎnr", but often used in written form.	我被绊了一下, 差点儿/几乎(没)摔倒。(没摔倒)
无此用法。 It cannot be used in this way.	表示接近某个数量、范围或程度。句中常带有表示数量、范围的词语, 有时含有夸张的含义。 It indicates closeness to a number, range or degree. In this case, it is used in sentences with words meaning number or range, with a sense of exaggeration.	1. 雨几乎下了一天。 2. 他最近很忙, 几乎一点儿休息时间都没有。

8. 常常、往往

常常 chángcháng	往往 wǎngwǎng	例句 Examples
指动作、行为的多次重复, 不一定有规律性, 可以用于主观意愿。 It indicates the repetition of an action or a behavior, with or without rules. It can indicate a subjective intention.	对到目前为止出现的情况或对以往经验的总结, 带有规律性, 不用于主观意愿。 It indicates the summary of current situation or past experience, usually with certain rules. It cannot indicate a subjective intention.	1. 我常常去那家餐馆吃饭。 2. 酒后开车往往造成交通事故。
无需在句中指明与动作有关的情况、条件或结果。 It's not necessary to point out the situation, condition or result concerning the action.	一般在句中要指明与动作有关的情况、条件或结果。 It's usually necessary to point out the situation, condition or result concerning the action.	1. 我常常去书店。 2. 我往往和她一起去书店。 3. 我往往去书店。(×)

可用于表示未来。 It can be used to indicate the future.	只可用于表示过去。 It can only be used to indicate past.	1．我希望你常常来玩。 2．他往往一个人来玩。
否定式为"不常"。 The negative form is "bù cháng" (not often).	一般之前不受否定副词的修饰。 Usually it cannot be modified by a negative adverb.	1．我们不常见面。 2．我们不往往见面。（×）

9. 从来、始终

从来 cónglái	始终 shǐzhōng	例句 Examples
表示从过去到现在一直都是如此,含有强调语气。 It indicates that something is always like this from the past until now, entailing a sense of emphasis.	表示某种情况或状态从开始到最后一直如此,没有任何变化。 It indicates that some situation or condition is always like this from the beginning to the end, without any change.	1．他从来不迟到。 2．他在会上始终不说话。
常用于否定句中,当否定副词是"没(有)"时,单音节动词、形容词后常带"过",双音节动词、形容词可带可不带。 It is often used in negative sentences. When the negative adverb is "méi (yǒu)", the monosyllabic verb or adjective is always followed by "guò", which is not necessary for disyllabic verbs or adjectives.	没有此用法。 It cannot be used in this way.	1．他从来没认真过。（从过去到现在一直不认真） 2．他从来没这么认真过。（现在认真的程度比以前任何时候都强）
少用于肯定句中，多修饰动词短语、形容词短语或小句,一般不修饰单个动词、形容词,常和"就""都"搭配使用,以加强语气。 It is seldomly used in positive sentences. It often modifies verbal phrases, adjective phrases or clauses instead of a single verb or adjective. It often matches "jiù" or "dōu" to reinforce the tone.	没有此用法。 It cannot be used in this way.	1．他们在生活中从来都是互相关心、互相帮助。 2．我们的老板从来就是一个人说了算,很少昕别人的意见。

10. 倒、反而

倒 dào	反而 fǎn'ér	例句 Examples
表示与预料的或与一般情理相反，出乎意料。语气比"反而"轻。 It indicates something unexpected. It is weaker in tone than "fǎn'ér".	表示不但没有按照常理进行，还走向了相反的方向，并且程度更深。有时构成"不仅没有／不仅不……反而……"的格式。 It indicates something is not only unexpected, but goes to the contrary with a deeper degree. It is sometimes used in the pattern "bùjǐn méiyǒu/bùjǐn bù... fǎn'ér...".	1. 雨没停，倒越下越大了。 2. 雨不仅没停，反而越下越大了。
表示事情不是那样，含有反说的语气。 It can indicate something is not as said, meaning something is on the contrary.	无此用法。 It cannot be used in this way.	你说得倒轻松，你来干呀！
动词／形容词＋倒＋动词／形容词，表示转折或让步。 The pattern "verb/adjective + dào + verb/adjective" indicates a transition or concession.	无此用法。 It cannot be used in this way.	1. 我跟他认识倒认识，就是不太熟。 2. 这件衣服的颜色好倒好，就是贵了点儿。
表示催促或追问，有不耐烦的语气。 It can indicate to urge or question, with a sense of impatience.	无此用法。 It cannot be used in this way.	你倒快点儿说话呀！

11. 多亏、幸亏

多亏 duōkuī	幸亏 xìngkuī	例句 Examples
表示由于某种有利条件或某人的帮助，避免了某种不好的结果或得到了某种好处，多用于主语前。 It indicates that due to some favorable conditions or somebody's help, certain bad result is avoided or something good happens. In this case, it is often used before the subject.	表示由于某种有利条件或某人的帮助，避免了某种不好的结果，多用于主语前。 It indicates that due to some favorable conditions or somebody's help, certain bad result is avoided. In this case, it is often used before the subject.	多亏／幸亏我带了身份证，我才拿到了挂号信。
多亏＋名词／代词＋了，…… It can be used in the pattern "duōkuī + noun/pronoun + le...".	无此用法。 It cannot be used in this way.	多亏你了，要不然我就来不及了。

12. 分明、明明

分明 fēnmíng	明明 míngmíng	例句 Examples
表示确实如此,常和反问句一起使用。为强调真实性,多用于复句的前一分句中,在主语前后均可。 It is often used with a rhetorical question, indicating something is true. In order to emphasize the authenticity, it is usually used in the first clause of a complex sentence, before or after the subject.	同"分明"。更加口语化。 It is similar to "fēnmíng", but is more colloquial.	你分明／明明看见了,可为什么说没看见呢?
形容词,表示清楚。 Adjective, meaning clear.	无此用法。 It cannot be used in this way.	这篇论文条理分明,写得很好。

13. 赶紧、赶快、赶忙、连忙

赶紧 gǎnjǐn	赶快 gǎnkuài	赶忙 gǎnmáng	连忙 liánmáng	例句 Examples
用于陈述句中,表示动作、行为迅速或急促。 When it is used in declarative sentences, it indicates the rapidity of an action or a behavior.	抓紧时机,加快速度。同"赶紧"。但更偏重于强调动作的快速、尽早。 It indicates to seize the chance and speed up, similar to "gǎnjǐn", but it emphasizes more on the high speed and promptness of an action.	表示抓紧时间急于做某事。 It indicates to take the time to do something urgently.	表示动作、行为紧接着前面的情况发生,更强调前后动作的连续关系。 It indicates some action or behavior follows the former action closely; it emphasizes the continual relationship between the actions.	外面突然刮起了大风,我赶紧／赶快／赶忙／连忙关上了窗户。
用于祈使句中,表示催促、命令、祈求或希望。含有"抓紧时间""尽快"的意思,用于还未发生的情况。 When it is used in imperative sentences, it indicates to urge, order, plead or hope. It is used to indicate actions not yet taken, containing the meaning of "take the time" and "do something as soon as possible".	可用于祈使句中,常用于还未发生的情况。 It can be used in imperative sentences, indicating actions not yet taken.	不能用于祈使句中,不能用于还未发生的情况。 It cannot be used in imperative sentences, and cannot indicate actions not yet taken.	不能用于祈使句中,不能用于还未发生的情况。 It cannot be used in imperative sentences, and cannot indicate actions not yet taken.	都 12 点了,咱们赶紧／赶快走吧。

14. 刚、刚刚、刚才

刚 gāng	刚刚 gānggāng	刚才 gāngcái	例句 Examples
副词，表示动作、行为或情况不久前发生。只能修饰动词和动词性短语。 Adverb, indicating some action or behavior just happened. It can only modify verbs or verbal phrases.	副词，表示动作、行为或情况不久前发生，但比"刚"更强调时间间隔的短促。只能修饰动词和动词性短语。 Adverb, indicating some action or behavior just happened, but emphasizing the briefness in time. It can only modify verbs or verbal phrases.	时间名词，可修饰名词做定语，也可做时间状语。 A noun indicating time. It can serve as an attribute for nouns as well as a time adverbial.	1. 这是我不久前刚／刚刚学会的一个词。 2. 刚才的事是我不对。 3. 你为什么刚才不说？
既可以和现在发生联系，也可以和过去的某一时刻发生联系。 It can connect with either present or past time.	同"刚"。 Same as "gāng".	只和现在发生联系。 It can only connect with present time.	1. 她刚／刚刚下火车。 2. 那一年，我刚／刚刚高中毕业就工作了。 3. 她刚才不太高兴，现在已经没事了。
说话人主观认为发生完成某个动作或事情的时间很短，但实际上并不一定很短。 The speaker subjectively thinks the referred action or thing was done a short time ago, but in fact it may not be short.	同"刚"。 Same as "gāng".	无此用法。 It cannot be used in this way.	1. 我去年刚／刚刚写了一本关于这个问题的书。 2. 我去年刚才写了一本关于这个问题的书。（×）
词后不能带否定词。 It cannot be followed by a negative word.	词后可带否定词。 It can be followed by a negative word.	词后可带否定词。 It can be followed by a negative word.	1. 她刚才／刚刚不说话是因为还在生气。 2. 她刚不说话是因为还在生气。（×）
词后可直接加数量短语。表示勉强达到，强调数量少，有"只""才"的意思。 It can be followed by a numeral phrase immediately, indicating a small number just reaching a certain level, similar to "zhǐ, cái".	词后可直接加数量短语。表示"正好""刚好"的意思。 It can be followed by a numeral phrase directly, indicating "zhènghǎo, gānghǎo".	无此用法。 It cannot be used in this way.	1. 我刚十八岁。 2. 我刚刚十八岁。 3. 我刚才十八岁。（×）

15. 果然、竟然、居然

果然 guǒrán	竟然 jìngrán	居然 jūrán	例句 Examples
表示事实与所说或所料的情况一样。 It indicates the fact is the same as said or expected.	表示出乎意料。 It indicates the fact is unexpected.	表示出乎意料,超出常理。多指不可能发生或不该发生的事情发生了,不容易做到的事做到了。 It indicates the fact is unexpected, and beyond common expectation. It usually refers that something impossible has happened or something difficult to do has been done.	1. 吃了药,他的病果然好了。 2. 没吃药,他的病竟然/居然好了。

16. 好像、似乎

好像 hǎoxiàng	似乎 sìhū	例句 Examples
表示说话人不十分有把握的想法或看法。有时可表示商量、劝告的语气。 It indicates the speaker is not very sure about what he says. It can also contain a tone of negotiation or persuasion.	同"好像"。多用于书面语。 It has the same usage with "hǎoxiàng", but is more often used in written language.	1. 听他的口音,好像/似乎是上海人。 2. 你决定以前好像/似乎该和父母商量一下。
用于比喻,有"仿佛、好似"的意思,常与"似的、一样"搭配使用。 When it is used in a metaphor, it has the same meaning with "fǎngfú, hǎosì", and often matches "shìde, yíyàng".	无此用法。 It cannot be used in this way.	她对我好像妈妈一样。

17. 突然、忽然

突然 tūrán	忽然 hūrán	例句 Examples
副词,表示情况发生得很快,而且出乎人们的意料。 Adverb, indicating something happens suddenly and beyond expectation.	同"突然"。 The same as "tūrán".	刚才还是大晴天,怎么突然/忽然下起雨来了。
形容词,可做定语,可接受程度副词的修饰。 Adjective. It can serve as an attribute, and can be modified by degree adverbs.	无此用法。 It cannot be used in this way.	1. 这件事发生得太突然了。 2. 面对突然事件,一定要沉着、冷静。

18. 千万、万万、万一

千万 qiānwàn	万万 wànwàn	万一 wànyī	例句 Examples
表示一定要……，用于祈使句，常和"要""不能""别"搭配使用。重叠使用后语气更强。 When it is used in imperative sentences, it usually matches "yào", "bù néng", "bié", indicating "must". Its reduplication form has a stronger tone.	表示劝阻、命令，含有一种极端强调的语气。用在否定形式前。 It is used before a negative statement, indicating dissuasion or order, containing a strong sense of emphasis.	表示假设的情况发生的可能性很小，多用于说话人不希望发生的事情。 It is often used to indicate a supposition is not likely to happen, and the speaker doesn't wish it to happen.	1. 你一个人在外地，千万要保重身体啊！ 2. 我万万没想到，他竟然这么快就去世了。 3. 万一时间来不及了，你就打的去吧。

19. 太、挺、真

太 tài	挺 tǐng	真 zhēn	例句 Examples
太＋形容词＋（了），带有感叹的语气。 The pattern "tài + adjective + (le)" has a tone of exclamation.	挺＋形容词＋（的），多用于口语，表示程度高。 The pattern "tǐng + adjective + (de)" is often used in spoken language, indicating a high degree.	真＋形容词，后一般不再修饰名词。表示程度高，含有一定的感情色彩。 The pattern "zhēn + adjective" is usually not followed by nouns; it indicates a high degree, usually in an emotional tone.	1. 这件衣服太肥了，我穿着不合适。 2. 这件衣服挺合适的。 3. 这件衣服真漂亮。
无此用法。 It cannot be used in this way.	无此用法。 It cannot be used in this way.	表示肯定客观情况的真实性，多修饰动词性成分。 It can be used to emphasize the authenticity of the objective situation, usually modifies verbal components.	我今天真不舒服，没骗你们。

20. 特别、尤其

特别 tèbié	尤其 yóuqí	例句 Examples
表示程度极高,有"非常"的意思。 It indicates a high degree, meaning "fēicháng".	表示程度极高,含有比较之意。 It indicates a high degree, with a sense of comparison.	1. 这里的物价特别高。 2. 这里的物价尤其高。(比其他地方的物价还高。)
表示专门为某一目的做某事,有"特地"的意思。 It indicates something is done for a certain purpose, meaning "tèdì".	无此用法。 It cannot be used in this way.	明天我就要回国了,今天特别来向你告别。
几件事或几个事物进行比较,指出突出的一个,常和"是"一起用。 It modifies the special one as compared with several things, usually matches "shì".	同"特别"。 The same with "tèbié".	他很喜欢运动,尤其 / 特别是游泳。
形容词,表示和别的不一样。 Adjective, indicating being different from others.	无此用法。 It cannot be used in this way.	你今天的发型很特别。

21. 偷偷、悄悄

偷偷 tōutōu	悄悄 qiāoqiāo	例句 Examples
强调怕被别人发现,秘密的程度比"悄悄"高,有时带有一定的贬义。 It emphasizes doing something secretly, and being afraid of being seen. It has a stronger sense than "qiāoqiāo" and sometimes has a derogatory sense.	强调不出声音,不引起别人的注意。 It emphasizes doing something without making a noise, so as not to arouse other's attention.	1. 看到大家都被骗了,他躲在房间偷偷地笑了。 2. 趁大家没有注意他,他一个人悄悄溜出了会场。

22. 一点儿、有点儿

一点儿 yìdiǎnr	有点儿 yǒudiǎnr	例句 Examples
不定量词,形容词 / 动词＋一点儿,表示数量少。 When it serves as an indefinite quantifier, it is usually used in the pattern "adjective/verb + yìdiǎnr", which means small in amount.	副词,有点儿＋形容词 / 动词,表示程度不高,多用于不如意的事。 Adverb. When it is used in the pattern "yǒudiǎnr + adjective/verb", it indicates something low in degree, usually something unpleasant.	1. 这次考试准备的时间短了一点儿。 2. 我们有点儿累了。

一点儿＋名词,相当于"一些"。 "Yìdiǎnr + noun" equals to "yìxiē" (some).	有点儿＋名词,此处的"有点儿"不是副词,而是"有＋一点儿"(动词＋量词)。 The "yǒudiǎnr" in the pattern "yǒudiǎnr + noun" is not an adverb, but the compound of "yǒu + yìdiǎnr" (verb + quantifier).	1. 我在地上洒了一点儿水。 2. 地上有点儿水。
一点儿＋(也／都)＋不／没＋动词,表示强调否定。 "Yìdiǎnr + (yě/dōu) + bù/méi + verb" emphasizes the negation of an action.	有点儿＋不＋形容词／动词,表示"不＋形容词／动词"的程度不高。 "Yǒudiǎnr + bù + adjective/verb" indicates the degree of "bù + adjective/verb" is not high.	1. 我一点儿也没听说过这个消息。 2. 他有点儿不喜欢这本小说。

23. 一直、总是

一直 yìzhí	总是 zǒngshì	例句 Examples
表示在一定的时间内,某种动作、行为持续进行没有间断,或情况、状态持续不变。有时"一直"的前后有"从""到"等词,表示时间的起止点。 It indicates some action or behavior continues without interruption. Sometimes "yìzhí" is used between "cóng" and "dào", which indicates the beginning and ending point of a period.	表示一直或经常如此,几乎没有例外。 It indicates something is always like that and almost without exception.	1. 这几年,我一直／总是想养小动物,只是一直／总是没有时间。(想法没有间断) 2. 奶奶总是咳嗽,而且越来越厉害。(经常)
强调所指的范围,常用在"到"或"动词＋到"的前面。 When it is used before "dào" or "verb + dào", it emphasizes the range referred to.	无此用法。 It cannot be used in this way.	买票的人太多了,从售票口一直排到大厅外。
表示动作、行为进行的方向不改变。 It indicates that the direction of an action or a behavior does not change.	无此用法。 It cannot be used in this way.	一直向前走,见到红绿灯右拐就到了。
无此用法。 It cannot be used in this way.	相当于"毕竟"。 Similar to "bìjìng".	和成年人相比,孩子总是力气小一些。

24. 只好、不得不

只好 zhǐhǎo	不得不 bùdébù	例句 Examples
表示没有其他选择,只能如此。所做的事并不是人们想做的。后带肯定式、否定式均可。 It indicates there are no other choices available, something unwanted has to be done. It can be followed either by a positive or negative phrase.	表示没有其他选择,只能如此。所做的事并不是人们想做的。后只能带肯定式。 It indicates there are no other choices available, something unwanted has to be done. It can only be followed by a positive phrase.	1. 外面的雨很大,孩子们只好不去踢球了。 2. 外面的雨很大,孩子们不得不留在家里。

强化练习 Exercises

■ 1—30 题,在每一个句子下面都有一个指定的词语,句中 ABCD 是供选择的四个不同位置,请判断这一词语放在句中哪个位置上恰当。

Please find the proper position out of the four choices of A, B, C, and D for the word below each sentence.

1. 他们 A 虽然 B 吃住在一起,可是 C 算不上知心的 D 朋友。
常常

2. 凡是自己 A 能做好 B 的事情,C 不要 D 麻烦别人。
就

3. A 把这项工作 B 交给谁呢? C 他 D 在认真地考虑着人选。
到底

4. A 我在教室里找不到你 B,C 原来 D 你上图书馆了。
怪不得

5. 这样的环境 A 我实在 B 受不了了,我 C 想 D 在这里住下去了。
不

6. 我 A 也 B 你 C 这么一个亲人了,D 我怎么会不惦记你呢?
就

7. 妈妈 A 把电视打开,还 B 没来得及看,就 C 被朋友 D 叫走了。
刚刚

8. A 读研究生时,我 B 想一个问题,我 C 读这么多书到底是 D 为了什么?
经常

9. 你的朋友 A 漂亮 B 是很漂亮,就 C 是懒得 D 不得了。
倒

10. 大家心里 A 都明白是怎么回事,B 他 C 一个人 D 还蒙在鼓里。
就

11. 它趴 A 在草坪上一动也 B 不动,C 没有这么 D 老实过。
从来

12. 外出旅游的弟弟 A 两个星期 B 没来电话了,妈妈真是 C 着急了 D。
有点儿

13. 别的体育项目我 A 都不喜欢，B 我 C 酷爱散步 D 这一项活动。
        就

14. 大家 A 都不好意思 B 发表意见，我就 C 先说说 D 自己的看法了。
        不得不

15. 她的消费档次 A 很高，她 B 不会 C 买这种 D 廉价的化妆品呢。
        才

16. 《红楼梦》我 A 读过两遍，B 有可能的话，C 想再 D 读一遍。
        才

17. 烫伤病人 A 吃鱼，B 不但不会引起发炎，C 能增加营养，D 促进愈合。
        反而

18. 你也觉得奇怪 A 不是？这是我们家 B 多年的习惯 C，夏天 D 要关窗户。
        反而

19. 爸爸是个外科医生，他 A 工作 B 很忙，C 一点儿娱乐、锻炼的 D 时间都没有。
        几乎

20. 母亲节，我想 A 送妈妈一套高级化妆品，来 B 到柜台前 C 犹豫 D 起来了。
        竟然

21. 为了 A 一张球票，B 兄弟俩 C 大打出手 D 起来。
        竟然

22. 我们一直 A 在客厅 B 看电视，C 没有 D 听见你们的敲门声。
        竟然

23. 朋友 A 精心挑选了一束鲜花 B 送给他，他 C 不 D 喜欢。
        偏偏

24. 我 A 不喜欢 B 猫狗，他 C 送给我 D 一对波斯猫。
        偏偏

25. 妹妹 A 不听妈妈的劝告，B 要一个人 C 骑自行车 D 周游世界。
        偏

26. 我 A 喜欢一个人生活，B 可是父母 C 不让我 C 搬出去。
        偏

27. 他 A 十分 B 尊重、孝顺父母，今天怎么会 C 和父母 D 吵起来了呢？
        向来

28. 远郊区 A 环境 B 很好，C 就是交通 D 太不方便了。
        倒

29. 她 A 特别 B 喜欢郊游,今天怎么 C 竟把自己关在屋子里 D 不参加郊游活动了呢?
    向来

30. A 分别了四十年的 B 小学同学,今天见了面 C,我还真 D 认不出来了。
    有点儿

■ 31—100 题,每个句子中有一个或两个空,请在 ABCD 四个答案中选择唯一恰当的一个。
  Please choose the correct answer for each blank from the four choices of A, B, C, and D.

31. 他一直不发言,大家谁也不知道他 _____ 是什么态度。
    A. 终于   B. 究竟   C. 于是   D. 曾经

32. 他们在工作中配合得很默契,多年来 _____ 没有出现过差错。
    A. 常常   B. 往往   C. 经常   D. 从来

33. 为了供弟弟妹妹上大学,我 _____ 退学,外出打工。
    A. 差点儿   B. 好容易   C. 不得不   D. 有点儿

34. 我盼望着妈妈 _____ 从国外回来,我们全家就可以过一个团圆年了。
    A. 赶快   B. 连忙   C. 急忙   D. 将要

35. 星期天,他 _____ 去北海玩儿了,却说自己一天都在家,没出门。
    A. 到底   B. 偏偏   C. 明明   D. 往往

36. 我 _____ 没有想到,养育了我二十多年的妈妈,竟不是我的亲生母亲。
    A. 千万   B. 万万   C. 万一   D. 万分

37. 他在发烧,_____ 他今天没有精神。
    A. 还是   B. 难怪   C. 明明   D. 连忙

38. 这两本书,你 _____ 要哪一本呢?
    A. 到底   B. 毕竟   C. 马上   D. 顿时

39. 这件衣服样子是有点儿过时了,但它 _____ 是妈妈亲手一针一线做出来的。
    A. 毕竟   B. 只好   C. 及时   D. 尽量

40. 李工程师的妈妈病 _____ 很厉害,他 _____ 请假回国去看看。
    A. 得……不得不……   B. 地……说不定……
    C. 的……不由得……   D. 了……差点儿……

41. 教室里全部安装了"探头",但 _____ 能解决考试作弊的问题。
    A. 未免   B. 未必   C. 不免   D. 免不得

42. 年轻时,他 _____ 学过三种外语,因为多年不用,现在 _____ 都忘光了。
    A. 曾经……差不多……   B. 已经……差不多……
    C. 曾经……差点儿……   D. 其实……好容易……

43. _____ 发生了什么事, _____ 你吓成这样?
    A. 到底……为……   B. 到底……把……
    C. 究竟……被……   D. 究竟……替……

44. _____ 救护船的到来, 我们才脱离了危险。
    A. 反正 B. 多亏 C. 只有 D. 即使

45. 别看他年纪小, _____ 我们做到的, 他都做到了。
    A. 将来 B. 已经 C. 凡是 D. 马上

46. _____ 参观过故宫的人, 无不赞叹中国古代劳动人民的智慧。
    A. 也许 B. 只好 C. 凡是 D. 永远

47. 擦地时, 我一不小心, 墩布碰了妹妹的脚, 我 _____ 说了声" _____ 对不起"。
    A. 赶紧……再三……   B. 赶快……实在……
    C. 赶忙……照样……   D. 连忙……首先……

48. 妈妈一进门, 儿子就 _____ 接过妈妈的提包, 递过拖鞋。
    A. 常常 B. 一直 C. 赶忙 D. 一定

49. 妈妈说 _____ 吵了, 女儿 _____ 把音响的声音调小了。
    A. 太……赶忙……   B. 真……赶忙……
    C. 很……连忙……   D. 怪……赶紧……

50. 大夫 _____ 给她扎过针灸, 她的胃痛 _____ 减轻了, 中国的银针真神啊!
    A. 刚……就……   B. 刚刚……才……
    C. 刚才……还……   D. 已经……才……

51. 他 _____ 就不懂外语, 怎么能看懂这些外文资料呢?
    A. 往往 B. 本来 C. 常常 D. 哪怕

52. 我把电话号码记错了, _____ 总打不通呢。
    A. 恨不得 B. 怪不得 C. 由不得 D. 不一定

53. 我忘了吃降压药, _____ 头这么晕呢。
    A. 不见得 B. 说不上 C. 怪不得 D. 尽可能

54. _____ 我们天天见面, 原来你也搬到这楼里来了。
    A. 虽然说 B. 眼看着 C. 怪不得 D. 好容易

55. 今天是教师节, _____ 学生们都给老师送鲜花和贺卡呢。
    A. 怪不得 B. 特别是 C. 不至于 D. 莫不是

56. 妈妈 _____ 把我们姐弟四个培养成人, 我们一定要好好孝顺她。
    A. 怪不得 B. 好容易 C. 差点儿 D. 恨不得

57. 她的情绪 _____ 平静 _____ , 你们千万别再刺激她了。

A．好容易……下来……　　　B．一会儿……回来……
C．说不定……起来……　　　D．好不容易……过来……

58．这两天,她总是一个人默默地坐在桌前发呆,_____ 有什么心事似的。
　　A．不料　B．只好　C．必须　D．好像

59．李航连续工作了三天三夜都没合眼,_____ 不知困倦似的。
　　A．好像　B．正在　C．马上　D．永远

60．三岁的刘源 _____ 把京剧"朔风吹"唱得如此字正腔圆,真让人赞叹不已!
　　A．曾经　B．竟然　C．所以　D．已经

61．我 _____ 想起今天下午儿子学校开家长会,我急忙请了假前往学校。
　　A．常常　B．往往　C．忽然　D．千万

62．这种情况发生得太 _____ 了,我一点儿思想准备都没有。
　　A．马上　B．突然　C．立刻　D．忽然

63．茫茫沙漠,荒无人烟,_____ 找不到一点儿水源。
　　A．地道　B．偏偏　C．几乎　D．明明

64．你怎么这样粗暴地对待自己的同学,_____ 太没有教养了。
　　A．仿佛　B．简直　C．几乎　D．偏偏

65．通过不懈的努力,刘阳 _____ 考上了梦寐以求的清华大学。
　　A．究竟　B．到底　C．将要　D．亲自

66．他昨天上了白班又加了一个夜班,_____ 显得很疲惫。
　　A．大约　B．幸好　C．难怪　D．有点儿

67．我自己认识路,你就 _____ 陪我去了。
　　A．应该　B．不必　C．象征　D．何必

68．妈妈一向和蔼可亲,今天 _____ 发这么大的脾气,这 _____ 是我们没想到的。
　　A．简直……再……　　　B．竟然……倒……
　　C．尽管……极……　　　D．曾经……好……

69．谢谢大夫,奶奶的病 _____ 这么快 _____ 治好了,医术真高!
　　A．竟然……才……　　　B．竟然……就……
　　C．究竟……仍……　　　D．简直……再……

70．下了楼 _____ 想起忘拿车钥匙了,_____ 上楼去取。
　　A．就……忽然……　　　B．才……连忙……
　　C．又……顺便……　　　D．乃……连忙……

71．这 _____ 是野草,你为什么坚持说它是麦苗呢?
　　A．明确　B．是否　C．明明　D．明白

72. 电视的图像已经很 _____ 了，你不用再调了。
    A. 清楚　B. 的确　C. 明明　D. 显然

73. 我就是想不通，我 _____ 有什么错？
    A. 难道　B. 居然　C. 究竟　D. 毕竟

74. 从五十年代到现在你一直居住在北京，居然不知"豆汁"为何物，_____ 不能让人相信。
    A. 难道　B. 曾经　C. 简直　D. 明明

75. 这是我们两个人之间的秘密，你 _____ 不能告诉别人。
    A. 显然　B. 千万　C. 万万　D. 明明

76. 前进的道路上尽管困难重重，他们 _____ 没有后退。
    A. 显然　B. 但是　C. 始终　D. 到底

77. 桑拿天 _____ 持续了半个月。
    A. 分别　B. 始终　C. 一直　D. 赶紧

78. 看你很眼熟，我们 _____ 在哪儿见过面。
    A. 一直　B. 似乎　C. 常常　D. 突然

79. 你这件上衣 _____ 漂亮，如果 _____ 配上一条白色的裤子，就更好看了。
    A. 特别……又……　　B. 十分……才……
    C. 特别……再……　　D. 尤其……还……

80. 大家 _____ 没有想到他走得这么突然。
    A. 一定　B. 万一　C. 万万　D. 千万

81. 你对当地的情况不太熟悉，_____ 遇到什么困难，可以找我的朋友帮助解决。
    A. 万一　B. 万万　C. 万分　D. 千万

82. 我们 _____ 忽略了身边的母爱，就因为她如同一杯白开水，在伸手可及的位置可以任意取用。
    A. 本来　B. 特别　C. 曾经　D. 往往

83. 夏季炎热，人们 _____ 喜食冰镇食品，如：冰棍、冰镇啤酒、冰镇西瓜等。其实，冰镇食品极易伤害人们的脾胃。
    A. 已经　B. 立即　C. 往往　D. 刚才

84. 出门时，_____ 带了雨具，_____ 没被突然降临的大雨淋着。
    A. 幸亏……却……　　B. 幸亏……好……
    C. 幸亏……才……　　D. 幸亏……就……

85. 这件事，你 _____ 不知道，_____ 不愿意说。
    A. 必须……到底……　　B. 未必……只是……
    C. 一定……只好……　　D. 反正……更加……

86. 他 _____ 说话算话,只要是他答应了的事情,一定能做到,你就放心吧。
    A．向来　B．继续　C．不时　D．马上

87. 她的体质太差了,_____ 一不注意就感冒。
    A．立刻　B．刚才　C．往往　D．已经

88. 天 _____ 下雨,_____ 我们带了雨具。
    A．赶紧……幸好……　　B．突然……幸亏……
    C．急忙……幸亏……　　D．幸亏……赶快……

89. 他学习非常好,门门优秀,_____ 是外语,每次考试都是第一。
    A．由于　B．尤其　C．始终　D．果然

90. 她 _____ 困了,让她先睡 _____ ,精神好了再学习,效率更高,磨刀不误砍柴工。
    A．有时候……一会儿……　B．有点儿……一会儿……
    C．差点儿……一口气……　D．有一些……一下子……

91. 学校八点 _____ 上课了,你现在还没出家门,是不是 _____ 晚了?
    A．就……好点儿……　　B．就……差点儿……
    C．就……一点儿……　　D．就……有点儿……

92. 你们一见面就聊得这么投机,_____ 你们几年前就认识了。
    A．原来　B．本来　C．经常　D．时常

93. _____ 两页台词,三天了你还没背下来。
    A．总体　B．总是　C．总数　D．总共

94. 每个人都需要感情的交流,_____ 是老年人,他们喜欢热闹,害怕孤独。
    A．原来　B．难怪　C．特别　D．常常

95. 我本想去李雨家,没想到她 _____ 先来我家了。
    A．就　B．也　C．倒　D．才

96. 香港回归十周年的纪念邮票发行了,我好不容易 _____ 买到一本。
    A．就　B．才　C．还　D．仍

97. 小李和小刘这两天在闹别扭,不知为什么,老师 _____ 让他们俩主持这场晚会。
    A．明明　B．万万　C．常常　D．偏偏

98. 这部电视剧的内容很好,只是节奏 _____ 太慢了点儿。
    A．难怪　B．未免　C．难免　D．未必

99. 小学同学聚会,分别四十年,今日一见,我们 _____ 认不出对方了。
    A．到底　B．简直　C．一直　D．马上

100. 老刘退休后身体 _____ 不好,自从参加了老年合唱团,不但精神好了,身体也一天比一天好。
    A．一直　B．曾经　C．更加　D．果然

Adverb

答疑解惑 Answers and Explanations

1. 选择 B。"常常"指动作、行为的多次重复，用于动词前。

The answer is B. "Chángcháng" indicates repetitive actions or behaviors; it is used before verbs.

2. 选择 C。"凡是……就……"是一个固定结构，"就"放在后一小句前。

The answer is C. "Fánshì... jiù..." is a fixed pattern; "jiù" is used before the second clause.

3. 选择 A。"到底"用于疑问句中，表示要求明确的答复，而且它要放在"把"引导的介词短语的前面。

The answer is A. When "dàodǐ" is used in an interrogative sentence, it requires a definite answer, and it should be put before the prepositional phrase led by "bǎ".

4. 选择 A。"怪不得"表示明白了原因后，不再觉得奇怪。这句话的意思是：因为"你去图书馆了"，所以"在教室里找不到你"就不觉得奇怪了。

The answer is A. "Guàibudé" indicates not feeling strange when getting to know the reason. The sentence means, because "you went to the library", it is not strange that "we can't find you in the classroom".

5. 选择 C。"不"是否定副词，用在动词或形容词前。"受不了"是否定形式，它的肯定形式是"受得了"。

The answer is C. "Bù" is a negative adverb used before verbs or adjectives. "Shòubuliǎo" is a negative form, and its positive form is "shòudeliǎo".

6. 选择 B。"就"在这里强调数量少，相当于"只有"的意思，表示"只有你一个亲人了"。"也"表示委婉的语气，去掉"也"，语气就显得直率，有时甚至生硬。这时"就"要放在"也"的后面，强调词语的前面。

The answer is B. "Jiù" here indicates the quantity is small, meaning "only", and in this sentence it means "I have only one relative, that is you". "Yě" indicates a tactful tone, and when "yě" is omitted, the tone becomes straightforward or even blunt. In this case, "jiù" should follow "yě" but precede the emphasized word.

7. 选择 A。"刚刚"表示动作、行为或情况不久前发生，强调时间间隔得短促。它只能修饰动词和动词性短语，要用在"把"引导的介词短语的前面。

The answer is A. "Gānggāng" indicates the action or behavior took place a while ago, emphasizing a short period of time. It can only modify verbs or verbal phrases, and be put before prepositional phrases led by "bǎ".

8. 选择 B。"经常"表示动作、行为的反复重复,用于动词前。

The answer is B. "Jīngcháng" indicates the repetitive actions or behaviors; it is used before verbs.

9. 选择 B。"形容词+倒(是)+形容词"是一个固定结构,表示转折关系。这句话的意思是:你的朋友虽然很漂亮,但是很懒。

The answer is B. "Adjective + dào(shì) + adjective" is a fixed structure, indicating transitional relation. The meaning of the sentence is "although your friend is beautiful, she is lazy."

10. 选择 B。"就"在这里强调数量少,相当于"只有"的意思,表示"只有他一个人蒙在鼓里"。"就"要放在强调词"他"的前面。

The answer is B. "Jiù" here indicates the quantity is small, meaning "only", and in this sentence it means "he is the only one who does not know it". "Jiù" should precede the emphasized word "tā".

11. 选择 C。"从来"表示从过去到现在都是如此,多用于否定句中,放在否定副词的前面。

The answer is C. "Cónglái" indicates something is always the same from past to present. It is often used in a negative sentence and before the negative adverb.

12. 选择 C。"有点儿"表示程度较低,相当于"稍微"。语法结构是"有点儿+形容词/表示内心情感的动词",多用于不如意的事。

The answer is C. "Yǒudiǎnr" indicates a low degree, the same as "shāowēi". The structure "yǒudiǎnr + adjective / verbs indicating emotion" is often used to indicate something is not as good as one wishes.

13. 选择 C。"就"在这里强调数量少,相当于"只",表示"只酷爱散步"。"就"应该放在强调词语的前面。

The answer is C. "Jiù" here indicates the quantity is small, simiar to "zhǐ", and in this sentence it means "only fond of walking". "Jiù" should precede the emphasized words or phrases.

14. 选择 C。"不得不"表示没有别的选择,只好这样做,多用于不如意的事。本题的意思是:因为"大家都不好意思发表意见",所以"我"只好"先说说自己的看法"。

The answer is C. "Bùdébù" means "having no other choices but to do this", usually indicating something is not as good as one wishes. The meaning of this sentence is "Since the others are shy to express their opinions, I have to say my viewpoint first."

15. 选择 B。"才"在本题中表示强调所说的事——她不会买这种廉价的化妆品,句尾常会搭配使用"呢"。

The answer is B. "Cái" in this sentence indicates the emphasis: She won't buy this kind of cheap cosmetics. In this case, "ne" is often used at the end of the sentence.

16. 选择 A。"才"在本题中,用于"动词+数量短语"的结构前,表示说话人认为动作进行的次数少。

The answer is A. When "cái" is used in the structure "verb + numeral phrase", it indicates the speaker thinks the number of the times of the action is too small.

17. 选择 C。"不但不……反而……"是一个固定结构,表示实际发生的事与预期的事正好相反。

The answer is C. "Búdàn bù... fǎn'ér" is a fixed structure, indicating the fact is totally contradictory to what is expected.

18. 选择 D。"反而"是一个副词,表示实际做法与一般常规做法相反。这句话的意思是:别人家夏天的时候都会开着窗户,但是我们家却要关窗户。"夏天关窗户"的做法与一般常规做法相反。所以"反而"放在实际做法的前面。

The answer is D. "Fǎn'ér" is an adverb indicating the actual way of doing things is contradictory to the norm. The meaning of this sentence is "In summer, other families will open their windows, while our family closes them instead." "Close the windows in summer" is contradictory to normal behavior, so "fǎn'ér" should precede the actual way of doing things.

19. 选择 C。"几乎"表示非常接近某个数量或程度。"几乎+名词性结构+都……"是一个固定结构。

The answer is C. "Jīhū" means very close to a certain number or degree. "Jīhū + noun structure + dōu..." is a fixed structure.

20. 选择 C。"竟然"表示出乎意料,用于动词性或形容词性短语前,在句中起加强语气的作用。这句话的意思是:我想送妈妈一套高级化妆品,但没想到来到柜台前却犹豫起来了。

The answer is C. "Jìngrán" means out of expectation; it is used before verbal or adjective phrases to reinforce the tone. The meaning of the sentence is "I wanted to buy a set of cosmetics for my mother, but I hesitated at the counter."

21. 选择 C。"竟然"表示出乎意料,用于动词性或形容词性短语前,在句中起加强语气的作用。这句话的意思是:为了一张电影票,没想到兄弟俩打架了。

The answer is C. "Jìngrán" means out of expectation; it is used before verbal or adjective phrases to reinforce the tone. The meaning of the sentence is "It's so strange that the brothers fought just for a movie ticket."

22. 选择 C。"竟然"表示出乎意料,用于动词性或形容词性短语前,在句中起加强语气的作用。"没有"是否定"听见"的,所以"竟然"要在 C 的位置。

The answer is C. "Jìngrán" means out of expectation; it is used before verbal or adjective phrases to reinforce the tone. "Méiyǒu" is to negate "tīngjiàn", so "jìngrán" should be used in the position of C.

23. 选择 C。"偏偏"在本题中表示事情的发生,与愿望、预料的相反,用于主语前后都可以。

The answer is C. "Piānpiān" in this sentence indicates what happened is contradictory to an expectation; it can be used before or after the subject.

24. 选择 C。"偏偏"在本题中表示主观上故意跟客观要求相反。这时的"偏偏"只能用在主语后、谓语前。"他送给我一对波斯猫"的实际做法与"我不喜欢猫狗"的客观要求是相反的。所以"偏偏"只能在 C 的位置。

The answer is C. "Piānpiān" in this sentence means the speaker deliberately opposes the objective requirement, and in this case it should be used after the subject and before the predicate only. "Tā sònggěi wǒ yí duì bōsī māo" is contradictory to the objective demand of "I don't like cats and dogs", therefore "piānpiān" should be in the position of C.

25. 选择 B。"偏"表示故意跟某人作对,一定要做某事,后常与"要"搭配使用。

The answer is B. "Piān" indicates to deliberately oppose somebody or do something, and it usually matches with "yào".

26. 选择 C。"偏"表示故意跟某人作对不做某事,后常与"不"搭配使用。

The answer is C. "Piān" indicates to deliberately oppose somebody by not doing something, and it usually matches with "bù".

27. 选择 A。"向来"表示某种情况或状态从过去到现在一直这样,保持不变。此句中"十分尊重、孝敬父母"是一直以来的情况,与"今天"的情况相对。所以"向来"在 A 的位置上。

The answer is A. "Xiànglái" indicates a certain situation or state remains unchanged from the past till present. In this sentence, the practice of "shífēn zūnzhòng, xiàojìng fùmǔ" is the usual situation, which is contradictory to the situation of "jīntiān", therefore "xiànglái" should be in the position of A.

28. 选择 B。"倒"表示转折,用于主语的后面。
The answer is B. "Dào" indicates transition, and it is used after the subject.

29. 选择 A。"向来"表示某种情况或状态从过去到现在一直这样,保持不变。此句中"喜欢郊游"是从过去到现在一直以来的情况,与"今天"的情况相反。所以"向来"在 A 的位置上。
The answer is A. "Xiànglái" indicates a certain situation or state unchanged from the past till present. In this sentence, the practice of "xǐhuan jiāoyóu" is the usual situation, which is contradictory to the situation of "jīntiān", therefore "xiànglái" should be in the position of A.

30. 选择 D。"有点儿"表示程度不高,用在动词"认"的前面。
The answer is D. "Yǒudiǎnr" indicates a low degree, and is used before the verb "rèn".

31. 选择 B。"究竟"表示进一步追究,含有强调的语气。
The answer is B. "Jiūjìng" indicates further questioning, with a tone of emphasis.

32. 选择 D。"从来"表示从过去到现在都是这样,常用于否定句中。
The answer is D. "Cónglái" indicates staying unchanged from the past till present, and is often used in the negative sentences.

33. 选择 C。"不得不"表示在没有其他选择的情况下,只能这样做。所做的事常是不愿做的事。"好容易"表示做某事难度很大,很不容易。
The answer is C. "Bùdébù" indicates having no other choices but to do so, often reluctantly. "Hǎoróngyì" means doing something is difficult or extremely hard.

34. 选择 A。"赶快"表示加快速度进行某个动作行为,可以用于祈使句,常用于还没有发生的情况。"连忙"和"急忙"只能用于陈述句中,不能用于表示命令、要求的祈使句中。
The answer is A. "Gǎnkuài" indicates to speed up doing something. It can be used in the imperative sentences to indicate things not happened yet. "Liánmáng" and "jímáng" can only be used in the declarative sentences, instead of imperative sentences which indicate an order or a demand.

35. 选择 C。"明明"表示事实的确如此,后面常有与事实相反的内容。
The answer is C. "Míngmíng" indicates what the truth is and is usually followed by an opposite fact.

36. 选择 B。"万万"表示一种极端的强调,含有"绝对"、"无论如何"的意思,后面是否定形式。"千万"表示恳切地嘱咐,用于祈使句中。"万一"表示发生某事的可能性极小,只用于不希望发生的事。

The answer is B. "Wànwàn" is used before a negative statement, indicating a dissuasion or an order with a strong sense of emphasis. "Qiānwàn" indicates to urge and is used in the imperative sentences. "Wànyī" is often used to modify things of little possibility and the speaker doesn't want it to happen.

37. 选择 B。"难怪"表示知道了原因之后,就不再觉得奇怪了。这类句子由两部分组成,一部分是说明原因,一部分是指出现象。"难怪"用在指出现象的小句中。

The answer is B. "Nánguài" means not feeling strange when getting to know the reason. Usually this kind of sentence consists of two parts, the first part explains the reason, and the second part points out the fact, and "nánguài" is used in the latter part.

38. 选择 A。"到底"可用于疑问句中,表示进一步追问,要得到确切的答案。"毕竟"表示事情不管怎样追根究底,结论只有一个,不能用在疑问句中。

The answer is A. "Dàodǐ" can be used in an interrogative sentence to indicate further questioning for the exact answer. "Bìjìng" indicates no matter how you get to the bottom of it, you can only get one conclusion, and it cannot be used in the interrogative sentences.

39. 选择 A。"毕竟"在本题中强调原因。

The answer is A. "Bìjìng" emphasizes the reason in this sentence.

40. 选择 A。"很厉害"是"病"的补语,它们之间需要用结构助词"得"连接;"不得不"表示在没有其他选择的情况下,只能这样做。所做的事常是不愿做的事。

The answer is A. "Hěn lìhài" is the complement of "bìng", and should be connected with the complement by the structural particle "de". "Bùdébù" indicates to have no other choices but to do so, often reluctantly.

41. 选择 B。"未必"表示委婉的否定,含有"不一定"的意思。"未免"多用于评价某种过分的行为或情况,并觉得不以为然,带有委婉的否定语气。

The answer is B. "Wèibì" indicates mild negation meaning "bù yídìng". "Wèimiǎn" is often used to evaluate some extreme actions or situations, indicating an indirect negation.

42. 选择 A。"曾经"表示某种动作行为或情况在以前发生或存在过,所修饰的动词或形容词的后面常有动态助词"过";"差不多"表示在程度上相差很少,相近。

The answer is A. "Céngjīng" indicates some actions or situations took place or existed before, and the modified verbs or adjectives are usually followed by the aspectual particle "guò". "Chàbùduō" indicates closeness in degree.

43. 选择 B。"到底"可用于疑问句中，表示进一步追问，要得到确切的答案。"你"是"吓"的受事，因而要用"把"把"你"提前到"吓"的前面。

The answer is B. "Dàodǐ" can be used in an interrogative sentence to indicate further questioning for the exact answer. "Nǐ" is the recipient of "xià", so it is necessary to use "bǎ" to put "nǐ" before "xià".

44. 选择 B。"多亏"表示由于别人的帮助，避免了不幸的发生。

The answer is B. "Duōkuī" indicates that due to some favorable conditions or somebody's help, a bad outcome is avoided.

45. 选择 C。"凡是"用在名词或名词性短语的前面，表示在某个范围内没有例外。用在主语前边，后面常有"都"和它搭配使用。此句中"我们做到的"是范围。这句话的意思是：我们做到的一切，他都做到了。

The answer is C. "Fánshì" is often used before nouns or noun phrases to indicate there is no exception within a certain scope. It is usually used before the subject followed by "dōu". In this sentence, "wǒmen zuòdào de" is the scope, and it means that whatever we have done, he has done it.

46. 选择 C。"凡是"用在名词或名词性短语的前面，表示在某个范围内没有例外。一般用在句首，后面常有"没有不/无不"和它搭配使用。

The answer is C. "Fánshì" is often used before nouns or noun phrases to indicate there is no exception within a certain range. It is usually used at the beginning of the sentence and matches with "méiyǒu bù/wú bù".

47. 选择 B。"赶紧"、"赶快"、"赶忙"、"连忙"四个词都可以用于陈述句中，且词义、用法相同；"实在"表示对某种情况加以确认或强调，有"的确"的意思。"再三"强调为了达到某种目的，多次重复某一动作行为。"照样"表示动作行为或状况维持原来的情况不变。"首先"表示最先、最早的意思。

The answer is B. "Gǎnjǐn", "gǎnkuài", "gǎnmáng" and "liánmáng" can all be used in declarative sentences and they have similar meaning and usage. "Shízài" indicates a confirmation or an emphasis of some situation, meaning "really". "Zàisān" emphasizes to repeat an action for a certain purpose. "Zhàoyàng" indicates some actions or situations remain unchanged. "Shǒuxiān" means "first".

48. 选择C。"赶忙"表示抓紧时间急于做某事，一般只用于陈述句中，只限于已经发生的情况。
The answer is C. "Gǎnmáng" indicates to take the time to do something urgently. It is only used in declarative sentences to indicate things that have happened.

49. 选择A。"太+形容词+了"是一个固定形式；"很"和"真"修饰形容词时，直接用于形容词前；"挺"修饰形容词时的结构是：挺+形容词+（的）。
The answer is A. "Tài + adjective + le" is a fixed structure. When "hěn" and "zhēn" modify adjectives, they are used immediately before the adjectives. The pattern of "tǐng" to modify the adjective is "tǐng + adjective + (de)".

50. 选择A。"刚"表示动作发生在不久以前，相当于"才"；"就"表示时间短，相当于"马上"。
The answer is A. "Gāng" indicates the action has just happened, similar to "cái". "Jiù" indicates the short time, similar to "mǎshàng".

51. 选择B。"本来"强调事实就是如此。"哪怕"是连词，表示姑且承认某个事实，后面多与"都""也""还"搭配使用。
The answer is B. "Běnlái" indicates that it's the truth. "Nǎpà" is a conjunction, indicating a recognition of something as the fact for the moment, and usually matches with "dōu", "yě" or "hái".

52. 选择B。"怪不得"表示明白了原因后，不再觉得奇怪。"恨不得"表示急切盼望做某事，多用于实际很难做到的事。"由不得"表示某人做不了主。
The answer is B. "Guàibùdé" means not feeling strange when getting to know the reason. "Hènbùdé" means to be eager to do something actually difficult to do. "Yóubùdé" means something is out of the control of somebody.

53. 选择C。"怪不得"表示明白了原因后，不再觉得奇怪。"不见得"表示不一定。"说不上"表示不能说达到了某个程度。
The answer is C. "Guàibùdé" means not feeling strange when getting to know the reason. "Bújiàndé" means not necessarily. "Shuōbúshàng" means not being sure.

54. 选择C。"怪不得"表示明白了原因后，不再觉得奇怪。"眼看着"有两个意思，一是亲眼看着某个动作行为发生，一是表示某种情况即将发生。
The answer is C. "Guàibùdé" means not feeling strange when getting to know the reason. "Yǎn kànzhe" has two meanings: one is seeing something happen, and the other is something is going to happen.

55. 选择 A。"怪不得"表示明白了原因后,不再觉得奇怪。"不至于"表示没有达到某种程度或发展到某个地步。"莫不是"表示"难道是……"的意思。

The answer is A. "Guàibùdé" means not feeling strange when getting to know the reason. "Bú zhìyú" means not having reached a certain degree yet. "Mòbúshì" means "nándào shì...?".

56. 选择 B。"好容易"表示做某事难度很大,很不容易。

The answer is B. "Hǎoróngyì" means doing something very difficult or extremely hard.

57. 选择 A。"好容易"和"好不容易"都表示做某事难度很大,很不容易。趋向动词"下来"用在形容词后表示程度由强到弱。

The answer is A. "Hǎoróngyì" and "hǎobùróngyì" both mean doing something difficult or extremely hard. Tendency verb "xiàlái" is used after the adjective to indicate the degree is from high to low.

58. 选择 D。本题中的"好像"表示说话人的想法或看法没有十足的把握。

The answer is D. "Hǎoxiàng" indicates the speaker is not very sure about his or her own view.

59. 选择 A。本题中的"好像"用于比喻,有"仿佛"的意思。

The answer is A. "Hǎoxiàng" in this sentence is used in a metaphor, same as "fǎngfú", meaning "as if".

60. 选择 B。"竟然"表示出乎意料,用于动词性或形容词性短语前,在句中起加强语气的作用。

The answer is B. "Jìngrán" means out of expectation; it is used before verbal or adjective phrases to reinforce the tone.

61. 选择 C。"忽然"表示某种情况迅速发生,而且常常出人意料。

The answer is C. "Hūrán" indicates something happens suddenly and out of expectation.

62. 选择 B。"突然"表示某种情况迅速发生,而且常常出人意料。它不仅做副词,而且还兼做形容词,可受程度副词的修饰。

The answer is B. "Tūrán" indicates something happens suddenly and out of expectation. It can not only be used as an adverb, but also serve as the adjective and be modified by degree adverbs.

63. 选择 C。"几乎"表示非常接近某个数量或程度。"地道"是一个形容词,表示"真正的、纯粹的"。

The answer is C. "Jīhū" indicates being very close to a certain number or degree. "Dìdào" is an adjective, meaning "true, pure".

64. 选择 B。"简直"表示达到或接近某种程度,带有强调的作用。"仿佛"是一个动词,表示像、类似的意思,常用于比喻。

The answer is B. "Jiǎnzhí" means reaching or being close to some degree, indicating an emphasis. "Fǎngfú" is a verb, often used in metaphors, indicating "as if".

65. 选择 B。"到底"在本题中表示经过某个过程以后最终出现的结果,有"终于"的意思。句中多有"了"或其他表示完成的词语。

The answer is B. "Dàodǐ" in this sentence indicates a result appeared after a certain process, meaning "finally". Usually there are words indicating completeness such as "le".

66. 选择 C。"难怪"表示知道了原因之后,就不再觉得奇怪了。这类句子由两部分组成,一部分是说明原因,一部分是指出现象。"难怪"用在指出现象的小句中。"大约"表示对数量的估计或对某种情况的推测。"幸好"表示由于某种有利条件存在而避免了不良后果的发生,相当于"幸亏"。

The answer is C. "Nánguài" means not feeling strange when getting to know the reason. Usually this kind of sentence consists of two parts, one part explains the reason, and the other points out the fact, and "nánguài" is used in the latter part. "Dàyuē" indicates an estimate of the number or situation. "Xìnghǎo" indicates that because of some favorable conditions, some unpleasant consequences are avoided, same as "xìngkuī".

67. 选择 B。"不必"表示事实上或情理上不需要,用于陈述句。"何必"表示"不必",是反问语气,语气比"不必"重。

The answer is B. "Búbì" is used in the declarative sentence to indicate something is not necessary either in fact or in reason. "Hébì" indicates "búbì", with the tone of a rhetorical question, though stronger than "búbì".

68. 选择 B。"竟然"表示出乎意料,用于动词性或形容词性短语前,在句中起加强语气的作用;"倒"在本题中表示发生的情况和预料的相反。

The answer is B. "Jìngrán" means out of expectation; it is used before verbal or adjective phrases to reinforce the tone. "Dào" in this sentence indicates something is contrary to what is expected.

69. 选择 B。"竟然"表示出乎意料,用于动词性或形容词性短语前,在句中起加强语气的作用;"就"在本题中表示说话人认为奶奶的病被治好所用的时间短。

The answer is B. "Jìngrán" means out of expectation; it is used before verbal or adjective phrases to reinforce the tone. "Jiù" in this sentence indicates the speaker thinks the time needed for curing grandma is short.

70. 选择 B。"才"在本题中表示说话人认为"想起"得晚；"连忙"表示动作行为紧接着前面的情况发生，特别强调前后动作的连续性。

The answer is B. "Cái" in this sentence indicates the speaker thinks it's too late for him to think of it. "Liánmáng" indicates an action immediately follows another, emphasizing the continuity of the actions.

71. 选择 C。"明明"表示事实的确如此，后面常有与事实相反的内容。"明确"是一个形容词，表示"清晰明白、非常确定"。"是否"是"是不是"的意思。

The answer is C. "Míngmíng" indicates what the truth is and is usually followed by an opposite fact. "Míngquè" is an adjective, meaning "clear, definite". "Shìfǒu" means "whether or not".

72. 选择 A。程度副词"很"的后面需要一个形容词，"清楚"和"显然"都是形容词，但"显然"表示容易看出或感觉到、非常明显的意思，不符合句意。

The answer is A. "Hěn" is an adverb indicating degree; it should be followed by an adjective. Although both "qīngchu" and "xiǎnrán" are adjectives, "xiǎnrán" means being easily seen and felt, and being evident, which does not match the topic.

73. 选择 C。"究竟"用于疑问句中，表示进一步追问，要求明确的答复。"难道"表示反问语气，句尾常有"吗"搭配使用。"居然"表示本来不应该或不可能发生的事出人意料地发生了。"毕竟"不能用于疑问句。

The answer is C. "Jiūjìng" is used in the interrogative sentence to indicate further questioning and demanding a definite answer. "Nándào" indicates a rhetorical tone and often matches with "ma" at the end of the sentence. "Jūrán" indicates something shouldn't have happened happens unexpectedly. "Bìjìng" cannot be used in the interrogative sentence.

74. 选择 C。"简直"表示达到或接近某种程度，带有强调的作用。

The answer is C. "Jiǎnzhí" indicates reaching or being close to some degree, with an emphasis.

75. 选择 B。"千万"表示恳切地嘱咐，用于祈使句中。"万万"表示一种极端的强调，含有"绝对""无论如何"的意思，后面是否定形式。

The answer is B. "Qiānwàn" indicates an urge, and is used in the imperative sentence.

"Wànwàn" is used before a negative statement, indicating absolutely or definitely, containing a strong sense of emphasis.

76. 选择 C。"始终"表示某种情况或状态从开始到最后一直如此,没有任何变化。
The answer is C. "Shǐzhōng" indicates some conditions or states remain unchanged from the beginning to the end.

77. 选择 C。"一直"表示在一定的时间内,某种动作、行为持续进行没有间断,或情况、状态持续不变。
The answer is C. "Yìzhí" indicates some actions or behaviors keep going or some conditions or states remain unchanged within a certain period.

78. 选择 B。"似乎"表示说话人对某种推测或判断不是十分肯定。
The answer is B. "Sìhū" indicates the speaker is not very sure of certain predication or judgment.

79. 选择 C。"特别""十分"和"尤其"都是程度副词,都可以修饰形容词。"再"在本题中表示追加补充,含有"另外"的意思。
The answer is C. "Tèbié", "shífēn" and "yóuqí" are all degree adverbs, and can modify adjectives. "Zài" in this sentence indicates an addition, containing the meaning of "in addition to".

80. 选择 C。"万万"表示一种极端的强调,含有"绝对、无论如何"的意思,后面是否定形式。
The answer is C. "Wànwàn" is used before a negative statement, indicating absolutely, containing a strong sense of emphasis.

81. 选择 A。"万一"表示发生某事的可能性极小,只用于不希望发生的事。"万分"是程度副词,比"十分"程度高。
The answer is A. "Wànyī" is often used to modify things of little possibility and the speaker doesn't want to see it happen. "Wànfēn" is a degree adverb but is higher in degree than "shífēn".

82. 选择 D。"往往"表示对到目前为止出现的情况或对以往经验进行总结,带有规律性,不用于主观意愿。
The answer is D. "Wǎngwǎng" indicates a summary of the situation up to now or of the past experience, which usually happens with certain pattern but does not contain the subjective will.

83. 选择 C。"往往"表示对到目前为止出现的情况或对以往经验进行总结,带有规律性,不用于主观意愿。句中一般常指明与动作有关的条件。在本题中，"喜食冰镇食品"是动作行为，"夏季炎热"是与动作行为有关的条件。

The answer is C. "Wǎngwǎng" indicates a summary of the situation up to now or of the past experience, which usually happens with certain pattern but does not contain the subjective will. Often there is some condition for the action. In this sentence, "xǐ shí bīngzhèn shípǐn" is the action, and "xiàjì yánrè" is the condition for the action.

84. 选择 C。"幸亏"表示由于某种有利条件或某人的帮助，避免了某种不好的结果，多用于主语前；"才"在句中强调结果。

The answer is C. "Xìngkuī" indicates that due to some favorable condition or somebody's help, a bad consequence is avoided. It is often used before the subject. "Cái" in this sentence emphasizes the result.

85. 选择 B。"未必"表示否定，相当于"不一定"、"不见得"，语气委婉；"只是"表示限定动作、事物的范围，相当于"仅是"，前后常有进一步说明或解释的语句。

The answer is B. "Wèibì" indicates a negation. It equals to "bùyídìng", "bújiàndé", but is more indirect in tone. "Zhǐshì" limits the range of an action or a matter, and equals to "jǐnshì". Usually it is preceded or followed by a clause for further explanation.

86. 选择 A。"向来"表示某种情况或状态从过去到现在一直这样，保持不变。"继续"是一个动词，表示动作行为连下去，不间断。"不时"表示时时、经常不断地，中间有间歇、停顿。

The answer is A. "Xiànglái" indicates some situations or states remain unchanged from the past till present. "Jìxù" is a verb, indicating some actions come in succession and continue. "Bùshí" means often and frequently, with pauses between the actions.

87. 选择 C。"往往"表示对到目前为止出现的情况或对以往经验进行总结，带有规律性，不用于主观意愿。句中一般常指明与动作有关的条件。在本题中，"感冒"是结果，"不注意"是条件。

The answer is C. "Wǎngwǎng" indicates the summary of the situation up to now or of the past experience, which usually happens with certain pattern but does not contain the subjective will. Often there is a condition for the action. In this sentence, "gǎnmào" is the result, and "bú zhùyì" is the condition.

88. 选择 B。"突然"表示某种情况迅速发生，而且常常出人意料；"幸亏"表示由于某种有利条件或某人的帮助，避免了某种不好的结果，多用于主语前。

The answer is B. "Tūrán" indicates something happens suddenly and unexpectedly. "Xìng kuī" indicates that due to some favorable condition or somebody's help, a bad consequence is avoided. It is often used before the subject.

89. 选择 B。"尤其"表示几件事或几个事物进行比较,指出突出的一个,常和"是"一起用。
The answer is B. "Yóuqí" refers to an outstanding one among several things or matters; it is usually followed by "shì".

90. 选择 B。"有点儿"表示程度不高,用在形容词"困"的前面;"一会儿"表示很短的时间。
The answer is B. "Yǒudiǎnr" indicates a low degree, and in this sentence, it is used before the adjective "kùn". "Yíhuìr" indicates a short time.

91. 选择 D。"就"在本题中表示强调、肯定的语气;"有点儿"表示程度不高,用在形容词"晚"的前面。
The answer is D. "Jiù" in this sentence indicates an emphasizing and affirmative tone. "Yǒudiǎnr" indicates a low degree and is used before the adjective "wǎn".

92. 选择 A。"原来"表示发现了以前不知道的情况,含有恍然大悟的意思,用于主语前后都可以。"本来"没有这种用法。
The answer is A. "Yuánlái" indicates to find out something unknown before, often in a sudden, and it can be used either after or before the subject. "Běnlái" cannot be used in this way.

93. 选择 D。"总共"表示几个方面数字的合计,一共。"总体"是一个名词,表示几个个体合成的事物。"总是"是一个副词,表示持续不变,经常。"总数"是一个名词,表示加在一起的数目。
The answer is D. "Zǒnggòng" indicates the total number adding up from several aspects. "Zǒngtǐ" is a noun, indicating a thing formed by several units. "Zǒngshì" is an adverb, indicating always and without change. "Zǒngshù" is a noun, indicating a total number.

94. 选择 C。"特别"表示几件事或几个事物进行比较,指出突出的一个,常和"是"一起用。
The answer is C. "Tèbié" refers to an outstanding one among several other things or matters; it is usually followed by "shì".

95. 选择 C。"倒"表示发生的事情和预料的相反。
The answer is C. "Dào" indicates something happened is contradictory to one's expectation.

96. 选择 B。"才"在本题中起强调作用,强调"买到一本"是很难的。
The answer is B. "Cái" in this sentence indicates an emphasis that it is very hard to "mǎidào yì běn".

97. 选择 D。"偏偏"表示主观上故意和客观要求不同,此时的"偏偏"必须用在主语后。

The answer is D. "Piānpiān" here indicates someone deliberately opposes the objective requirement, and must be used after the subject.

98. 选择 B。"未免"多用于评价某种过分的行为或情况,并觉得不以为然,带有委婉的否定语气。

The answer is B. "Wèimiǎn" is often used to evaluate some actions or situations that are overdone, indicating an indirect negation.

99. 选择 B。"简直"表示达到或接近某种程度,带有强调的作用。

The answer is B. "Jiǎnzhí" means reaching or being close to some degree, indicating an emphasis.

100. 选择 A。"一直"表示在一定的时间内,某种动作、行为持续进行没有间断,或情况、状态持续不变。

The answer is A. "Yìzhí" indicates some actions or behaviors going without interruption or some conditions or states remain unchanged within a certain period.

③ 介词 Preposition

- 介词的作用主要是用来介绍与动作行为相关的时间、处所、方向、对象、依据以及原因、目的等。介词最主要的特点是使用时后面一定要有宾语,而且宾语多为名词性成分,通常把"介词 + 宾语"称为介词结构。介词结构可以在句中做状语、定语及补语。
- 学习的时候,要注意它们常和哪些动词搭配使用以及近义介词之间的差别。

The function of preposition is mainly for introducing factors related to actions and behaviors, including time, location, direction, object, basis, reason and purpose. The most important feature of preposition is that an object, mainly nominal, must follow. The structure of "preposition + object" is known as the preposition structure, wihch can be used as adverbials, attributes and complements in the sentence.

Attention should be paid to the matching verbs and the differences among similar prepositions.

考点精讲 Examination Points

1. 按照 ànzhào
① 表示遵循某种准则或标准。它的宾语不能是单音节词语。

"Ànzhào" means to follow some principles or standards; its object can't be monosyllabic words.

例:按照他介绍的方法,我们终于做好了。

② 可以与"说""来说""来讲""来看"等词语搭配使用,表示根据某种事理来判断,但"按照"的后面一定要有名词性成分。

"Ànzhào" can be matched with "shuō", "láishuō", "láijiǎng", "láikàn" etc. to indicate a judgment based on certain reasons. There must be a nominal element after "ànzhào".

例:按照现在的进度看,按时完工没问题。

2. 朝 cháo
① 表示动作的方向。宾语一般是表示方位、处所的词语。"朝"有时还可以表示抽象意义的方向。

"Cháo" shows the direction of an action. Its object is usually words for directions or locations. "Cháo" sometimes indicates directions of abstract things.

例：出了门一直朝东走就到了。

我们在朝这个目标努力。

② 表示动作、行为的对象。宾语多是表示人的词语。

"Cháo" shows the object of an action or behavior. Its object is usually a word indicating person.

例：他朝我挥了挥手。

特别提示 *Special Tips*

☆ "朝"有时后面带"着"，这时的宾语不能是单音节方位词，一般是多音节词语或短语。

"Cháo" is sometimes followed by "zhe"; in this case, the object can't be monosyllabic words for directions or locations, but multisyllabic words or phrases.

例：我们朝着大海边跑去。

3. 趁 chèn

表示所利用的机会或条件。后面的宾语如果是双音节以上的词语时，"趁"后可加"着"。

"Chèn" shows a chance or condition being taken use of. If the following object is a phrase with two or more syllables, "chèn" can be followed by "zhe".

例：这是刚做好的饭菜，你快趁热吃吧。

我们应该趁（着）年轻多学点儿本领。

4. 从 cóng

① 介绍起点。常常和"到""往""向"等词语搭配使用。"从……"后可以加"起""开始"等词语，以此来强调和突出起点。

"Cóng" shows the starting point. It often matches with "dào", "wǎng", "xiàng", etc. "Cóng" can be followed by "qǐ" and "kāishǐ" to emphasize and highlight the starting point.

A. 表示时间。

Showing the time.

例：我们每天上课的时间是从八点到十二点。

他从昨天起就没出过家门。

B. 表示范围。

Showing the range.

例：这本书我已经从头到尾看了好几遍了。

C. 表示处所、来源。

Showing the location or source.

例：我刚从书店回来。

这个消息是我从报纸上看到的。

D. 表示发展和变化。

Showing development and change.

例：这家公司从无到有，从弱到强，短短几年，发展得很快。

② 介绍动作行为的凭借或依据。后面有时会跟"看""看来""来看""来说"等词语。

Showing the basis of an action. It is sometimes followed by "kàn", "kànlái", "lái kàn" or "lái shuō".

例：从你的体检结果来看，你的身体很健康。

③ 介绍动作行为经过的路线、处所。后面常会出现"过"或其他表示趋向的词语。

Showing the route or location of an action. It is often followed by "guò" or other tendency words.

例：小鸟从我们的头上飞过。

汽车从我们身边开过去了。

④ 介绍动作行为的着眼点。含有从某个方面或角度考虑的意思。

Showing the focus of an action. It implies to consider from a certain aspect or angle.

例：我们应该从工作出发，团结一致把工作做好。

特别提示 Special Tips

☆ "打"做介词时，意义和用法与"从"基本相同，多用于口语中。

When "dǎ" is used as a preposition, its meaning and usage are similar to "cóng", and it is more used in spoken Chinese.

5. 当 dāng

① 介绍事情发生的时间。多用于书面语。

Introducing the time when something happens. It is often used in written language.

A. "当……时/的时候"。表示事情发生在另一件事或另一状态出现的时候，多用于句首。

"Dāng... shí/de shíhòu" shows something happens while another event or state appears. It is often used at the beginning of a sentence.

例：当我正要出门的时候，电话铃响了。

特别提示 *Special Tips*

☆ 在口语表达中,"当"可以省略。

"Dāng" can be omitted in spoken language.

例:我大学毕业的时候,他才五岁。

☆ "当"的前面可加"每"或"正","每当"表示"每一次到……的时候","正当"表示"正在……的时候"。

"Měi" or "zhèng" can be put before "dāng". "měidāng" indicates "every time when…", "zhèng dāng" indicates "while…".

例:每当我看到我们的这张合影,我都会想起我们过去一起读书时的情景。

正当我要离开,他推门进来了。

B. "当……以前/之前/以后/之后"。表示事情发生在另一件事之前或之后。

"Dāng…yǐqián/zhīqián/yǐhòu/zhīhòu" shows that something happens before or after another event.

例:当我来之前,妈妈反复叮嘱我。

当天气暖和了以后,大雁飞往了北方。

② 介绍事情或行为发生的时间、处所或方位等。

Introducing the location or direction of a thing or behavior.

A. "当+单音节名词"。

"dāng + monosyllabic noun"

例:他们当众宣布下个月结婚。

B. "当+(着)+面"或"当着……的面"。表示面对面。

"Dāng + (zhe) + miàn" or "dāngzhe… de miàn" means "face to face".

例:有事当面说,背后议论别人不好。

刚才当着大家的面,我没好意思说。

6. 对 duì

① 介绍出动作行为的对象或目标,相当于"朝""向"的意思。"对"一定放在主语的后面。

Introducing the object or target of an action or a behavior, similar to "cháo" and "xiàng". "Duì" must be put after the subject.

例:我对大家点了点头。

② 引出与动作行为有关系的人或事物,表示对待。

Introducing a person or thing related to an action or a behavior to show relationship.

A. 表示人与人之间的对待关系。多修饰表示态度的词语。

Showing relationship between people. It usually modifies phrases concerning attitude.

例：他对我很热情。

B. 表示事物与人之间的对待关系。

Showing relationship between a thing and a person.

例：这件事对我打击很大。

C. 表示人与事物之间的对待关系。"对"构成的短语放在主语的前后都可以。

Showing relationship between a person and a thing. "Duì" can be put before or after the subject.

例：我对这个问题不感兴趣。

对这个问题我不感兴趣。

特别提示 Special Tips

☆ 有时为了突出或强调宾语，可以用"对"把宾语提前。

Sometimes for the sake of highlighting or emphasizing the object, "duì" can be used to lead the object before the verb.

例：他每天都很忙，不太关心孩子的学习。

他每天都很忙，对孩子的学习不太关心。

7. 对于 duìyú

介绍出与动作行为有关系的事物。

Introducing something related to an action or a behavior.

① "对于"用在主语前，一般有停顿。

The phrase of "duìyú" is used before the subject, and there is often a pause between the phrase and the subject.

例：对于这个问题，我有几点看法。

② "对于"用在主语后，不需停顿。

The phrase of "duìyú" is used after the subject, and there is no pause between it and the subject.

例：我对于当时的情况不太清楚。

特别提示 Special Tips

☆ 凡是能用"对于"的时候都能用"对"，但是能用"对"的时候不能都用"对于"。

Where "duìyú" is used, "duì" can replace it, not vice versa.

☆ 当"对"介绍动作行为的对象或目标时,"对"不能用"对于"替换。

When "duì" is used to introduce an object or the target of an action or a behavior, it can't be replaced by "duìyú".

> 例:他对我笑了笑。 (√)
>
> 他对于我笑了笑。 (×)

☆ 当"对"表示人与人之间的对待关系时,"对"不能用"对于"替换。

When "duì" is used to introduce the relationship between people, it can't be replaced by "duìyú".

> 例:大家对我很热情。 (√)
>
> 大家对于我很热情。 (×)

☆ 句中有能愿动词或副词时,"对"用在能愿动词或副词的前后都可以。"对于"只能用在能愿动词或副词的前面。

When there is a modal verb or adverb, "duì" can be put either before or after them. "Duìyú" can only be put before the modal verb or adverb.

> 例:大家会对你很热情的。 (√)
>
> 大家对你会很热情的。 (√)
>
> 他对于这个决定可能有意见。 (√)
>
> 他可能对于这个决定有意见。 (×)

8. 关于 guānyú

引出动作行为涉及的人或事。

Introducing people or things related to an action or a behavior.

① "关于+名词/名词性短语+的",做定语。

"Guānyú + noun/nominal phrase + de" is used as the attribute.

> 例:我非常喜欢看关于中国历史的书。

② "关于+名词/动词/小句",做状语。多放在句首或主语前,后面有停顿。

"Guānyú + noun/verb/clause", used as the adverbial, is often put at the beginning of a sentence or before the subject, and there is a pause following it.

> 例:关于这个问题,我还要再考虑考虑。

③ 由"关于"组成的介词短语用在"是……的"句式里,强调事物涉及的范围或包含的内容。

The prepositional phrase of "guānyú" used in the pattern of "shì... de" emphasizes the range or the content of something.

> 例:我们今天的议题都是关于环保的。

④ 由"关于"组成的介词短语单独使用,用来做文章的标题。

The prepositional phrase with "guānyú" is used individually as the title of an article.

例:《关于现代汉语语法》

特别提示 *Special Tips*

☆ "关于"表示动作行为关联、涉及的事物或范围;"对于"介绍出动作行为的对象。两种意思都有时,用"关于"或"对于"都可以。

"Guānyú" introduces a matter or range related to an action or a behavior; "duìyú" introduces the object of an action or a behavior. When showing the above two meanings, both "guānyú" and "duìyú" can be used.

例:关于这个问题,我们已经下发了一个通知。

对于这个问题,我们已经想出了解决办法。

关于 / 对于这个问题,我们都表示有信心解决。

☆ "关于"做状语时,只能用在主语的前面;"对于"用在主语的前后都可以。

When "guānyú" is used as an adverbial, it can only be put before the subject; while "duìyú" can be put before or after the subject.

例:关于这个地方,我了解得不多。　　(√)

我关于这个地方了解得不多。　　(×)

对于这件事,我不想再说什么了。(√)

我对于这件事不想再说什么了。　(√)

☆ 由"关于"组成的介词短语可以单独做文章的标题;由"对于"组成的介词短语的后面必须加上中心词才可以做文章的标题。

The prepositional phrase of "guānyú" can be the title of an article itself; while the phrase of "duìyú" can serve as the title of an article only when followed by a noun serving as the subject matter.

例:《关于中国历史》

《对于中国历史的研究》

9. 就 jiù

① 介绍出动作的对象或范围。

Introducing the object or range of an action or a behavior.

例:两国领导人就双边问题交换了意见。

② 表示从某一方面进行论述。多用于与其他人或事进行比较,常用"就……来看/来说/而言/而论"结构。

Showing a statement made from a certain aspect. It's often used to make comparison

Preposition

with other people or things, "jiù... láikàn / láishuō / éryán / érlùn" is the commonly used pattern.

例：就学习成绩来说，他不如玛丽，但就能力而言，他可比玛丽强多了。

就我看，他是个可以信赖的朋友。

特别提示 *Special Tips*

☆ "就……而言/而论"多用于书面语。

"Jiù... éryán/érlùn" is often used in written language.

10. 据 jù

引出某种结论的凭据或依据。

Introducing the basis of a conclusion.

①. "据+双音节动词"。

"jù + disyllabic verb"

例：据统计，今年来华留学的人数比去年大幅增加。

②. "据+（……）+说/讲/看/传"。

"jù + (...)+shuō/jiǎng/kàn/chuán"

例：据他说，他很快就要出国留学去了。

据说，他很快就要出国留学去了。

11. 靠 kào

引出动作行为依靠的对象或关系。

Introducing the object or relation on which an action or a behavior relies.

例：全家人靠他一个人的工资生活。

他靠朋友的关系进了这家公司。

12. 凭 píng

引出动作行为的凭借、依靠或根据。一般其后跟名词或名词性短语。

Introducing the basis of an action or a behavior. It's often followed by a noun or nominal phrase and can be put before the subject and there is a pause.

例：我们要凭自己的真本事吃饭。

大家请凭票入场。

特别提示 *Special Tips*

☆ 如果后面的名词性短语较长时，"凭"后可加"着"。

If the following nominal phrase is a long one, "zhe" can be put after "píng".

例：凭着多年的经验，他绕过了一个又一个的暗礁。

☆ "凭什么"是一个固定格式,表示质问。

"Píngshénme" is a fixed phrase showing questioning.

例:你凭什么管我的事?

☆ 当介绍动作行为的依靠时,"靠"和"凭"同义,但"靠"多用于口语,"凭"多用于书面语。

When introducing the basis of an action or a behavior, "kào" and "píng" have the same meaning. While "kào" is used more in spoken language, "píng" in written language.

13. 随着 suízhe

① "随着+名词+的+动词"。表示某事物发展变化的前提条件或原因,常在句首。

"Suízhe + noun + de + verb" shows a precondition or reason of development or change, often put at the beginning of a sentence.

例:随着科学的发展,人们的生活越来越方便。

② "随着+名词性短语"。表示某动作行为紧跟在另一事件之后,常在句首。

"Suízhe + nominal phrase" shows an action or a behavior closely following another event, often put at the beginning of a sentence.

例:随着一阵急促的脚步声,他慌慌张张地跑了进来。

14. 往 wǎng

表示动作行为的方向。

Showing direction of an action or a behavior.

① "往+方位词/处所词/抽象意义的词语+动词"。

"wǎng + words of direction/location/words of abstract meaning + verb"

例:往前走就看见了。

凡事都要往好处想。

② "某些单音节动词+往+处所词"。

"certain monosyllabic verb + wǎng + words of location"

例:这是开往上海的班机。

特别提示 Special Tips

☆ 当表示"面对某个方向移动"时,用"往"或"朝"都可以。

When showing "to move towards some direction", either "wǎng" or "cháo" can be used.

例:往前走、朝前走

☆ 当只有"面对",没有动作"移动"的意思时,只能用"朝";当只有"移动",没有"面对"的意思时,只能用"往"。

When showing "to face" but not "to move", only "cháo" can be used; when showing "to move" but not "to face", only "wăng" can be used.

例：这是朝南的房子。　　（√）

这是往南的房子。　　（×）

我每天都往家里打电话。（√）

我每天都朝家里打电话。（×）

☆ "往"只能表示动作的方向，不能表示动作的对象；"朝"既可以表示动作的方向，又可以表示动作的对象。

"Wăng" can only be used to indicate the direction of an action, but not the object of it; while "cháo" can indicate both the direction and the object.

例：往我这儿看　　　（√）

朝我这儿看　　　（√）

朝我点了点头　　（√）

往我点了点头　　（×）

15. 为 wèi

① 介绍出动作行为的服务对象。

Introducing the object of an action or a behavior.

例：学校为社会培养出合格的人才。

② 介绍出关心或注意的对象，其后的动词多是表示心理情感类的词语。

Introducing the object of care or attention, verbs are often these showing emotions and feelings.

例：父母总为儿女操心。

③ 表示目的。"为"后一般可以加"了"，多用于主语前，有语音停顿。基本格式如下：

Showing purpose. "Le" can be put after "wèi" and used often before the subject. There is a phonetic pause. The basic patterns include:

A. "为+名词/动词性短语+(而)……"强调做某事的目的。"为"后可以加"了"，一般用在主语后。

"Wèi + noun/verbal phrase + (ér)..." emphasizes the purpose of doing something. "Le" can be put after "wèi" and used often after the subject.

例：我们为（了）大家的健康干杯！

我们为维护世界和平而努力。

B. "为……起见"一般用在主语前，"为"后可以加"了"。

"Wèi... qǐjiàn" is often used before the subject, "le" can be put after "wèi".

例:为(了)安全起见,我们大家一起走吧。

16. 为了 wèile

① 引出目的,有以下常用格式:

Introducing purposes. The basic patterns include:

A. "为了+名词/动词性短语"。

"wèile + noun/verbal phrase"

例:为了孩子,我决定不去国外工作了。

他为了早点儿买上自己的汽车和房子,每天都在拼命地工作。

B. "为了……而……"强调目的,一般放在主语的后面。

"Wèile... ér..." emphasizes the purpose and is often put after the subject.

例:他为了父母而努力学习。

C.在"为了……起见"结构中,"为了"后多加双音节词,一般用于主语前。

In the struture "wèile... qǐjiàn", "wèile" is often followed by disyllabic words and used before the subject.

例:为了方便起见,他每天吃住在学校。

② 引出原因,用在主语前后都可以,也可不加"了"。

Introducing reason, it can be used either before or after the subject, "le" can be omitted.

例:我们为了郊游准备了一个晚上。(√)

为了郊游,我们准备了一个晚上。(√)

为了一件小事,他和妻子吵架了。(√)

他为了一件小事和妻子吵架了。(√)

特别提示 Special Tips

☆ "为了"没有"为"的①②用法。

"Wèile" doesn't have the above usages of ① and ② of "wèi".

17. 向 xiàng

① 表示动作的方向。

Showing the direction of an action.

A. "向+方位词/处所词+动词"。

"xiàng + word of direction/location + verb"

例:晕车的时候向外看,你会觉得好一点儿。

B. "某些单音节动词+向+方位词/处所词"。单音节动词只限于"走""奔""冲""飞""通""转""流""涌""滚""指""投""划""飘""射""刺""杀""引""偏"等。

"monosyllabic verb + word of direction/location".

These monosyllabic verbs are limited to "zǒu", "bēn", "chōng", "fēi", "tōng", "zhuǎn", "liú", "yǒng", "gǔn", "zhǐ", "tóu", "huá", "piāo", "shè", "cì", "shā", "yǐn", "piān", etc.

例:一群大雁飞向了远方。

② 表示动作行为的对象。宾语通常是表示人或事物的词语。

Showing the object of an action or a behavior. Its object is usually words indicating people or things.

例:请代我向他问好。

特别提示 *Special Tips*

☆ 所有用"朝"的句子都可以用"向"替换。

Wherever "cháo" is used in a sentence, "xiàng" can replace it.

例:这是朝南的房子。　　(√)

这是向南的房子。　　(√)

☆ "向"可以用在动词后,"朝"只能用在动词前。

"Xiàng" can be put after a verb, while "cháo" is only put before a verb.

例:向远处飞　　(√)

飞向远方　　(√)

朝远处飞　　(√)

飞朝远方　　(×)

☆ 表示动作行为的对象时,"朝"只能和与身体动作姿态有关的动词性短语组合;"向"没有这样的限制。

When showing the object of an action, "cháo" can only be combined with the verbal phrases concerning body actions and postures; while "xiàng" can be used without such a limit.

例:朝他挥了挥手　　(√)

向他挥了挥手　　(√)

向老师请教问题　(√)

朝老师请教问题　(×)

18. 依照 yīzhào

引出动作、事件所凭借的依据。一般用在双音节或多音节的词语前,多用于书面语。

Introducing the basis of an action or event. It is usually used before disyllabic or multisyllabic words in written language.

例：依照学校的规定，考试作弊者开除学籍。

特别提示 Special Tips

"按照"偏重于介绍动作行为的原则、根据或凭借，在执行的过程中可根据实际情况略作变动。"依照"偏重于强调完全照办，不能变动，所以多用于法律条文或政府文件。

"Ànzhào" introduces the principle or basis of an action or a behavior, which can be adjusted based on the specific situation. "Yīzhào" indicates to abide by and not to make any change, often used in legal or governmental documents.

19. 以 yǐ

① 引出动作行为的依据或凭借，多用于书面语，有如下常用格式：

Showing the basis of an action or a behavior, often used in written language. The basic patterns include:

A. "以+名词性短语"。表示依据或凭借。

"Yǐ + nominal phrase" indicates the basis of an action.

例：他以优异的成绩考入了北京大学。

B. "以……而论/来说"。表示举例。

"Yǐ... érlùn/láishuō" gives an example.

例：以学习成绩而论，大卫不如你，但以能力来说，你就比不上大卫了。

② 表示动作行为进行的程度或方式，有"按照""依照"的意思。

Showing the degree or way of an action, with the meaning of "according to".

例：据说，杨晨以 70 万马克的身价转会到法兰克福队。

两国以和平谈判的方式解决了边境问题。

③ 表示原因或理由，有"因为""由于"的意思，有时后面有"而"相呼应。

Showing reason, similar to "yīnwèi", "yóuyú". It sometimes matches with "ér".

例：黄山一向以奇松、怪石、云海而闻名。

④ 表示补充和说明。"以"通常用在动词后，动词多为表示"给予"意义的单音节动词。多用于书面语。

Showing a supplement and exposition. "Yǐ" is often used after the verb, which is often monosyllabic with the meaning of "giving". It is often used in written language.

例：我代表学校向大家致以节日的问候。

⑤ "以……为"结构的用法

The usage of "yǐ... wéi" structure

A. "以+名词/名词性短语+为+名词"。表示"拿……作为""把……当做"的意思。

"Yǐ + noun/nominal phrase + wéi + noun" means "ná... zuòwéi", "bǎ... dāngzuò".

例：你真是以校为家啊！

B. "以+名词/名词性短语+为+形容词"。表示"要数""要算"的意思。当多种事物进行对比时，"为"前常常加"最"。

"Yǐ + noun/nominal phrase + wéi + adjective" shows "yàoshǔ", "yàosuàn". When used in comparison with many other people or things, "zuì" is often put before "wéi".

例：在我们班同学当中，以大卫最为聪明。

C. "以+动词/动词性短语+为+名词"。表示"认为""觉得"的意思。

"Yǐ + verb/verbal phrase + wéi + noun" means "rènwéi", "juéde".

例：他以热心助人为乐事。

⑥ "以+方位词"。表示空间、数量或范围的界限。

"Yǐ + word of direction" shows the boundary of space, quantity or range.

例：北京在黄河以北。

新生都在 18 岁以上。

这几天的气温一直在 32℃以上。

20. 由 yóu

① 介绍出动作行为的发出者。动作的受事可以放在主语前。

Introducing the doer of an action or a behavior. The object can be put before the subject.

例：客人们由我陪同参观了颐和园。

② 介绍原因、来源或构成成分、方式。

Introducing a reason, a source, a part or a way.

例：拉肚子是由吃了不干净的食品引起的。

这个评审组由七个专家组成。

班长由全班同学投票选出。

③ 表示起点，相当于"从"。

Showing the starting point, similar to "cóng".

A. 表示时间的起点。

Showing the starting point of time.

例：由今天开始我们放假一周。

B. 表示空间或处所的起点。

Showing the starting point of space or location.

例：飞机由北京出发，飞往香港。

C. 表示范围或发展、变化的起点。

Showing the starting point of range or of development and change.

例：我们准备把房子由里到外装修一下。

她由普通职员提升为部门经理。

④ 表示事物的由来或出处。

Showing the source of something.

例：这几句话我是由这篇文章中找来的。

21. 自 zì

① 介绍时间、空间或处所的起点，相当于"从"。多用于书面语。

Showing the starting point of time, space or location. It's similar to "cóng" and often used in written language.

A. 表示时间的起点。

Showing the starting point of time.

例：她自小就很聪明。

B. 表示空间或处所的起点。

Showing the starting point of space or location.

例：黄河自西向东，流经九个省，最后流入渤海。

狼群自山上冲了下来。

C. "自……而……"。表示空间的起点，强调变化或范围。可用于此结构的词是意义相对的单音节词。

"Zì... ér..." shows the starting point of space and highlights the change or range. The monosyllabic words with opposite meanings can be used in this structure.

例：马蹄声自远而近，越来越清脆。

特别提示 Special Tips

☆ 此结构常见的词语还有：自上而下、自前而后、自左而右、自内而外……

Other phrases with such structure include: zìshàng'érxià, zìqián'érhòu, zìzuǒ'éryòu, zìnèi'érwài, etc.

---

② "某些动词+自+……"。表示动作发生的由来或原因。

"Some verbs + zì+..." shows the origin or reason of something happened.

例：这段话摘自《中国日报》。

特别提示 *Special Tips*

☆ 能够用于此结构的动词还有：出、抄、来、录、寄、选、译、引、源、转引……

Other verbs used in this structure include: chū, chāo, lái, lù, jì, xuǎn, yì, yǐn, yuán, zhuǎnyǐn, etc.

22. 自从 zìcóng

介绍时间的起点，仅限指过去的时间。

Introducing the starting point of time, limited to the time in the past.

例：自从来到中国，玛丽越来越喜欢中餐了。

自从练瑜伽以来，我的身体好多了。

自从她出国以后，我们再没见过面。

特别提示 *Special Tips*

☆ "从"后面可以是时间的起点，也可以是地点、范围或发展变化的起点；"自从"后只能是时间的起点。

The starting point after "cóng" can be of time, place, range or development and change; while the starting point after "zìcóng" can only be of time.

例：他从屋里走了出来。　　　　（√）

他自从屋里走了出来。　　　（×）

从老人到孩子都喜欢他。　　（√）

自从老人到孩子都喜欢他。　　（×）

公司从无到有，从弱到强，发展很快。（√）

公司自从无到有，自从弱到强，发展很快。（×）

从有了孩子以后，他们觉得更加幸福了。（√）

自从有了孩子以后，他们觉得更加幸福了。（√）

☆ "从"后的时间可以是将来的，也可以是过去的；"自从"只能是过去的时间。

The time after "cóng" can be either future or past time, while the time after "zìcóng" can only be in the past.

例：从有了孩子以后，他们觉得更加幸福了。（√）

自从有了孩子以后，他们觉得更加幸福了。（√）

从明天开始，我们放假。　　　　（√）

自从明天开始，我们放假。　　　（×）

☆ "从"还可以介绍动作行为经过的地点;"自从"没有此用法。

"Cóng" can introduce the place that an action passes by; but "zìcóng" doesn't have this usage.

例:她从我身边过去了。　　　　(√)

她自从我身边过去了。　　　　(×)

23. 在……上 zài... shàng

中间加名词或名词性短语,一般不能加动词性短语。介绍方面、空间范围或条件。

In "zài... shàng" structure, there should be a noun or nominal phrase between "zài" and "shàng", instead of a verbal phrase. This is to introduce the aspect, spacial scope or condition.

例:大卫在学习上很有一套方法。(方面)

科学技术在历史上起过重要作用。(时间)

在实验的基础上,他进行了理论的总结。(前提条件)

24. 在……中 zài... zhōng

中间加动词或动词性短语时,表示动作行为正在进行。中间加名词或名词性短语时,表示范围。

In "zài... zhōng" structure, when there is a verb or verbal phrase between "zài" and "zhōng", it shows an action in progress. When there is a noun or nominal phrase between them, it shows the scope.

例:两国首脑正在谈判中。(正在进行)

他在教学工作中取得了显著的成绩。(范围)

25. 在……下 zài... xià

中间加可兼做动词的名词或名词性短语,表示前提条件。

In "zài... xià" structure, there can be a noun or nominal phrase, which can also be used as a verb, between "zài" and "xià" to show a precondition.

例:在大家的帮助下,他进步很快。(条件)

在老师的鼓励下,他终于敢于在课堂上回答问题了。(前提条件)

Preposition

1—17 题, 在每一个句子下面都有一个指定的词语, 句中 ABCD 是供选择的四个不同位置, 请判断这一词语放在句中哪个位置上恰当。

Please find the proper position out of the four choices of A, B, C, and D for the word below each sentence.

1. 河水 A 欢快地 B 流 C 远方 D。
                      向

2. A 一到圣诞节 B 大卫都要 C 孩子买 D 点儿礼物。
                      给

3. A 我要付款时, B 一摸兜 C 突然发现 D 没带钱。
                      正当

4. A 我要上车时, B 老总突然 C 打来电话, D 原定计划取消了。
                      正当

5. 这么复杂的 A 环境 B 一个十几岁的孩子 C 来说, 怎么应付得 D 了呢?
                      对

6. A 安娜喜欢上京剧以后, B 就 C 天天 D 早起吊嗓子, 练身段。
                      自从

7. A 秋天的到来, B 树叶纷纷 C 落下, D 飘向四面八方。
                      随着

8. A 这是 B 一本 C 颐和园长廊彩画故事的 D 小册子。
                      关于

9. A 他的性格是 B 家庭环境 C 决定 D 的。
                      由

10. A 北方一天比一天冷了, 大雁排着队 B 温暖 C 的南方飞去 D。
                      向

11. 向李老师学汉语已经两年了, A 我们 B 他的 C 教学内容、D 教学态度都很满意。
                      对

12. 目前, 全世界人们 A 用于交流的 B 语言主要 C 英语 D 为主。
                      以

13. 大卫他们 A 正在 B 参加 C 汉语朗读比赛作 D 准备。
                      为

14. 他 A 惊人的毅力,B 克服病痛,C 刻苦练习,D 终于又站了起来。
　　　　以

15. A 去美国 B 考察的机会,我正好 C 看看 D 在那里读书的女儿。
　　　　趁

16. 病床上的周导演 A 让夫人 B 替自己 C 观众们表示感谢 D。
　　　　　　向

17. A 明天 B 开始,我们 C 每天早晨 D5:30 起床跑步锻炼身体。
　　　从

■ 18—50 题,每个句子中有一个或两个空,请在 ABCD 四个答案中选择唯一恰当的一个。

Please choose the correct answer for each blank in the sentences from the four choices of A, B, C, and D.

18. ＿＿＿＿＿＿＿ 天气预报,今明两天将有大到暴雨。
　　A.凭　B.由　C.按　D.据

19. 留学回国的大卫 ＿＿＿＿＿＿＿ 自己的发展前景充满信心。
　　A.对　B.问　C.把　D.跟

20. ＿＿＿＿＿＿＿ 自身条件来说,小李不如小赵,但是小李比小赵刻苦。
　　A.由　B.对　C.自　D.就

21. 李教授走进教室 ＿＿＿＿＿＿＿ 同学们点了点头,开始上课。
　　A.朝　B.就　C.往　D.当

22. 教练对孩子们说:"学会水中憋气 ＿＿＿＿＿＿＿ 你们学会游泳是很重要的。"
　　A.对　B.为　C.关于　D.使

23. 大卫 ＿＿＿＿＿＿＿ 自己的要求太高了,同学们佩服得不得了。
　　A.对　B.给　C.让　D.在

24. 你有什么困难,可以 ＿＿＿＿＿＿＿ 学校提出来。
　　A.请　B.向　C.使　D.拿

25. ＿＿＿＿＿＿＿《北京晚报》报道,北京将推行不合格食品主动召回制度。
　　A.据说　B.据　C.依靠　D.靠

26. 他一直想 ＿＿＿＿＿＿＿ 自己的努力让老总相信自己的能力。
　　A.据　B.凭　C.让　D.把

27. 在燕莎购物商城,售货员 ＿＿＿＿＿＿＿ 我详细地介绍了如何正确使用化妆品。
　　A.和　B.给　C.对　D.从

28. 救护车快速到来，_____ 抢救病人提供了宝贵的时间。
    A. 把 B. 跟 C. 为了 D. 为

29. 我考上了中国传媒大学，_____ 新疆来到了北京。
    A. 向 B. 以 C. 往 D. 从

30. 我们只有坚持 _____ 着北斗星的方向走，才能走出这片茂密的森林。
    A. 到 B. 向 C. 对 D. 在

31. 活动内容 _____ 同学们商量决定。
    A. 从 B. 由 C. 被 D. 向

32. 学校 _____ 我们提供了良好的学习环境。
    A. 为了 B. 就 C. 给 D. 至于

33. 进入深山区，_____ 安全起见，大家一定要紧紧跟着向导。
    A. 为 B. 从 C. 就 D. 以

34. 高尚的人格、精湛的演技 _____ 她赢得了无数观众的心。
    A. 给 B. 从 C. 把 D. 为

35. 事业有成，全 _____ 自己的努力。
    A. 依 B. 靠 C. 指 D. 论

36. _____ 四川省汶川大地震的报道引起了全国乃至全世界人民的广泛关注。
    A. 随着 B. 由于 C. 关于 D. 对于

37. _____ 这两天天气好，赶快把被褥晒一晒。
    A. 凭 B. 趁 C. 靠 D. 据

38. 飞机就要起飞了，_____ 大家的安全，请旅客系好安全带。
    A. 基于 B. 因为 C. 为了 D. 由于

39. 这个班的学生来 _____ 世界各国，但是他们相处得很好。
    A. 从 B. 自 C. 在 D. 出

40. 李教授 _____ 自己渊博的知识、严谨的教学态度赢得了学生的好评。
    A. 借 B. 靠 C. 据 D. 以

41. _____ 我出国进修的事情，领导已经作出了决定。
    A. 鉴于 B. 关于 C. 由于 D. 至于

42. 我们这个班是 _____ 六个国家的留学生组成的。
    A. 被 B. 为 C. 受 D. 由

43. 如果不是大家的帮助与支持，_____ 他个人的本事是完不成这项任务的。
    A. 凭 B. 从 C. 由 D. 用

44. 这几位老先生在学科建设 _____ 作出了巨大的贡献。
    A．内 B．下 C．上 D．中

45. 只有 _____ 天气好的情况 _____ ，飞机才能正点起飞。
    A．在……中   B．在……上
    C．在……里   D．在……下

46. 无论坐飞机还是坐火车，_____ 规定都要进行安全检查。
    A．随着 B．按照 C．经过 D．由于

47. _____ 教育孩子的问题 _____ ，我和父母的意见始终是一致的。
    A．在……中   B．在……上
    C．在……里   D．在……下

48. 中国古代劳动人民 _____ 自己的聪明才智和勤劳的双手，修建了举世闻名的万里长城。
    A．让 B．凭 C．把 D．给

49. 乘飞机要 _____ 身份证购买飞机票。
    A．据 B．靠 C．凭 D．由

50. 在我的记忆 _____ ，我的家乡是一个山清水秀的地方。
    A．中 B．内 C．上 D．下

答疑解惑 Answers and Explanations

1. 选择 C。"向"在句中表示动作的方向，其中一种格式是：动词+向+方位词。本句"向"用在动词"流"的后面，后带方位词"远方"告诉我们水的流向。

The answer is C. "Xiàng" indicates the direction of an action. One of the patterns is: verb + xiàng + the word of direction. In this sentence "xiàng" should be put after the verb "liú", and followed by "yuǎnfāng" to tell the direction the water flows to.

2. 选择 C。"给"在句中介绍动作"买"给予的对象。本句中"大卫"是主语，"买点礼物"是动宾结构，"给"介绍的对象是"孩子"。

The answer is C. "Gěi" introduces the object of the action "mǎi". "Dàwèi" is the subject of the sentence, "mǎi diǎn lǐwù" is a "verb + object" structure. The object of "gěi" is "háizi".

3. 选择 A。"正当……时"在句中表示事情发生正是在另一件事或另一状态出现的时候，多用于句首，介绍出事情发生的时间。本句"正当"用在句首，介绍出"付款"这一事情发生的时间是在"没带钱"这一事情出现的时候。

The answer is A. "Zhèngdāng... shí" indicates something happens when another event or state appears. It's often used at the beginning of a sentence to introduce the time of an action. "Zhèngdāng" in this sentence introduces the time of "fùkuǎn" when "méi dài qián" appears.

4. 选择 A。"正当……时"在句中表示事情发生正是在另一件事或另一状态出现的时候,多用于句首,介绍出事情发生的时间。本句的意思是"我正在上车的时候,老总突然打来电话"。
The answer is A. "Zhèngdāng... shí" indicates something happens while another event or state appears. It's often used at the beginning of a sentence to introduce the time of an action. This sentence indicates "The boss called suddenly when I was about to get on the bus".

5. 选择 B。"对……来说"在句中表示从某人的角度来看问题。"对"的后面应该加上某人。
The answer is B. "Duì... láishuō" indicates to view from someone's angle. Somebody should follow "duì".

6. 选择 A。"自从"在句中介绍时间的起点,仅限指过去的时间。本句中"安娜喜欢上京剧"已经是过去的事情了。
The answer is A. "Zìcóng" introduces the starting point of a past time. In this sentence, "Ānnà xǐhuan shang Jīngjù" is something happened in the past.

7. 选择 A。"随着+名词性短语"在句中表示某动作行为紧跟在另一事件之后,本句"树叶纷纷飘落"是紧跟在大风之后的。
The answer is A. "Suízhe + nominal phrase" indicates one action follows closely another action. In this sentence "shùyè fēnfēn piāoluò" happens just after "fēng".

8. 选择 C。"关于"在句中介绍动作行为涉及的人或事。"关于+名词/名词性短语",可以做定语。本句中"关于+颐和园长廊彩画故事"做"小册子"的定语。
The answer is C. "Guānyú" is to introduce a person or an event related to an action or a behavior. "Guānyú + noun/nominal phrase" can be an attribute. In this sentence, "guānyú + Yíhéyuán chángláng cǎihuà gùshì" is the attribute of "xiǎo cèzi".

9. 选择 B。"由"在句中介绍原因、来源或构成成分、方式。本句中的"由"介绍了他性格形成的原因。
The answer is B. "Yóu" is to introduce a reason, a source, a part or a way. In this sentence, "yóu" introduces the reason for the formation of his character.

10. 选择 B。"向"在句中表示动作的方向,常用的句式:向+方位词+动词。本句"向"+方位词"南方"+动词"飞",表明大雁飞的方向。

The answer is B. "Xiàng" shows the direction of an action. The commonly used sentence structure is "xiàng + words of location + verb". In this sentence, "xiàng"+ word of location "nánfāng"+ verb "fēi" shows the direction of wild geese flying to.

11. 选择 B。"对"在句中介绍出与动作行为有关系的人或事物,表示对待。本句的"对"表示人与人之间的对待关系,即学生对李老师的态度是"满意"的。

The answer is B. "Duì" introduces a person or an event related to an action or a behavior. It shows a relationship of treatment. In this sentence, "duì" indicates a relationship between people, that is, the student is "satisfied" with Mr./Ms. Li.

12. 选择 C。"以"在句中表示动作行为进行的方式。本句的意思是"人们"主要"用于交流的语言"是"英语"。

The answer is C. "Yǐ" shows the way an action is progressing. In this sentence, "rénmen" use "Yīngyǔ" as "jiāoliú de yǔyán".

13. 选择 B。"为"在句中表示原因。句中"参加汉语朗读比赛"是"作准备"的原因。

The answer is B. "Wèi" shows the reason. In this sentence, "cānjiā hànyǔ lǎngdú bǐsài" is the reason for "zuò zhǔnbèi".

14. 选择 A。"以"在句中介绍出动作行为的依据或凭借,多采用"以+名词性短语"的形式。本句动作行为"站"的依据是"惊人的毅力"。

The answer is A. "Yǐ" introduces the basis of an action or a behavior. It often takes the form of "yǐ + nominal phrase". Here the basis for the action "zhàn" is "jīngrén de yìlì".

15. 选择 A。"趁"在句中表示所利用的机会或条件。本句所表示利用的机会是"去美国考察"。

The answer is A. "Chèn" shows the chance or condition being taken. In this sentence, the chance taken is "qù Měiguó kǎochá".

16. 选择 C。"向"在句中表示动作行为的对象,宾语通常是表示人或事物的词语。本句中动作行为的对象是"观众们",宾语是"感谢"。

The answer is C. "Xiàng" shows the object of an action or a behavior, usually about people or events. In this sentence, the recipient of the action is "guānzhòngmen" and the object is "gǎnxiè".

17. 选择 A。"从"在句中介绍起点。"从"后边可以加"开始"等词语,以此来强调和突出起点。本句"明天"就是锻炼身体的起点。

The answer is A. "Cóng" is to show the starting point. "Cóng" can be followed by "kāishǐ" to emphasize and highlight the starting point. In this sentence, "míngtiān" is the starting point of physical exercises.

18. 选择 D。"据"在句中引出某种结论的凭据或依据。本句中的"据"引出"今明两天将有大风"的依据是"天气预报"。

The answer is D. "Jù" is to show the basis of a conclusion. "Jù" introduces the basis of the conclusion "jīn míng liǎng tiān jiāng yǒu dàfēng" is "tiānqì yùbào".

19. 选择 A。"对"在句中引出与动作行为有关系的人或事物,表示对待。本句的"对"表示人"大卫"与事物"发展前景"的对待关系。

The answer is A. "Duì" introduces a person or an event related to an action or a behavior and shows a relationship of treatment. "Duì" in this sentence shows the relationship between the person "Dàwèi" and the event "fāzhǎn qiánjǐng".

20. 选择 D。"就"在句中表示从某一方面进行论述。多用于与其他人或事进行比较。本句就是把小李和小赵的身体情况和学习的态度进行对比。

The answer is D. "Jiù" shows a statement from a certain aspect. It is often used to make a comparison with other people or things. This sentence compares Xiao Li with Xiao Zhao on their physical conditions and learning attitudes.

21. 选择 A。"朝"在句中表示动作、行为的对象。宾语多是表示人的词语。本句中的"朝"表示李教授点头的对象是"学生们"。

The answer is A. "Cháo" shows the object of an action or a behavior. Its object is often words indicating persons. In this sentence, "cháo" shows the recipients of Professor Li's nodding is "xuéshēngmen".

22. 选择 A。"对"在句中表示事物与人之间的对待关系。本句中的"对"表示事物"学会憋气"与人"你们"之间的对待关系。

The answer is A. "Duì" shows a relationship of treatment between people and things. In this sentence, "duì" shows the relationship between the thing "xuéhuì biēqì" and the people "nǐmen".

23. 选择 A。"对"在句中可以表示人与人之间的对待关系。本句表示的是大卫与自己的对待关系。

The answer is A. "Duì" shows a relationship of treatment between people. In this sentence, it shows a relationship between "Dàwèi" and "zìjǐ".

24. 选择 B。"向"在句中表示动作行为的对象,宾语通常是表示人或事物的词语。本句中的"向"所表示的对象是"学校"。

The answer is B. "Xiàng" shows the recipient of an action. Its object is usually a word indicating a person or thing. In this sentence, the recipient of "xiàng" is "xuéxiào".

25. 选择 B。"据"在句中介绍出得出某种结论的凭据或依据,采用格式:据+(……)+说/讲/看/传,引出结论"北京将推行不合格食品主动召回制度"的凭据或依据是《北京晚报》。

The answer is B. "Jù" introduces the basis of a conclusion. The pattern is "jù + (...) + shuō/jiǎng/kàn/chuán". It introduces the basis of the conclusion "Běijīng jiāng tuīxíng bù hégé shípǐn zhǔdòng zhàohuí zhìdù" is "*Běijīng Wǎnbào*".

26. 选择 B。"凭"在句中介绍出动作行为的凭借、依靠或根据,一般后跟名词或名词性短语。本句中的"凭"介绍出让老总相信自己能力的根据是"自己的努力"。

The answer is B. "Píng" introduces the basis of an action or a behavior. It is followed by a noun or nominal phrase. In this sentence, "píng" introduces the basis that makes the boss believe him is "zìjǐ de nǔlì".

27. 选择 B。本句中的"给"介绍出讲解的对象是"我"。

The answer is B. "Gěi" introduces the recipient of explaining is "wǒ".

28. 选择 D。本句"为"介绍出动作行为的对象是:抢救病人。

The answer is D. In this sentence, "wèi" introduces the recipient of the action is "qiǎngjiù bìngrén".

29. 选择 D。本句中的"从"表示地点发生变化。

The answer is D. In this sentence, "cóng" shows the change of location.

30. 选择 B。"向"在句子中表示动作的方向。常用的格式是:向+方位词/处所词+动词。本句中"向"+方位词"北斗星"+动词"走",表明走的方向。

The answer is B. "Xiàng" indicates the direction of an action. The common pattern is: "xiàng + word of direction/location + verb", showing the direction of walking.

31. 选择 B。"由"可在句子中介绍动作行为的发出者。本句的意思是:活动内容是同学们商量决定的。

The answer is B. "Yóu" may introduce the doer of an action. The meaning of the sentence is that the content of the activity is decided by the students.

32. 选择 C。"给"在句中介绍出动作或行为的对象是"我们"。

The answer is C. "Gěi" introduces the object of the action is "wǒmen".

33. 选择 A。"为……起见"表示目的,多用于主语前,有语音停顿。

The answer is A. "Wèi... qǐjiàn" shows the purpose, and is often used before the subject with a phonetic pause.

34. 选择 D。"为"在句子中介绍出动作行为的服务对象是"她"。

The answer is D. "Wèi" introduces the recipient of the action or the behavior is "tā".

35. 选择 B。"靠"在句子中介绍出动作行为依靠的对象是"努力"。

The answer is B. In this sentence, "kào" introduces the object that the action depends on is "nǔlì".

36. 选择 C。"关于"在句中介绍动作行为涉及的人或事。本句中的"关于"+名词性短语"四川省汶川大地震"做"报道"的定语。

The answer is C. "Guānyú" introduces a person or an event related to an action or a behavior. In this sentence, "guānyú"+ nominal phrase "Sìchuān Shěng Wènchuān dà dìzhèn" is the attribute of "bàodào".

37. 选择 B。"趁"在句子中表示所利用的机会或条件。后面的宾语如果是双音节以上的词语时,"趁"后面可以加"着"。本句中的"趁"所表示的是"晒被褥"所利用的条件。

The answer is B. "Chèn" shows the chance or condition being used. If the following object is a disyllabic or multisyllabic word, "chèn" can be followed by "zhe". In this sentence, "chèn" introduces the condition for "shài bèirù".

38. 选择 C。"为了"在句中介绍目的,它通常用的格式是:为了+名词/动词性短语。本句中"为了"介绍的目的是"大家的安全"。

The answer is C. "Wèile" introduces the purpose. Its common pattern is: "wèile" + noun/ nominal phrase. In this sentence, the purpose of "wèile" is "dàjiā de ānquán".

39. 选择 B。"某些动词+自+……"表示动作发生的由来或原因,本句中动词"来"+自+"世界各国",表明这班学生的由来。

The answer is B. "Some verbs + zì +..." is to show the reason of an action. In this sentence, "lái" + "zì"+"shìjiè gèguó" shows where the students come from.

40. 选择 B。"靠"在句中介绍出动作行为依靠的对象或关系。本句中"靠"引出李教授 "赢得学生的好评"是因为"自己渊博的知识、严谨的教学态度"。

The answer is B. "Kào" introduces the object or relation that an action or a behavior depends on. In this sentence, "yíngdé xuéshēng de hǎopíng" is because of Professor Li's "zìjǐ yuānbó de zhīshí, yánjǐn de jiàoxué tàidù".

41. 选择 B。"关于"在句中引出动作行为涉及的人或事。本句的"关于"引出行为涉及的事是 "我出国进修的事情",采用的格式是:关于+短语。

The answer is B. "Guānyú" introduces a person or an event related to an action or a behavior. In this sentence, the event introduced by "guānyú" is "wǒ chū guó jìnxiū de shìqing". The format is "guānyú" + phrase.

42. 选择 D。"由"在句中介绍原因、来源或构成成分、方式。本句中的"由"介绍了这个班级的构成成分——来自六个国家的留学生。

The answer is D. "Yóu" introduces a reason, a source or a composing part, or a way. In this sentence, "yóu" introduces the composing parts of this class—foreign students from six countries.

43. 选择 A。本句中的"凭"后跟名词性短语"他个人的本事",引出动作行为的依据。

The answer is A. In this sentence, "píng" followed by the nominal phrase "tā gèrén de běnshì" introduces the basis of the action.

44. 选择 C。"在……上"在句子中引出方面、空间范围或条件。中间可以加名词或名词性短语,一般不能是动词性短语。本句中的"在……上"中间加了名词性短语"学科建设",引出"这几位老先生"在"学科建设"方面的贡献。

The answer is C. "Zài... shàng" introduces an aspect, a spacial scope or a condition. In between, there can be a noun or nominal phrase, but not verbal phrase. In this sentence, "xuékē jiànshè" is put between "zài" and "shàng", introducing the contribution made by "zhè jǐ wèi lǎoxiānsheng" to "xuékē jiànshè".

45. 选择 D。"在……下"在句中表示前提条件。中间可以加可兼作动词的名词或名词性短语。本句"飞机正点起飞"的前提条件是"天气好"。

The answer is D. "Zài... xià" shows a precondition. A noun or nominal phrase which can also be used as a verb can be put in between. In this sentence, the precondition for "fēijī zhèngdiǎn qǐfēi" is "tiānqì hǎo".

46. 选择 B。"按照"在句中表示遵循某种准则或标准,它的宾语不能是单音节词语。本句中的"按照"后面的宾语是双音节词语"规定",它表示的是无论坐飞机还是坐火车都要遵循的规则。

The answer is B. "Ànzhào" indicates to follow some principles or standards. Its object can't be monosyllabic words. In this sentence, the object after "ànzhào" is the disyllabic word "guīdìng", regulation one must follow whether taking a train or flight.

47. 选择 B。"在……上"在句中介绍方面、空间范围或条件。中间可以加名词或名词性短语，一般不能是动词性短语。本句以"在……上"句式介绍在教育孩子问题方面。

The answer is B. "Zài... shàng" introduces the aspect, spacial scope or condition. A noun or nominal phrase, not a verbal phrase, can be put between "zài" and "shàng". In this sentence, it introduces the aspect of educating the children.

48. 选择 B。本句"凭"介绍出动作行为"修建长城"凭借、依靠的是"聪明才智和勤劳的双手"。

The answer is B. In this sentence, "píng" introduces the basis of the action "xiūjiàn chángchéng" is "cōngmíng cáizhì hé qínláo de shuāngshǒu".

49. 选择 C。本句中的"凭"表示"购买飞机票"的根据是身份证。需要注意的是，当证件或票据作为凭借时，只能用"凭"，不能用"靠"。

The answer is C. In this sentence, "píng" introduces the condition of "gòumǎi fēijīpiào" is "the ID card". Special attention should be paid when a certificate/card or receipt is the basis for doing a certain thing, only "píng" is used, not "kào".

50. 选择 A。如果"在……中"的中间加动词或动词性短语时，表示动作行为正在进行；如果中间加名词或名词性短语时，表示范围。本句"在……中"中间加上了名词性短语"我的记忆"，表示范围。

The answer is A. If a verb or verbal phrase is put between "zài" and "zhōng", it indicates an action is in progress; if a noun or nominal phrase is put between them, it indicates a range. In this sentence, the nominal phrase "wǒ de jìyì" is used, so it indicates a range.

④ 连词 Conjunction

● 连词是用来连接词、短语或小句的。但有的连词只能用来连接词或短语，如"和"；有的连词既可以连接词或短语，也可以连接小句，如"而"；大部分连词用来连接小句，而且要有另一连词或起关联作用的副词与之搭配，如"因为……所以"等。

Conjunction is used to connect words, phrases or clauses. Some conjunctions can only connect words or phrases like "hé"; others can connect words, phrases and clauses like "ér"; most of the conjunctions are used to connect clauses together with other conjunctions or adverbs like "yīnwèi...suǒyǐ".

考点精讲 Examination Points

1. 并 bìng

① 连接双音节动词，按动作行为进行的先后顺序排列。

Connecting disyllabic verbs which are ordered according to the time sequence of the actions.

例：大会讨论并通过了这一法案。

② 连接做状语的双音节词语。

Connecting disyllabic words used as the adverbial.

例：大家认真并努力地工作着。

③ 用于后一小句前，后一小句主语省略。

Being used before the second clause, whose subject is omitted.

例：他扶起了老人，并把老人送到了医院。

2. 并且 bìngqiě

表示同时并存或动作行为先后进行。

Showing two actions existing at the same time or happening one after another.

① 连接并列的动词、动词性短语、能愿动词、形容词、小句等。常用以下格式：

Connecting juxtaposed verbs, verbal phrases, modal verbs, adjectives and clauses.

The following two patterns are most commonly used.

例:国民们都熟悉并且遵守交通规定。

他的话风趣并且幽默。

学生应该并且必须认真学习。

为了迎接朋友的到来,他粉刷了房屋,并且添置了许多新家具。

A. "并且+还+……"。

"bìngqiě + hái +..."

例:这本汉语书有丰富的例句,并且还配有大量的漫画。

B. "并且+……+也……"。

"bìngqiě +... + yě..."

例:时间晚了,并且您的眼睛也不好,您就别送了。

② 连接句子,"并且"后可以有停顿。

Connecting sentences. There can be a pause after "bìngqiě".

例:使用信用卡购物可以不需要随身携带大量现金,并且,避免了准备零钱的麻烦。

特别提示 Special Tips

☆ "并且"一般不连接名词或名词性短语。

"Bìngqiě" usually doesn't connect nouns or nominal phrases.

例:老师并且学生 (×)

☆ "并且"一般不连接单音节形容词。

"Bìngqiě" usually doesn't connect monosyllabic adjectives.

例:他的眼睛又大又亮。 (√)

他的眼睛大并且亮。 (×)

3. 不然 bùrán

① 用于后一小句前,表示对前一小句的假设性否定,引出结论。"不然"后可以带"……的话",常用于口语。

Being used before the second clause for the supposed negation of the first clause, introducing a conclusion. "Bùrán" can be followed by "... dehuà" and used in spoken language.

例:我们最好带一张地图,不然很容易迷路的。

我得把这件事记在本子上,不然的话,一会儿就忘了。

② 用于后一小句前,表示选择,即对前一小句假设性否定后,引出另一种可能。

Being used before the second clause to indicate a choice. Another possibility is introduced after a supposed negation for the first clause.

例:年轻人都叫他李老师,不然,就叫李老。

每周三我一般都在学校,不然,就是临时出去开会了。

4. 从而 cóng'ér

用于后一小句的句首。前一小句介绍原因、方法等,"从而"引出结果、目的,有"因此就""于是""以便"的意思。多用于书面语。

Being used at the beginning of the second clause. The first clause introduces the reason or way and "cóng'ér" introduces the result or purpose, which has the meaning of "yīncǐ jiù", "yúshì", "yǐbiàn". It's usually used in written language.

例:中国调整了经济政策,从而加快了发展的步伐。

老师同学都向他伸出了援助之手,从而使他走出了困境。

5. 而 ér

① 连接语义相对或相反的成分,表示转折。

Connecting elements of semantic contrast or opposition to indicate a transition.

A. 连接语义相对或相反的形容词或形容词性短语、动词或动词性短语及小句,有"但是""却""然而""倒"等意思。

Connecting adjectives, adjective phrases, verbs or verbal phrases and clauses with opposite meanings. It has the meaning of "dànshì", "què", "rán'ér", and "dào".

例:我们的新房布置得简单而温馨。

今天是他毕业的日子,而他一点儿也不高兴。

B. 连接肯定和否定的成分,对比着说明一件事。

Connecting elements of affirmation and negation to explain one thing through comparison.

例:在暑热的季节,我们应该多吃清淡的,而少吃油腻的。

C. 用于前一小句的主语和谓语之间,含有假设的意味,有"如果""要是"的意思,后面要有表示结论的句子。

"Ér" is used between the subject and predicate of the first clause, means "rúguǒ" or "yàoshi", indicating a hypothesis. It should be followed by a clause showing a conclusion.

例:企业家而不了解市场营销情况,必然会失败。

② 连接语义上互相补充的词、短语或小句。表示并列或递进关系。

　　Connecting words, phrases or clauses supplementing each other, and showing juxtaposition or a furthering relation.

　　A. 连接并列的形容词或形容词性短语。

　　Connecting juxtaposed adjectives or adjective phrases.

　　　　例：我们的教室宽敞而明亮。

　　B. 连接承接或递进关系的动词短语或小句。

　　Connecting verbal phrases or clauses of connecting or furthering relation.

　　　　例：中国各地的小吃各有特色，而山西以面食闻名。

③ 连接表示目的、原因、依据、方式、状态的动词或动词性短语。

　　Connecting verbs or verbal phrases of purpose, reason, basis, way or state.

　　　　例：她为了不辜负妈妈的期望而拼命努力学习。

　　　　　　我们应该排队上车，不应该一拥而上。

④ "由+名词/形容词+而+名词/形容词"。表示由一个阶段或状态到另一个阶段或状态。

　　"Yóu + noun/adjective + ér + noun/adjective" shows to change from one stage or state to another stage or state.

　　　　例：他气得脸由红而变白，又由白而变红，一句话都说不出来了。

⑤ 用于一些固定用法中。

　　Being used in fixed expressions.

　　A. "一而再，再而三"，表示重复，常做状语。

　　"Yī'érzài, zài'érsān" indicates repetition and is often used as an adverbial.

　　　　例：我一而再，再而三地嘱咐你要注意安全，可你就是不听。

　　B. "不得而知"，表示不知道。

　　"Bùdé'érzhī" means "don't know".

　　　　例：到底发生了什么，大家都不得而知。

特别提示 *Special Tips*

☆ "而"多用于书面语。

　　"Ér" is used more in written language.

6. 而且 érqiě

① 用于后一小句前，常有"还""也""又""更"等配合使用，表示递进关系。

　　Being used in the second clause, and often combined with "hái", "yě", "yòu", "gèng" to show a furthering relation.

例:这个女孩多才多艺,歌唱得好,而且漫画画得也很好。

② 连接句子。如果句子较长,"而且"后边可以有停顿。

Connecting sentences. If the sentence is long, there will be a pause after "érqiě".

例:这个假期除打算学习外语以外,我还打算外出旅游,而且,有可能的话,我也想去学车。

③ 连接意思相关的形容词、动词或副词,表示递进关系。

Connecting adjectives, verbs or adverbs of related meaning to show a furtheing relation.

例:妹妹美丽而且善良。

大会讨论而且通过了这项决定。

这个周末应该而且必须完成这个报告。

7. 反之 fǎnzhī

表示转折,引出与上文相反的另一个意思或从正反两个方面说明同一个道理。可以连接小句或句子,多用于书面语。当意思明确时,可以有某些省略。有时会说"反之也一样""反之亦然"。

Showing a transition and introducing another meaning contrary to the previous contents, or accounting for the same thing from both positive and negative sides. It connects clauses or sentences and is used more in written language. When the meaning is explicit, there can be some omissions. Sometimes "fǎnzhī yě yíyàng" or "fǎnzhīyìrán" can be used, meaning vice versa.

例:我认为听力的好坏与词汇量的大小很有关系,词汇量大,听力就好;反之,词汇量小,听力就差。

8. 固然 gùrán

① 表示承认某个事实,引起下文的转折。多用于主语后,后一小句常有"但是""可是""不过""而""却"等词与之呼应。

Showing the acceptance of some facts and introducing a transition in the following text. It is often used after the subject, and echoes with "dànshì" "kěshì" "búguò" "ér" "què" in the second clause.

例:小李固然聪明,但是对工作极不负责任。

② "形容词+固然+形容词"。表示转折。

"Adjective + gùrán + adjective" shows a transition.

例:住在郊区,环境固然好,就是交通不太方便。

③ 表示承认某个事实,同时也承认另一个事实。前后不是转折关系,而是递进。后常跟"更"

"也"配合使用。

Showing the acceptance of one fact and another at the same time. The relation of the former and the latter is not transitional, but furthering. It is usually followed by "gèng" or "yě".

例：自己在家做饭固然麻烦些，但是比起饭店的菜更卫生可口。

9. 还是 háishi

① 用在疑问句中，表示选择。

Being used in interrogative sentences to show choices.

例：明天的会是两点还是三点？

我们是先坐飞机，还是先坐火车？

② 用在陈述句中，表示不确定的看法。

Being used in declarative sentences to show uncertain ideas.

A. 句中有"不知道"等表示不确定意思的词语。

There are words indicating uncertainty like "bùzhīdào" in the sentence.

例：我也不知道他是今天来还是明天来。

B. 先提出选择的内容，再说出说话人的观点。

First stating the content of choices, then stating the speaker's own idea.

例：你的话是真的，还是假的，现在已不重要了。

③ 用于"不管/无论/不论……还是……，都……"结构中，表示不受所说情况的影响。

Being used in "bùguǎn/wúlùn/búlùn... háishi..., dōu..." structure to show not being influenced by the said conditions.

例：不管你对我好还是不好，我对你都是真诚的。

10. 好 hǎo

用于后一小句，引出动作行为的目的。多用于口语。

Being used in the second clause to introduce the purpose of an action. It's often used in spoken language.

例：请你大一点儿声音，好让在座的每个人听清楚。

大卫希望多交几个中国朋友，他好有机会多练习口语。

11. 何况 hékuàng

① 用于后一小句，引出更进一层的意思，带有反问的语气。"何况"前可以加"更""又"，后可以加"又"。前一小句中常有"都""还""尚且"等词。

Being used in the latter clause to introduce a furthering meaning with the tone of a rhetorical question. "Gèng" and "yòu" can be put before "hékuàng"; "yòu" can be put after "hékuàng". There are often "dōu", "hái", "shàngqiě" in the first clause.

例：刚才经理跟他说他都没同意，更何况你呢？

这种天气坐在屋里不动都觉得热，何况又是露天作业呢？

② 用于后一小句，补充说明更进一步的理由，相当于"况且"。

Being used in the second clause to supplement further reasons, similar to "kuàngqiě".

例：我来这儿已经不止一次了，何况我又不是孩子，我怎么会迷路呢？

12. 或者 huòzhě

① 表示选择，提出多种选项。

Showing choices.

例：你有问题给我打电话或者发短信都可以。

② 表示多种情况交替出现。

Showing situations appearing alternately.

例：每个周末，我或者在家看书，或者和朋友一起去逛街。

③ 表示等同。

Showing equivalence.

例：马铃薯，或者说土豆，在北方是一种很普通的农作物。

④ 用于"无论/不论/不管……或者……，……"结构中，表示包括所有的情况。

Being used in "wúlùn/búlùn/bùguǎn... huòzhě...,..." structure to show all the situations are included.

例：不管刮风或者下雨，他从没有迟到过。

13. 既 jì

① 用于前一小句，表示承认某一事实或前提，后一小句根据这个事实或前提做出推断或结论，多与"就"搭配使用，只能用于主语后。多用于书面语，相当于"既然"。

Being used in the first clause to show the acceptance of a fact or precondition, based on which there is an inference or a conclusion in the second clause starting with "jiù". It can only be used after the subject and often in written language, similar to "jìrán".

例：你既来上课，就要专心听讲。

② 连接两个结构相同或相似的并列成分，表示两种情况同时存在。常用"既……也/又……"结构。

Connecting juxtaposed elements to show two coexisting situations. "Jì... yě/yòu..." is a commonly used structure.

例：大卫既精通汉语，也精通英语。

这个姑娘既稳重又大方。

14. 鉴于 jiànyú

用于表示因果关系的复句中，引出动作行为的原因或理由。一般用于句首。

Being used in complex sentences of cause and effect to introduce reasons of an action or a behavior. It's often used at the beginning of the sentence.

例：鉴于你的身体原因，我们建议你住院观察。

鉴于近日异常的天气变化，气象台提醒人们提防山洪暴发。

15. 可见 kějiàn

用于后一小句前，引出根据前一小句的现象所做出的判断或结论。可以连接小句、句子或段落

Being used before the second clause to introduce a judgment or conclusion based on the facts in the first clause. It can connect clauses, sentences or paragraphs.

例：他主动把捡到的钱包交还了失主，可见他是一个拾金不昧的好孩子。

现在无论男女老幼都在积极学外语，可见人人都想当好奥运东道主。

16. 况且 kuàngqiě

表示进一步说明理由或补充新的理由。常与副词"也""又""还"等配合使用。

Showing a further or new reason. It is often used together with adverbs like "yě" "yòu" and "hái".

例：他是我的朋友，我必须帮助他，况且，在我最困难的时候他帮助过我。

特别提示 *Special Tips*

☆ "况且"没有"何况"的第一种用法，也就是说"况且"不能用反问的语气引出进一步的理由。

"Kuàngqiě" does not have the first usage of "hékuàng", that is to say, "kuàngqiě" can't introduce a further reason with the tone of a rhetorical question.

例：这个问题孩子都会回答，何况你呢？ （√）

这个问题孩子都会回答，况且你呢？ （×）

17. 免得 miǎnde

用于后一小句的句首，表示避免不希望的事情发生。

Being used at the beginning of the second clause meaning to avoid something unwanted to happen.

例：请你早作决定，免得到时来不及。

你一到就给我们来电话，免得让我们着急。

18. 难怪 nánguài

表示在知道了原因之后，对发生的某种情况就不觉得奇怪了。

Showing after getting to know the reason, one doesn't feel strange about something happened.

例：原来你们以前学的是一个专业，难怪你们谈得这么投机。

难怪他身体这么好，原来他每天都坚持锻炼身体，风雨无阻。

19. 宁可 nìngkě

在比较了两方面的利害得失以后，选择"宁可"后的一方面。常用以下格式：

After comparing gains and losses of two aspects, one chooses the one after "nìngkě". The following patterns are commonly used:

① "宁可……，也不/决不……"。"也不/决不"引出舍弃的一方面。

In the structure "nìngkě..., yěbù/juébù...", "yYěbù/juébù" introduces the choice being given up.

例：宁可我被饿死，也决不接受你的施舍。

② "与其……，宁可……"。"与其"引出舍弃的一方面。

In the structure "yǔqí..., nìngkě...", "yǔqí" introduces the choice being given up.

例：与其让我和他一起出去玩，我宁可留在家里。

③ "宁可……，也要……"。"也要"引出选择的目的。

In the structure "nìngkě..., yěyào...", "yěyào" introduces the purpose of a choice.

例：妈妈宁可自己省吃俭用，也要供孩子读书。

④ "……，宁可……"。前一小句引出舍弃的原因。

In the structure "..., nìngkě...", the first clause introduces the reason of giving up.

例：跟旅行社旅游限制太多，我说咱们宁可自己去。

特别提示 Special Tips

☆ "宁肯"和"宁愿"的意义、用法和"宁可"基本相同，只是更加强调个人的意愿。

The meaning and usage of "nìngkěn" and "nìngyuàn" are similar to "nìngkě", but more emphasize individual will.

例：我宁肯自己吃亏，也不能让别人吃亏。

这个时间路上太堵了，我宁愿走着去。

20. 任 rèn

表示"不管""无论""不论"的意思，也就是"在任何条件下都如此"的意思。

Showing the meaning of "bùguǎn", "wúlùn", "búlùn", that is, "under any circumstances".

例：任你是谁，都要遵守国家的法律。

任天气如何，他每天都是最早一个到校。

21. 甚至 shènzhì

连接多项词、短语、小句，"甚至"放在最后一项的前面，含有更进一层的意思。

Connecting several words, phrases and clauses. It's put before the last item with a furthering meaning.

例：我走遍了中国的大江南北，东北、内蒙古、云南、海南，甚至西藏我都去过。

大多数人，甚至幼儿园的小朋友，都知道要爱护环境。

这次运动会，不但学生参加了，甚至老师也参加了。

22. 省得 shěngde

避免不好的或不希望的事情发生。用于后一小句前，相当于"免得"，多用于口语。

It is used to avoid bad or unwanted things to happen. It's used before the latter clause, similar to "miǎnde". It is often used in spoken language.

例：你到了以后马上给我们打电话，省得大家担心。

我们一定要注意饮食卫生，省得吃坏肚子。

23. 要么 yàome

① 用于"……，要么……"结构中，表示如果前面所说的情况不能实现，就选择后者，有让步的意思。

The structure "..., yàome... "shows that if the former situation can't be realized, the latter can be chosen. It indicates a concession.

例：你太累了，干脆让别人干吧，要么你歇会儿再干。

② 用于"要么……，要么……"结构中，表示从二者之间选择其中的一个，前后两项是互相排斥的。

"Yàome..., yàome..." indicates to choose one between two mutually exclusive choices.

例：要么你去，要么我去，反正不能两个人一起去。

24. 以 yǐ

用于后一小句前,表示动作行为的目的。有"为了""以便"的意思。

Being used before the second clause to show the purpose of an action or a behavior. It has the meaning of "wèile", "yǐbiàn".

例:每个小区都安装了健身器材,以方便人们锻炼身体。

大家平时应多看中文电视、多听中文广播,以提高自己的汉语听说水平。

25. 以便 yǐbiàn

用于后一小句前,表示前一小句所说的容易使后一小句所说的目的实现。

Being used before the second clause to show that the purpose expressed in it is likely to be realized based on what is said in the first clause.

例:大卫旅游时总爱带着摄像机,以便随时把美景记录下来。

请大家把手机号码留给我,以便有事的时候及时通知大家。

26. 以免 yǐmiǎn

用于后一小句前,表示前一小句所说的可以使后一小句所说的情况不发生,后一小句所说的常常是不好的或不希望发生的情况。相当于"免得",多用于书面语。

Being used before the first clause to show that something expressed in the second clause will not happen due to what is said in the first clause. Something in the second clause is usually bad or unwanted. It's similar to "miǎnde", and often used in written language.

例:天气多变,我们要随时添减衣服,以免感冒。

外出时一定要看管好自己的物品,以免丢失。

27. 以至 yǐzhì

① 表示时间、数量、程度、范围上的延伸。可连接两项或多项词或短语,"以至"用于最后一项前

Showing the extension of time, quantity, degree or range. It can connect two or more words or phrases, while "yǐzhì" is put before the last item.

例:老人、中年人、青年人,以至孩子,不同年龄段都有书法爱好者。

玛丽反复读课文,一遍、两遍、三遍,以至十几遍,最后终于读得语音标准、十分流畅了。

② 用于后一小句前,表示因为前一小句所说的情况而产生后一小句的结果。

Being used before the latter clause in which a result appears due to what is said in the first clause.

例：她是个可爱的姑娘，以至人人都喜欢她。

　　他太累了，以至坐在椅子上不知不觉就睡着了。

28. 以致 yǐzhì

用于后一小句前，表示因为前一小句所说的原因而使后一小句所说的结果产生，这一结果是说话人不希望发生的。

Being used before the second clause in which a result appears due to what is said in the first clause. The result is unwanted.

例：她总是算计别人，以致没有一个朋友。

　　老李常常暴饮暴食，以致越来越胖。

特别提示 *Special Tips*

☆ "以致"不能表示时间、数量、程度、范围的延伸。

"Yǐzhì (以致)" can't show the extension of time, quantity, degree or range.

例：进行改革以后，工作效率提高几倍，以至十几倍。(√)

　　进行改革以后，工作效率提高几倍，以致十几倍。(×)

☆ "以致"所说的结果是说话人不希望发生的；"以至"所说的结果是因为前一小句所说的情况程度深而产生的。

The result indicated by "yǐzhì(以致)" is something unwanted; the result indicated by "yǐzhì (以至)" appears due to the strong influence of the situation in the first clause.

例：他学习起来非常专注，以至常常忘了吃饭。

　　由于事前没有作好准备，以致在工作中出了差错。

☆ "以至"可以连接词、短语和小句；"以致"一般只连接小句。

"Yǐzhì (以至)" can connect words, phrases and clauses, while "yǐzhì (以致)" usually connects clauses.

29. 再说 zàishuō

用于后一小句前，进一步补充说明原因，多用于口语。

Being used before the second clause to further explain a reason, it's often used in spoken language.

例：他第一次来北京，再说还带了很多行李，我们当然得去接他。

　　这家酒店的服务一般，再说房价太贵了，我们还是换一家吧。

☆ "再说"还可做动词使用,表示等以后再处理或考虑。

"Zàishuō" can be used as a verb to indicate to deal with or consider at a later time.

例:我现在很忙,这事以后再说吧。

我们先吃饭,有什么事吃了饭再说好吗?

30. 至于 zhìyú

表示提出另一件事,常用于小句或句子的句首。

It is used to mention another thing, often put at the beginning of a clause or sentence.

例:我只知道他回国了,至于什么时候走的就不清楚了。

这只是大家的建议,至于是否可行,还请您再考虑考虑。

☆ "至于"还可做副词使用,表示达到了某种程度。常用于否定句或反问句中。

"Zhìyú" can also be used as an adverb to show reaching a certain degree. It's often used in negative sentences or rhetorical questions.

例:你不至于连这么简单的题都不会做吧?

你要是早点儿注意身体,哪至于病得这么严重啊?

强化练习 Exercises

■ 1—10题,在每一个句子下面都有一个指定的词语,句中 ABCD 是供选择的四个不同位置,请判断这一词语放在句中哪个位置上恰当。

Please find the proper position out of the four choices of A, B, C, and D for the word below each sentence.

1. A 安娜今天 B 这么高兴, C 原来她的毕业论文通过 D 了。
　　　　　　　　　　　　难怪

2. 这里 A 景色 B 优美, C 空气也新鲜, D 我们就多住几天吧。
　　　　　　　　　　　　并且

3. A 这本书 B 明天就要还, C 我可以 D 借给你。
　　　　　　　　　　　　不然

4. 他 A 晚饭后, B 不是读书, C 就是看报纸, D 就是搞创作。
　　　　　　　　　　　　要么

5. 大卫不仅会 A 开汽车，B 还会 C 修理汽车 D。
$$而且$$

6. 这 A 是 B 一项 C 伟大 D 艰巨的任务。
$$而$$

7. 步行上班 A 耽误一些时间，B 但是 C 对身体 D 有好处。
$$固然$$

8. A 这么长时间 B 看不见大卫，C 原来他 D 回国了。
$$难怪$$

9. A 你的表现，B 我们 C 决定 D 辞退你。
$$鉴于$$

10. A 他在家里 B 都不爱说话，更 C 在这么多生人面前 D 唱歌了。
$$何况$$

11—50 题，每个句子中有一个或两个空，请在 ABCD 四个答案中选择唯一恰当的一个。
Please choose the correct answer for each blank from the four choices of A, B, C, and D.

11. 小王 _____ 接受能力与反应能力都较慢，但他学习刻苦，次次考试都名列前茅。
   A. 甚至　B. 固然　C. 可见　D. 至于

12. 我不知道安娜是喜欢中国古典音乐，_____ 不喜欢中国古典音乐。
   A. 并且　B. 从而　C. 还是　D. 或者

13. 松鼠的窝通常搭在树枝分叉的地方，_____ 干净 _____ 暖和。
   A. 既……又……　　　B. 一面……一面……
   C. 虽然……但是……　D. 或者……或者……

14. 图书馆的书是供大家使用的，借了书籍一定要按时归还，_____ 妨碍别人使用。
   A. 以　B. 免　C. 省　D. 以免

15. 这部电视剧今天播 _____ 明天播？
   A. 还是　B. 或者　C. 并且　D. 以便

16. 请把字写得工整规范些，_____ 让别人看清楚。
   A. 为　B. 好　C. 而　D. 任

17. 你 _____ 知道自己做错了，就应该及时纠正。
   A. 因为　B. 既然　C. 虽然　D. 不但

18. 大卫希望在中国多待几年，_____ 有更多的机会了解中国。
   A. 好　B. 并且　C. 而且　D. 反之

19. 这样做 _____ 稳妥, _____ 太费事,恐怕时间来不及。
    A．如果……那么…… 　　B．不仅……而且……
    C．固然……可是…… 　　D．与其……不如……

20. 爸爸妈妈已经 _____ 搬到北京,和我们住在一起,安度晚年。
    A．决定并商量 　　B．商量并决定
    C．决定又商量 　　D．商量又决定

21. 你不愿意乘车去颐和园, _____ 咱们坐游艇去?
    A．要是　B．要么　C．要求　D．要

22. 你们叫我张老师, _____ 叫我小张都可以。
    A．以便　B．而且　C．可见　D．或者

23. 到了北京要及时给家里打电话 _____ 父母担心。
    A．不要　B．省得　C．省　D．不让

24. 不管刮大风 _____ 下大雪,明天出行的计划都不变。
    A．还是　B．要么　C．固然　D．况且

25. 用钢笔写字我都写不好,更 _____ 写毛笔字了。
    A．并且　B．何况　C．除非　D．难道

26. 咱们快去吧, _____ 大家等急了。
    A．可以　B．省得　C．以　D．可

27. 朱老师 _____ 学识渊博,又亲切和蔼。
    A．何况　B．还是　C．既　D．要么

28. 星期天我有个重要的会, _____ 我可以陪妈妈去外地旅游。
    A．所以　B．不然　C．不过　D．就

29. 这只是我个人的想法, _____ 是否可行,大家提提意见。
    A．不过　B．甚至　C．至于　D．至少

30. 大卫 _____ 喜欢中国的京剧,也喜欢中国的书法。
    A．既　B．而且　C．固然　D．要么

31. 这几年人们的收入增加了,很多人买新房,买别墅, _____ 买汽车的人就更多了。
    A．至于　B．至少　C．不过　D．至今

32. 北京的地方这么大, _____ 你连个电话号码也没有,这找起来可就太困难了。
    A．鉴于　B．况且　C．宁可　D．至于

33. 夏天各海滨城市消夏避暑的游人甚多,我 _____ 待在家里。
    A．宁可　B．省得　C．要么　D．以免

34. 动物园里的鸟种类很多,_____ 究竟有多少种,我就说不清了。
   A. 关于   B. 对于   C. 至于   D. 至少

35. 大卫专心致志地看报纸,做摘抄,_____ 妈妈进屋来他都不知道。
   A. 以免   B. 以致   C. 以至   D. 以及

36. 小李是个爽快的人,说话直来直去,_____ 别人是否接受得了,他没考虑。
   A. 至少   B. 至于   C. 至上   D. 甚至

37. 科学发展得真快,_____ 很多人跟不上时代的步伐。
   A. 以免   B. 以致   C. 以至   D. 以及

38. 大卫 _____ 不睡觉,也要把这篇文章背下来。
   A. 并且   B. 从而   C. 再说   D. 宁可

39. _____ 你的表现与工作能力,老总决定提升你为总经理助理。
   A. 况且   B. 何况   C. 至于   D. 鉴于

40. 这次参加京剧票友比赛盛况空前,有五六岁的小朋友,有中青年,_____ 80多岁的老人也来参赛。
   A. 鉴于   B. 甚至   C. 以免   D. 以便

41. 任何时候我们都必须按客观规律办事,_____ 就会受到客观规律的惩罚。
   A. 反之   B. 从而   C. 并且   D. 免得

42. 你叫它土豆,_____ 叫马铃薯都对,因为前者是人们的俗称,后者是它的学名。
   A. 是   B. 还是   C. 要么   D. 或者

43. 你有不明白的问题,找李老师 _____ 找张老师都可以。
   A. 并且   B. 不然   C. 宁可   D. 或者

44. 雨 _____ 停了,我们就快点儿赶路吧!
   A. 并且   B. 从而   C. 既   D. 好

45. 保护环境和生态平衡已是当务之急,_____ 我们人类将失去生存的家园。
   A. 而且   B. 反之   C. 鉴于   D. 可见

46. 夏天千万不要到非游泳区游泳,_____ 发生意外。
   A. 免得   B. 不得   C. 值得   D. 难得

47. 他歌唱得很好,可是他不认识五线谱,_____ 连简谱都不认识。
   A. 何况   B. 或者   C. 甚至   D. 从而

48. 现在给他打电话,恐怕来不及了,_____ 他也不一定喜欢划船。
   A. 再见   B. 再回   C. 再说   D. 说说

49. 顾客一定要保留好购物凭证,发现问题 _____ 退换。
    A. 以免   B. 以便   C. 以至   D. 以

50. 他酒后驾车回家的路上,撞了前边正常行驶的车,_____ 酒后驾车有多危险!
    A. 可见   B. 可以   C. 看见   D. 知道

答疑解惑 Answers and Explanations

1. 选择 A。"难怪"表示在知道了原因之后,对发生的某种情况就不觉得奇怪了。本句的意思是:当知道了安娜毕业论文通过了以后,对她的高兴也就不觉得奇怪了。所以,选择 A 是正确的。

The answer is A. "Nánguài" indicates one doesn't feel strange after getting to know the reason. In this sentence, after knowing that Anna's thesis has passed, one doesn't feel surprised at her happiness.

2. 选择 C。"并且"表示同时并存或动作行为先后进行。通常所用的句式是:并且+……+ 也……。本句是"并且+空气+也新鲜",表示"景色优美"和"空气新鲜"这两种情况同时并存。

The answer is C. "Bìngqiě" indicates two things existing at the same time or one after another. A common pattern is: "bìngqiě +... + yě...". In this sentence, coexist "bìngqiě + kōngqì + yě xīnxiān" shows "jǐnsè yōuměi" and "kōngqì xīnxiān" coexist.

3. 选择 C。"不然"在句子中用于后一小句前,表示对前一小句的假设性否定,引出结论。本句中的"不然"用于后一小句"我可以借给你"的前边,表示对前一小句"这本书明天就要还"的假设性否定,引出结论——不能借给你。

The answer is C. "Bùrán" is used before the second clause of the sentence to show a supposed negation to the first clause and give a conclusion. In this sentence, "bùrán" is put before the second clause to show the supposed negation to the first clause and draw the conclusion that I can't lend it to you.

4. 选择 D。"要么"表示从多种情况之间选择其中的一个,前后几项是互相排斥的。本题的意思是:他晚饭后,常常看书、看报纸或是搞创作。

The answer is D. "Yàome" indicates to choose one from many choices, which are exclusive. The implication of this sentence is: After dinner, he usually either reads books or magazines, or writes something.

5. 选择 B。"而且"用于后一小句,常有"还""也""又""更"等配合使用,表示递进关系。本句的意思是:大卫既会开汽车,又会修汽车。
The answer is B. "Érqiě" is used in the second clause, and combined with "hái", "yě",

"yòu","gèng". It shows a furthering relation. The meaning of this sentence is David can both drive and repair a car.

6. 选择 D。"而"在句子中连接语义上互相补充的词、短语或小句,表示并列或递进关系。本句中的"而"连接的是形容词"伟大"和"艰巨",二者是并列关系。

The answer is D. "Ér" connects semantically complementary words, phrases or clauses to show a juxtaposition or furthering relation. In this sentence, "ér" connects the adjectives "wěidà" and "jiānjù" which are juxtapositional.

7. 选择 A。"固然"表示承认某个事实,引起下文的转折。多用于主语后,后一小句常有"但是""可是""不过""而""却"等词与之呼应。"步行上班"是本句的主语,所以应该选择 A。

The answer is A. "Gùrán" indicates the acknowledgement of some facts and introduces a transition. It's often used after the subject and combined with"dànshì,""kěshì","búguò", "ér" or "què" in the second clause. "Bùxíng shàngbān" is the subject of the sentence, so A is correct.

8. 选择 A。"难怪"表示在知道了原因之后,对发生的某种情况就不觉得奇怪了。本句的意思是:知道大卫回国了,对长时间看不见他也就不奇怪了。所以,选择 A 是正确的。

The answer is A. "Nánguài" indicates one doesn't feel strange after getting to know the reason. The meaning of this sentence is: When the fact that David has gone back to his country is known, it's not strange that people haven't seen him for a long time.

9. 选择 A。"鉴于"用于表示因果关系的复句中,引出动作行为的原因或理由。一般用于句首。本句的意思是:因为你的表现不好,所以辞退你。

The answer is A. "Jiànyú" is used in the complex sentence of cause and effect to show the reason of an action or a behavior. It's often used at the beginning of a sentence. The meaning of this sentence is: Because of your poor performance, we have decided to fire you.

10. 选择 C。"何况"用于后一小句,引出更进一层的意思,带有反问的语气。"何况"前可以加"更"或"又",后可以加"又"。前一小句中常有"都""还"和"尚且"等词。

The answer is C. "Hékuàng" is used in the second clause to show a furthering meaning with the tone of a rhetorical question. "Gèng" or "yòu" can be put before "hékuàng", and "yòu" can be used after it. There are often "dōu", "hái" and "shàngqiě" in the first clause.

11. 选择 B。"固然"表示承认某个事实,引起下文的转折。多用于主语后,后一小句常有"但是"、"可是""不过""而""却"等词与之呼应。本题中首先承认"小王接受能力与反应能力都较慢",再引起转折——"他学习刻苦,次次考试都名列前茅"。

The answer is B. "Gùrán" indicates the the acknowledgement of some facts and introduces a transition. It's often used after the subject, "dànshì", "kěshì", "búguò", "ér", or "què" are often used in the latter clause. In this sentence, first is the acknowledgement of the fact "Xiǎo Wáng jiēshòu nénglì yǔ fǎnyìng nénglì dōu jiào màn", then is the transition: "tā xuéxí kèkǔ, cì cì kǎoshì dōu míngliè–qiánmáo".

12. 选择 C。"还是"用在陈述句中,表示不确定的看法。本句中有"不知道"一词,表示"我对安娜喜欢什么"并不确定。
The answer is C. "Háishi" is used in declarative sentences to show uncertain ideas. In this sentence, "bù zhīdào" shows I am not sure about what Anna likes.

13. 选择 A。"既"在句子中连接并列成分,表示两种情况同时存在。常用句式有:既……又……。连接结构和音节数都相同或相似的形容词、动词或动词性短语。本句中的"既……又……"连接结构和音节数都相同的形容词"干净、暖和",表示并列关系。因此,选择 A 是正确的。
The answer is A. "Jì" connects elements of juxtaposition to show two situations exist at the same time. The common pattern is: "jì... yòu...". It connects adjectives, verbs or verbal phrases of similar structures and syllables. In this sentence, "jì... yòu..." connects "gānjìng", "nuǎnhuo", two adjectives with the same structures and syllables to show juxtaposition.

14. 选择 D。"以免"在句子中用于后一小句前,表示前一小句所说的可以使后一小句所说的情况不发生,后一小句所说的常常是不好的或不希望发生的情况。相当于"免得",多用于书面语。本句中的前一小句所说的"书籍要按时归还"是不希望"妨碍别人使用"这一情况发生。所以,选择 D 是正确的。
The answer is D. "Yǐmiǎn" is used before the second clause to show what is said in the first clause can help avoid the situation in the second. What is said in the second is usually bad or unwanted. It's similar to "miǎnde" and often used in written language. In this sentence, what is said in the former clause "shūjí yào ànshí guīhuán" indicates "fáng'ài biérén shǐyòng" is not expected to happen.

15. 选择 A。"还是"用在疑问句中,表示选择。本句是一个疑问句,表示在"今天播"和"明天播"之间做一选择。
The answer is A. "Háishi" is used in interrogative sentences to show choices. This sentence is an interrogative sentence, showing to make a choice between "jīntiān bō" and "míngtiān bō".

16. 选择 B。"好"在句子中用于后一小句,引出动作行为的目的,多用于口语。本句中的"好"用于后一小句之前,引出"写得工整规范"的目的是"让别人看清楚"。

The answer is B. "Hǎo" is used in the second clause to introduce the purpose of an action or a behavior. It's often used in spoken language. In this sentence, "hǎo" is used before the second clause to introduce the purpose of "xiě de gōngzhěng guīfàn" is "ràng biérén kàn qīngchu".

17. 选择 B。"既然"在句子中用于前一小句,表示承认某一事实或前提,后一小句根据这个事实或前提做出推断或结论。只能用于主语后。本句中的"既然"表示"知道自己做错"这一事实,后一小句根据这个事实做出结论"应该及时纠正"。所以,选择 B 是正确的。

The answer is B. "Jìrán" is used in the first clause to show the acknowledgement of a fact or precondition, on which an inference or a conclusion is based. It can only be put after the subject. In this sentence, "jìrán" shows the fact "zhīdào zìjǐ zuòcuò", and a conclusion "yīnggāi jíshí jiūzhèng" is drawn according to the fact.

18. 选择 A。"好"在句子中用于后一小句,引出动作行为的目的。多用于口语。本句中的"好"用于后一小句之前,引出"在中国多待几年"的目的是"有更多的机会了解中国"。

The answer is A. "Hǎo" is used in the second clause to introduce the purpose of an action. It's often used in spoken language. In this sentence, "hǎo" is used in the second clause to introduce the purpose of "zài Zhōngguó duō dāi jǐ nián" is "yǒu gèng duō de jīhuì liǎojiě Zhōngguó".

19. 选择 C。"固然"表示承认某个事实,引起下文的转折。多用于主语后,后一小句常有"但是""可是""不过""而""却"等词与之呼应。本句中的"固然"表示首先承认"这样做稳妥"的事实,再引起下文转折,后面的小句有"可是"一词与之呼应,所以选择 C 是正确的。

The answer is C. "Gùrán" indicates the acknowledgement of a certain fact and introduces a transition. It's often used after the subject and combined with "dànshì", "kěshì" and "búguò", "ér" or "què" in the second clause. In this sentence, "gùrán" shows the acknowledgement of the fact "zhèyàng zuò wěntuǒ" first, then introduces the transition. There is "kěshì" in the second clause to echo with it, so C is correct.

20. 选择 B。"并"可以连接双音节动词,按动作行为进行的先后顺序排列。本题中的两个动词"商量"和"决定"如果按照动作行为进行的先后顺序排列,应该先"商量",然后"决定"。所以,B 是正确答案。

The answer is B. "Bìng" can connect disyllabic verbs, which are arranged in time sequence. In this sentence, if the two verbs "shāngliang" and "juédìng" are arranged in time sequence, "shāngliang" should come first, followed by "juédìng". Therefore, B is correct.

21. 选择B。"要么"在使用时,有一个常见格式:……,要么……。表示如果前面所说的情况不能实现,就选择后者,有让步的意思。本句中"要么"前面说"不愿意乘车去颐和园",后面一句让步"坐游艇"。所以,选择B是正确的。

The answer is B. When "yàome" is used, there is a common pattern: "..., yàome...". It shows if what is said first can't be realized, one can choose the latter, with a sense of concession. In this sentence, "bú yuànyì chéng chē qù Yíhéyuán" is before "yàome", followed by "zuò yóutǐng". So B is correct.

22. 选择D。"或者"在句子中可以表示二者等同。本句中的"张老师"和"小张"其实是一个人,所以应该选择D。

The answer is D. "Huòzhě" indicates two choices are the same. In this sentence, "Zhāng lǎoshī" and "Xiǎo Zhāng" refer to the same person, so D is the correct answer.

23. 选择B。"省得"表示避免不好的或不希望的事情发生,用于后一小句前,相当于"免得"。多用于口语。本句中的"省得"表示不要让父母担心。因此,选择B是正确的。

The answer is B. "Shěngde" indicates to avoid bad or unwanted things. It's used before the second clause, similar to "miǎnde". It's often used in spoken language. In this sentence, "shěngde" shows not to have parents worry. So B is correct.

24. 选择A。"还是"在句子中的常见的格式之一是:无论/不论/不管……还是……,……。表示包括所有的情况。本句中的"还是"表示包括"刮大风,下大雪"等所有恶劣天气。

The answer is A. A common pattern of "háishi" is: "wúlùn/búlùn/bùguǎn... háishi..., ...", showing all is included. In this sentence, "háishi" shows all bad weathers are included, like "guā dàfēng", "xià dàxuě".

25. 选择B。"何况"在句子中用于后一小句,引出更进一层的意思,带有反问的语气。"何况"前可以加"更"或"又",后可以加"又"。前一小句中常有"都""还""尚且"等词。本句中的"何况"前面加一"更",表示更进一层的意思。本题的意思是:钢笔字都写不好,怎么能把毛笔字写好呢?所以,选择B是正确的。

The answer is B. "Hékuàng" is used in the second clause to introduce a furthering meaning. It has the tone of a rhetorical question. "Gèng" or "yòu" can be put before "hékuàng", and "yòu" after it. There are often "dōu", "hái", "shàngqiě" in the former clause. In this sentence, "gèng" is put before "hékuàng" to show a furthering meaning. The meaning of this sentence is: I cannot write well in pen, not to mention in brush. So, B is correct.

26. 选择B。"省得"表示避免不好的或不希望的事情发生,用于后一小句前,相当于"免得",多用于口语。本句中的"省得"表示不希望发生让"大家等急了"的事情。所以,选择B是正确的。

The answer is B. "Shĕngde" shows to avoid something bad or unwanted. It's used in the second clause, similar to "miănde". It is often used in spoken language. In this sentence, "shĕngde" shows one doesn't hope the happening of "dàjiā dĕng jí le".

27. 选择 C。"既"在句子中连接并列成分,表示两种情况同时存在。常用的句式有:既……又……。本句中的"既"和"又"连接的是"学识渊博"和"亲切和蔼"。

The answer is C. "Jì" connects two juxtaposed elements to show two things exist at the same time. A common pattern is "jì... yòu...". In this sentence, it connects "xuéshí yuānbó" with "qīnqiè hé'ǎi".

28. 选择 B。"不然"在句子中用于后一小句前,表示对前一小句的假设性否定,引出结论。"不然"后可以带"的话",常用于口语。本句中的"不然"用于后一小句"我可以陪妈妈去外地旅游"前,表示对前一个小句"星期天我有个重要的会"的假设性否定。因此,选择 B 是正确的。

The answer is B. "Bùrán" is used before the second clause to show the supposed negation of the first clause and introduce a conclusion. "Dehuà" can be put after "bùrán" and often used in spoken language. In this sentence, "bùrán" is used before the second clause "wǒ kěyǐ péi māma qù wàidì lǚyóu". It shows the supposed negation to the first clause "xīngqītiān wǒ yǒu gè zhòngyào de huì". So B is the correct answer.

29. 选择 C。"至于"表示提出另一件事,常用于小句或句子的句首。本句中"至于"前说的是一件事,即"这只是我个人的想法","至于"后提出的是另一件事,即"大家提意见"。所以,选择 C 是正确的。

The answer is C. "Zhìyú" shows to raise another thing. It's often used in a clause or at the beginning of a sentence. In this sentence, one thing is stated before "zhìyú", that is, "zhè zhǐshì wǒ gèrén de xiǎngfǎ". Another thing is mentioned after "zhìyú", that is, "dàjiā tí yìjiàn". So C is correct.

30. 选择 A。"既"在句子中连接并列成分,表示两种情况同时存在。常用的句式是:既……也……。本句中的"既"和"也"连接两个结构相同的短语:"喜欢中国的京剧"和"喜欢中国的书法"。

The answer is A. "Jì" connects two juxtaposed elements to show two things exist at the same time. A common pattern is: "jì... yě...". In this sentence, it connects two phrases of the same structure: "xǐhuan Zhōngguó de Jīngjù" and "xǐhuan Zhōngguó de shūfǎ".

31. 选择 A。"至于"表示提出另一件事,常用于小句或句子的句首。本句中"至于"前说的是"买新房,买别墅"的事,"至于"后说的是"买汽车"。

The answer is A. "Zhìyú" shows to raise another thing. It's often used in a clause or at the beginning of a sentence. In this sentence, the thing before "zhìyú" is "mǎi xīnfáng, mǎi biéshù", while another thing after "zhìyú" is "mǎi qìchē".

32. 选择 B。"况且"表示进一步说明理由或补充新的理由。常与副词"也""又""还"等配合使用。本句中的"况且"与"又"配合使用,补充新的理由"连个电话号码也没有"。

The answer is B. "Kuàngqiě" shows to further explain the reasons or to supplement a new reason. It's often used together with adverbs like "yě", "yòu" and "hái". In this sentence "kuàngqiě" and "yòu" are used together to give a new reason, "lián gè diànhuà hàomǎ yě méiyǒu".

33. 选择答案 A。"宁可"表示在比较了两方面的利害得失以后,选择"宁可"后的一方面。常用的句式有:……,宁可……。本句在比较了"海滨城市游客多"和"待在家里"二者的利害得失以后,选择后一方面:待在家里。

The answer is A. "Nìngkě" shows that after comparing the advantages and disadvantages of the two aspects, one chooses the one after "nìngkě". A common pattern is "..., nìngkě...". In this sentence, after comparing the advantages and disadvantages of "hǎibīn chéngshì yóukè duō" and "dāi zài jiāli", one chooses the latter.

34. 选择 C。"至于"表示提出另一件事,常用于小句或句子的句首。本句中"至于"前说的是"动物园里的鸟种类多"一事,"至于"后说的是"究竟多少种"。

The answer is C. "Zhìyú" shows to raise another thing. It's often used in a clause or at the beginning of a sentence. In this sentence, the thing before "zhìyú" is "dòngwùyuánli de niǎo zhǒnglèi duō", another thing after "zhìyú" is "jiūjìng duōshǎo zhǒng".

35. 选择 C。"以至"用于后一小句前,表示因为前一小句所说的情况而产生后一小句的结果。本句中的"以至"用于后一小句前,表示因为前一小句"专心看报纸,做摘抄"而产生后一小句"妈妈进屋来他都不知道"的结果。

The answer is C. "Yǐzhì" is used before the second clause to show a result from what is stated in the first clause. In this sentence, "yǐzhì" is used before the second clause to show the result "māma jìn wū lái tā dōu bù zhīdào" because of "zhuānxīn kàn bàozhǐ, zuò zhāichāo".

36. 选择 B。"至于"表示提出另一件事,常用于小句或句子的句首。本句中"至于"前说的是"小李说话直来直去"一事,"至于"后说的是"别人是否接受得了"。

The answer is B. "Zhìyú" shows to raise another thing. It's often used in a clause or at the beginning of a sentence. In this sentence, the thing before "zhìyú" is "Xiǎo Lǐ shuōhuà zhílái–zhíqù", while another thing after "zhìyú" is "biérén shìfǒu jiēshòu de liǎo".

37. 选择 B。"以致"在句子中用于后一小句前,表示因为前一小句所说的原因而使后一小句所说的结果产生,这一结果是说话人不希望发生的结果。本句中的"以致"用于后一小句前,表示因为前一小句"科学发展得很快"这一原因而使后一小句所说的结果"很多人跟不上时代的步伐"产生,而这一结果是说话人不希望发生的。

The answer is B. "Yǐzhì" is used before the second clause to show a result is produced due to the reason in the first clause. The result is not wanted by the speaker. In this sentence, "yǐzhì" is used before the second clause, which shows the reason in the clause "kēxué fāzhǎn de hěn kuài". This result "hěnduō rén gēnbúshàng shídài de bùfá" is not wanted by the speaker.

38. 选择答案 D。"宁可"表示在比较了两方面的利害得失以后,选择"宁可"后的一方面。常用的句式是:宁可……,也要……。"也要"引出选择的目的。本句比较了"睡觉"和"背文章"的利害得失以后,用"也要"引出选择的目的——把这篇文章背下来。

The answer is D. "Nìngkě" shows after comparing the advantages and disadvantages of the two aspects, one choose the one after "nìngkě". A common pattern is: "nìngkě... yěyào...". "Yěyào" introduces the purpose of choosing. This sentence compares the advantages and disadvantages of "shuìjiào" and "bèi wénzhāng", "yěyào" is used to introduce the purpose of choosing "bǎ zhè piān wénzhāng bèi xiàlai".

39. 选择 D。"鉴于"用于表示因果关系的复句中,引出动作行为的原因或理由。一般用于句首。本句中的"鉴于"用于句首,表示"提升你为总经理助理"是因为"你的表现与工作能力"。

The answer is D. "Jiànyú" is used in the complex sentence of cause and effect to introduce the reason of an action or a behavior. It's often used at the beginning of a sentence. In this sentence, "jiànyú" is used at the beginning to show the reason for "tíshēng nǐ wéi zǒngjīnglǐ zhùlǐ" is "nǐ de biǎoxiàn yǔ gōngzuò nénglì".

40. 选择 B。"甚至"在句子中可以连接多项词、短语、小句,"甚至"放在最后一项的前面,含有更进一层的意思。本句用"甚至"连接"五六岁的小朋友"、"中青年"和"80 多岁的老人"三个并列项。

The answer is B. "Shènzhì" connects several words, phrases or clauses in a sentence. It is put before the last item and has the meaning of furthering the relation. In this sentence "shènzhì" connects three juxtaposed elements "wǔ–liù suì de xiǎo péngyou", "zhōng-qīng nián" and "bāshí duō suì de lǎorén".

41. 选择 A。"反之"表示转折，引出与上文相反的另一个意思或从正反两个方面说明同一个道理。可以连接小句或句子，多用于书面语。本句中"反之"表示转折，它从"遵循客观规律"和"违背客观规律"正反两方面说明一个道理：一定要按客观规律办事。

The answer is A. "Fǎnzhī" shows a transition. It introduces an opposing idea to the first clause or states the same truth from two opposing perspectives. It can connect clauses or sentences and is often used in written language. In this sentence, it illustrates the truth "yídìng yào àn kèguān guīlǜ bànshì" from two perspectives, "zūnxún kèguān guīlǜ" and "wéibèi kèguān guīlǜ".

42. 选择 D。"或者"表示等同。本句中的"或者"表示"土豆"和"马铃薯"是一种事物的两个名称，它们实际上是等同的。

The answer is D. "Huòzhě" shows an equivalence. In this sentence, "huòzhě" shows "tǔdòu" and "mǎlíngshǔ" are two names for one thing, and they are in fact the same.

43. 选择 D。"或者"表示选择，提出多种选项，选择其中的一个。本句中的"或者"提出两种选项，也就是两个供选择的人：李老师和张老师。

The answer is D. "Huòzhě" shows choices. There are several choices, among which one is made. In this sentence, there are two choices, namely, two people: "Lǐ lǎoshī hé Zhāng lǎoshī".

44. 选择 C。"既"在句子中用于前一小句，表示承认某一事实或前提，后一小句根据这个事实或前提做出推断或结论。只能用于主语后。多用于书面语。相当于"既然"。本句中的"既"用于前一小句表示承认"雨停了"这一事实，后一小句根据这一事实做出结论——"快点赶路"。

The answer is C. "Jì" is used in the first clause to show the acknowledgement of some facts or preconditions, on which an inference or a conclusion is made. It can only be used after the subject and often in written language. It equals to "jìrán". In this sentence, "jì" is used in the former clause to show the acknowledgement of the fact "yǔ tíng le", on which the conclusion "kuàidiǎn gǎnlù" is made.

45. 选择 B。"反之"表示转折，引出与上文相反的另一个意思或从正反两个方面说明同一个道理。本句是从正反两个方面说明一个道理，即保护环境和生态平衡的重要性。

The answer is B. "Fǎnzhī" shows a transition. It introduces an opposing idea to the first clause or states the same truth from two opposing perspectives. In this sentence, the importance of environmental protection and ecological balance is illustrated from the two opposing sides.

46. 选择 A。"免得"在句子中用于后一小句的句首，表示避免不希望的事情的发生。本句中的

Conjunction

"免得"用于后一小句"发生意外"前,表示不希望"意外"发生。

The answer is A. "Miǎnde" is used at the beginning of the second clause, showing to avoid something unwanted. In this sentence, "miǎnde" is used before the second clause "fāshēng yìwài", showing not to expect any "yìwài".

47. 选择 C。"甚至"在句子中连接后两个分句。"甚至"放在最后一项的前面,含有更进一层的意思。

The answer is C. "Shènzhì" connects two clauses. "Shènzhì" is put before the last clause to show a furthering meaning.

48. 选择 C。"再说"在句子中用于后一小句前,进一步补充说明原因,多用于口语。本句中的"再说"引出另一个原因——"他不一定喜欢划船"。

The answer is C. "Zàishuō" is used before the second clause to show a supplementary reason and often used in spoken language. In this sentence, "zàishuō" introduces another reason: "tā bù yídìng xǐhuan huá chuán".

49. 选择 B。"以便"在句子中用于后一小句前,表示前一小句所说的容易使后一小句所说的目的实现。本句中的"以便"用于后一小句"退换"前,表示前一小句所说的"保留好购物凭证"容易使后一小句所说的目的"发现问题退换"实现。

The answer is B. "Yǐbiàn" is used before the second clause to show what is stated in the first clause makes what is stated in the second clause likely to happen. In this sentence, "yǐbiàn" is used before "tuìhuàn" in the second clause to show "bǎoliú hǎo gòuwù píngzhèng" makes the purpose "fāxiàn wèntí tuì-huàn" easier to realize.

50. 选择 A。"可见"在句子中用于后一小句前,引出根据前一小句的现象所做出的判断或结论。它可以连接小句、句子或段落。本句中的"可见"用于后一小句前,引出根据前一小句"他撞了前边正常行驶的车"的现象,连接后一小句并做出结论"酒后驾车有多危险"。

The answer is A. "Kějiàn" is used before the second clause to introduce a judgment or conclusion based on the fact in the first clause. It can connect clauses, sentences or paragraphs. In this sentence, "kějiàn" is used before the second clause to introduce the fact "tā zhuàngle qiánbiān zhèngcháng xíngshǐ de chē" and based on which, a conclusion is drawn that "jiǔhòu jià chē yǒu duō wēixiǎn".

5 助词 Particle

● **助词不能独立使用，必须用在其他词语的后面或句尾。它们在句中只起一种辅助作用。助词可以分为三类：结构助词、动态助词和语气助词。**

Particle can not be used independently. It must follow other words or be used at the end of a sentence to play an auxiliary role. There are three kinds of particles, namely structural particle, aspectual particle and modal particle.

考点精讲 Examination Points

一、结构助词 Structural particle

1. 的 de

① 用在某些词或短语的后面，构成"的"字短语，可在句子中做定语、谓语、补语、主语和宾语。

"De" is used after some words or phrases to form "de" phrases, which can serve as the attribute, predicate, complement, subject and object in the sentence.

A. 做定语

Being used as the attribute.

a. "双音节形容词/多音节形容词+的"。

"disyllabic adjective/multisyllabic adjective + de"

例：干净的教室、热乎乎的饭菜

b. "形容词重叠形式+的"。

"adjective duplication + de"

例：大大的眼睛、雪白雪白的墙壁

c. "动词+的"。

"verb + de"

例：听的音乐、写的字

d. "短语+的"。

"phrase + de"

例：我买的书、关于比赛的结果

e. "名词/代词+的"。

"noun/pronoun + de"

例：学校的环境、我们的课本

特别提示 *Special Tips*

☆ 单音节形容词做定语时，名词前不加"的"，如：小手、新问题。

When monosyllabic adjective serves as an attribute, "de" is unnecessary before the noun it modifies, such as xiǎo shǒu, xīn wèntí.

☆ 名词做定语时，如果表示的是所修饰成分的质地、属性、产地、用途时，定语与中心语之间不加"的"，如：木头桌子、汉语书、新疆哈密瓜、乒乓球拍子。

When a noun serves as an attribute indicating quality, property, place of origin or function, "de" is unnecessary between the attribute and the word modified: mùtóu zhuōzi, Hànyǔ shū, Xīnjiāng hāmìguā, pīngpāngqiú pāizi.

☆ 代词做定语修饰表示亲属称谓的词语时，"的"可省略，如：我妈妈、他哥哥。

When a pronoun serves as an attribute to modify words indicating kinship, "de" is unnecessary: wǒ māma, tā gēge.

☆ 复数代词修饰表示集体的名词（人或单位）时，"的"可省略，如：我们老师、他们公司。

When a plural pronoun modifies a collective noun (people or organization), "de" is unnecessary: wǒmen lǎoshī, tāmen gōngsī.

☆ 说明职业的定语后面不加"的"，如：中文老师、网络工程师。

"De" doesn't follow attributes indicating profession: zhōngwén lǎoshī, wǎngluò gōng-chéngshī.

B. 做谓语或补语

Being used as the predicate or complement.

a. "名词/代词+的"。

"noun/pronoun + de"

例：这张桌子木头的。

b. "形容词+的"。

"adjective + de"

例：手脏乎乎的。

c. "动词/小句+的"。

"verb/clause + de"

例：这个问题他答的。

d. "固定结构+的"。

"fixed structure + de"

例：他们有说有笑的。

C. 做主语或宾语

Being used as the subject or object.

a. "名词/代词+的+（名词）"。

"noun/pronoun + de + (noun)"

例：我的（成绩）比他高。

b. "形容词+的+（名词）"。

"adjective + de + (noun)"

例：我喜欢鲜艳的（衣服）。

c. "动词/小句+的+（名词）"。

"verb/clause + de + (noun)"

例：这是她送给你的（书）。

② 用在句尾，加强肯定的语气。

"De" can be used at the end of a sentence to strengthen the positive tone.

A. 用于还没有发生的事情，表示一种推测或判断。

When "de" modifies things that have not happened yet, it indicates a prediction or judgment.

例：把这件事告诉他，他会着急的。

B. 用于已经发生的事情，表示强调，常与"是"搭配使用。

When "de" modifies things already happened, it indicates an emphasis and often matches with "shì".

例：我是 1973 年 10 月出生的。

③ 其他用法

Other usages

A. 用于并列关系的同类词语的后面，表示没有列举完。

When "de" is used after a list of words with parallel relation, it indicates the list continues.

例：什么叔叔、舅舅、姑姑、姨的，中国的亲属称谓复杂极了。

B. 用在两个相同的动词性成分之间，表示对某种情况的概括。

When "de" is used between two verbal components, it indicates a generalization of certain situations.

例：打球的打球，打太极拳的打太极拳，跳舞的跳舞，老人们都喜欢在公园里锻炼身体。

C. 在某些动宾短语的中间，插入"指人的名词/代词+的"，表示动作的对象。

When "noun/pronoun concerning people + de" is used within verb + object phrase, it indicates the object of an action.

例：帮我的忙、生孩子的气

D. 用在"大+时间词语+的"的格式中，强调原因、条件、情况等，隐含有另一种与此不相称的情况存在。

The pattern "dà + time phrase + de" emphasizes the reason, condition or situation, implying it's inappropriate for certain situations.

例：大白天的，睡什么觉啊？（白天不应该睡觉）

2. 地 de

用在某些词语的后面，构成"地"字短语，在句子中做状语。

"De" is used after some words to form "de" phrase; it can serve as an adverbial modifier in the sentence.

① "某些双音节副词+地"。

"bisyllabic adverb + de"

例：渐渐（地）熟悉起来、反复（地）强调

② "形容词性成分+地"。

"adjective component + de"

例：很快地跑、舒舒服服（地）睡一觉

③ "各种短语+地"。

"phrase + de"

例：有计划地进行、手拉手地出去了

④ "拟声词+地"。

"onomatopoeia word + de"

例：呜呜地哭了、哗哗地下起雨来

⑤ "某些双音节动词+地"。

"disyllabic verb + de"

例：同情地看了看、理解地点了点头

⑥ "某些名词+地"。

"noun + de"

例：历史地见证了这一伟大时刻

⑦ "数量词+地"。

"quantifier + de"

例：一个一个地写、一句句地说

☆ 单音节形容词或副词做状语时,动词前不加"地",如:慢走、刚来。

When a monosyllabic adjective or adverb serves as an adverbial modifier, "de" is unnecessary before the verb it modifies, such as, màn zǒu, gāng lái.

☆ 在某些副词、双音节形容词、形容词重叠形式或某些固定格式后,"地"都可以省略,如上面的例子中带括号的"地"。

"De" in the brackets of sample sentences of ① and ② can be omitted when it follows some adverbs, disyllabic adjectives, reduplicated adjectives or some fixed structures.

3. 得 de

用在动词或形容词后,连接补语。

"De" is used after verbs or adjectives, connecting the complement.

① 连接可能补语。做补语的只限于单个的动词或形容词,否定形式是"动词+不+补语"。

"De" connects the possible complement, which can only be a single verb or adjective. The negative form is "verb + bù + complement".

例:听得见——听不见、清洗得干净——清洗不干净

② 连接程度补语。

"De" connects the degree complement.

A. "动词/形容词+得+形容词"。

"verb/adjective + de + adjective"

例:写得快、胖得可爱。

B. "形容词+得+很"。

"adjective + de + hěn"

例:好得很、清楚得很。

C. "动词/形容词+得+短语/小句"。

"verb/ adjective + de + phrase/clause"

例:看得一清二楚、乱得谁也进不去。

☆ 带补语的动词,不能再带"了""着""过",也不能重叠。

The verbs with complement cannot be followed by "le", "zhe", "guo" and cannot be reduplicated either.

例:写了得快　　　(×)

清洗清洗不干净　(×)

☆ 学习的时候,注意和普通动词"得 (dé)"、能愿动词"得 (děi)"区分。

Please pay attention to the differences with the verb "dé" and the modal verb "děi".

4. 所 suǒ

用在及物动词的前面,使"所+动词"成为名词性短语。多用于书面语。在口语中,"所"可以省略,表达的意思一样。

"Suǒ" is used before a transitive verb to make "suǒ + verb" a noun phrase. It is often used in written language. In spoken language, "suǒ" can be omitted and the meaning will not change.

① "(名词/代词) +所+动词"的用法

The usages of the structure "(noun/pronoun) + suǒ + verb"

A. 加"的"修饰名词。被修饰的名词/代词是前面动词的受事。

When "de" is put to modify the noun, the noun/pronoun modified is the recipient of the verb.

例:我所认识的人、他所熟悉的环境

B. 加"的"代替名词。

When "de" is put after "suǒ", it can replace a noun phrase.

例:他所学的不一定没用。 (= 他所学的本领)

我所说的是有一定根据的。 (= 我所说的话)

C. 不加"的"代替名词,动词限于单音节,多用于固定词语。

"Suǒ" can substitute nouns without "de", and the relevant verbs are monosyllabic. It is more aften used in fixed phrases.

例:所闻所见、各取所需

② "为+名词+所+动词"的用法

The usage of the structure "wéi + noun + suǒ + verb"

A. 表示被动。

It indicates the passive voice.

例:为表面现象所蒙蔽

B. 不表示被动。

It doesn't indicate the passive voice.

例:为前人所不知

③ "所+动词"做"有"或"无"的宾语

"Suǒ + verb" serves as the object of "yǒu" or "wú".

例:有所创造、若有所思

无所不知、无所作为

☆ 请记住下面的习惯用语：

Please remember the following idioms:

闻所未闻　　为所欲为　　各有所长　　大失所望

众所周知　　无所不用　　无所不包　　所答非所问

二、动态助词 Aspectual particle

1. 了 le

① "动词+了+宾语"的用法

　　The usage of the structure "verb + le + object"

A. 一般表示动作完成。

　　It generally indicates an action is completed.

　　　　例：我已经洗了衣服。

　　　　　　我看了三遍这部电影。

B. 不独立成句,后面有小句时,表示前一动作完成后再发生后一动作,或前一情况是后一情况的假设条件。

　　When it doesn't form a complete sentence but is followed by a clause, it indicates the previous action is done before the latter action takes place or is the precondition of the latter action.

　　　　例：下了课我就回家了。

　　　　　　你写完了作业再去玩吧。

　　有些动词后的"了"表示动作的结果。这类动词有：忘、丢、关、喝、吃、咽、吞、泼、洒、扔、放、涂、抹、擦、碰、砸、摔、磕、撞、踩、伤、杀、切、冲、卖、还、毁……

　　　　Sometimes "le" after some verbs indicates the result of an action. This kind of verbs include: wàng, diū, guān, hē, chī, yàn, tūn, pō, sǎ, rēng, fàng, tú, mǒ, cā, pèng, zá, shuāi, kē, zhuàng, cǎi, shāng, shā, qiē, chōng, mài, huán, huǐ....

　　　　例：卖了旧的买新的

　　这时的"了"可以用于命令句和"把"字句中,还可以在动词前加能愿动词。

　　In this case, "le" can be used in imperative sentences and "bǎ" sentences, and modal verbs can be added before the verb.

　　　　例：你可以把它关掉了。

　　　　　　你放了他吧。

Particle

☆ 如果动词不表示变化时,动词的后面不能加"了",如:是、姓、好像、属于、觉得、认为、希望、需要、作为……

If the verb doesn't indicate any change, it cannot be followed by "le", e.g.: shì, xìng, hǎoxiàng, shǔyú, juéde, rènwéi, xīwàng, xūyào, zuòwéi....

例:我是留学生。（√）

我是了留学生。(×)

☆ 句子中有表示经常性动作的修饰词时,动词的后面不能加"了"。

When the verb indicates a regular action, it cannot be followed by "le".

例:我经常六点起床。（√）

我经常六点起了床。(×)

☆ 宾语是动词时,"了"不能加在谓语动词后,可加在句末。

When the object is a verb, the first verb cannot be followed by "le", but "le" can be put at the end of the sentence.

例:他答应参加。　　（√）

他答应参加了。　　（√）

他答应了参加。　　（×）

☆ 连动句、兼语句中的"了"一般在后一动词后。

"Le" in serial verbal sentences or pivotal sentences generally follows the second verb.

例:我去书店买了几本书。

老师叫他找来了一份参考资料。

② "动词+宾语+了"。肯定情况出现了变化。

"Verb + object + le" indicates there has been a certain change.

例:外面下雨了。(已经开始下雨)

③ "动词+了+宾语+了"。既表示动作已经完成,又表示事态有了变化。

"Verb + le + object" indicates an action has been completed and meanwhile there has been a certain change.

例:我已经写了作业了。

☆ 动词是结束性动作时,后面紧跟的"了"可以省略。

When the verb indicates a finished action, the following "le" can be omitted.

例:他已经到(了)上海了。

④ "动词+了(不带宾语)"的用法

The usage of "verb + le (without the object)"

A. 只表示事态有了变化，不表示动作的完成。也常表示情况将有变化，前面常有"快""要""该"或"可以"等词。

It only indicates the change of a situation instead of the finish of an action. It often indicates a situation will change, there are often "kuài", "yào", "gāi" or "kěyǐ" before it.

例：他又哭了。（还在哭）

水快开了。（将要开）

B. 表示动作完成并且事态已经有了改变。前面不能用"快""要"等词，可用"已经"。

It indicates an action is finished and a situation is changed. "Kuài", "yào" cannot be used before it, but "yǐjīng" can.

例：他已经知道了。

C. 不独立成句，表示这个动作完成后出现另一动作或某一状态。

"Le" cannot form an independent sentence; it indicates another action or state appears after one action is finished.

例：他听了很高兴。

⑤ 形容词+了。表示已经或即将出现新情况；或肯定已经出现的情况，不表示有过变化。

"Adjective + le" indicates a situation that already occurred or a new situation that is about to occur. It can also indicate the confirmation of a situation, but not any change.

例：人老了，精神就差了。

这件大衣太长了。

天快黑了。

⑥ 句中有时量短语和动量短语的用法：

When there are time quantifier phrases or verb quantifier phrases in the sentences; the usages are as follows:

A. "动词/形容词+了+数量"。表示动作开始到完成时的量。

"Verb/adjective + le + numeral" indicates the quantity of an action from the beginning to the end.

例：我只睡了两个小时。

这个月只晴了三天。

B. "动词/形容词+了+数量+了"。表示动作持续的时间，且动作行为还可继续下去。动词后的"了"有时可省略。

"Verb/adjective + numeral + le" indicates the period of time of the action from the beginning to the end. "Le" after the verb sometimes can be omitted.

例：我已经学了半年了。

C. "动词+了+数量+宾语"。表示动作开始到结束时的量。

"Verb + le + numeral + object" indicates the quantity of an action from the beginning to the end.

例：我学了两年中文。

D. "动词+了+数量+宾语+了"。表示到说话时为止动作延续的量,动作可继续下去。

"Verb + le + numeral + object + le" indicates the quantity of an action up to the moment, and the action may continue.

例：我教了十年对外汉语了。

E. "动词+宾语+动词+了+数量"。表示到说话时为止动作延续的量。

"Verb + object + verb + le + numeral" indicates the quantity of an action up to the moment.

例：我教对外汉语教了十年。

F. "动词+宾语+动词+了+数量+了"。不独立成句时,表示前一动作经历了一段时间后开始了后一动作或形成某一状态,前一动词可继续下去。

When "verb + object + verb + le + numeral + le" doesn't form an independent sentence, it indicates after some time the first action begins, another action or a state begins. The first may continue.

例：我排队排了三次了,可还是没有买到。

G. "宾语+动词+了+数量+了"。表示到说话时为止动作延续的量。

"Object + verb + le + numeral + le" indicates the quantity of the action up to the moment.

例：我冬泳已经坚持了三年了。

⑦ "名词/数量词语+了"。表示已经或将要出现某种新情况。

"Noun/numeral phrase + le" indicates a new situation has already appeared or will appear.

例：周末了。

半个月了,还是没有任何消息。

2. 着 zhe

① 用于动词或形容词之后,表示动作或状态持续。

When "zhe" is used after verbs or adjectives, it indicates an action or a state continues.

A. "动词/形容词+着+宾语+(呢)"。

verb/adjective + zhe + object + (ne)

例：天上挂着一轮明月。

妹妹红着眼睛出去了。

B. 用于动词之间。

Being used between the verbs.

a. 表示后一动作进行时前一动作在继续，前一动作可看作是后一动作进行的状态或方式。

It indicates the latter action carries on while the previous action continues, and the previous one can be seen as the state or way of the latter one.

例：我喜欢听着音乐吃饭。

b. 表示第一个动作持续进行时出现了第二个动作，第一个动词和"着"必须重复使用。

It indicates the second action begins while the first one is still carrying on, and the first verb and "zhe" must be used in duplication.

例：他听着听着睡着了。

② 用于动词后，表示动作正在进行，前面可以加"正""正在""在"，句尾可以加"呢"。

When "zhe" is used after verbs, it indicates the action is carrying on. It can follow "zhèng", "zhèngzài" or "zài", and the sentence can end with "ne".

例：大家正上着课呢，小点儿声。

3. 过 guo

① 在动词或形容词后，表示行为或状态已经成为过去，成为一种经验。

When "guo" is used after verbs or adjectives, it indicates some actions or states have passed and become a kind of experience.

A. "动词+过"。动词前常有表示时间的词语，如"曾（经）""已经""从来""以前"等。

"Verb + guo". In this case, there is usually time phrases before the verbs, such as "céng(jīng)", "yǐjīng", "cónglái" and "yǐqián", etc.

例：我们曾经一起聊过天。

特别提示 Special Tips

☆ 动作性不强的动词，如"知道""以为""认为""在""属于""使得"等，不能带"过"。

Some verbs without a strong sense of action cannot be followed by "guò", such as "zhīdào", "yǐwéi", "rènwéi", "zài","shǔyú", "shǐdé", etc.

例：我曾以为他是南方人。 （√）

我以为过他是南方人。 （×）

B. "形容词+过"。其否定形式是：(从来)没+形容词+过。

Adjective + guò. The negative form is (cónglái) méi + adjective + guò.

例：我也年轻过，我能理解。

他的作业(从来)没错过。

② 表示想象中将要发生的事情或假设要发生的事情已经完成，或成为过去。

It can indicate something imagined or supposed to happen has finished or passed.

例：这篇论文等我看过了，你再看。

三、语气助词 Modal particle

罢了 bàle

用于陈述句尾，表示仅此而已，有把事情往小里说的意味。常和"只不过""只是""无非"等词语搭配使用。

It is used at the end of a declarative sentence, indicating no more than what should have been done, containing a sense of underestimation. It often matches with "zhǐbúguò", "zhǐshì" and "wúfēi".

例：不用客气，这只是我应该做的罢了。

强化练习 Exercises

■ 1—15 题，在每一个句子下面都有一个指定的词语，句中 ABCD 是供选择的四个不同位置，请判断这一词语放在句中哪个位置上恰当。

Please find the proper position out of the four choices of A, B, C, and D for the word below each sentence.

1. 反复思考后 A，我决定 B 大学毕 C 业就考研究生 D。
   了

2. 爸爸是个外交官 A，他 B 多次 C 出访过 D 欧洲十几个国家。
   曾

3. 小船儿轻轻 A 飘荡 B 在水中，迎面吹来 C 了凉爽 D 风。
   的

4. 成双成对 A 鸳鸯和一些野鸭 B 在湖面上 C 自由自在地游着 D。
   的

5. 这篇文章 A 一发表 B 立刻产生 C 非同一般的 D 反响。
了

6. 他看 A 眼前的景色 B,陷入 C 了深深的回忆 D。
着

7. 大卫是我 A 留学 B 时期最知心 C 朋友 D。
的

8. 他 A 一眼 B 也没看 C 就把报纸扔 D。
了

9. 爷爷一下 A 飞机就热泪盈眶地抱 B 爸爸 C 说 D:"我可见到你们了!"
着

10. 在清华大学 A 学习 B 的四年中,他从来没 C 请 D 一次假。
过

11. 任务重,时间紧 A,我们吃 B 晚饭 C,马上回办公室 D 加班。
了

12. 图书馆刚进 A 一批新书 B,我们赶紧去 C 借 D。
了

13. 他正看 A 书 B,忽然听 C 见妈妈叫 D 他去吃饭。
着

14. 听 A 到大家的赞扬 B,安娜不好意思地低下头 C 摆弄 D 手指头。
着

15. 安娜一向身体很好 A,从没得 B 病,今天突然发 C 高烧,她害怕 D 了。
过

■ 16—35 题,每个句子中有一个或两个空,请在 ABCD 四个答案中选择唯一恰当的一个。

Please choose the correct answer for each blank from the four choices of A, B, C, and D.

16. 起风了,大海波涛汹涌,浪头大 _____ 吓人。
A. 的 B. 地 C. 得 D. 了

17. 颐和园那美丽 _____ 景色真让人流连忘返。
A. 的 B. 地 C. 得 D. 了

18. 你们看我儿子将来能胜任 _____ 了总经理的工作吗?
A. 的 B. 地 C. 得 D. 了

19. 风轻轻 _____ 吹着,好像在告诉我们,春天来了。
A. 的 B. 地 C. 得 D. 了

20. 小河潺潺地流 _____ ，几块石头横在水面，算是桥。
    A．着　B．了　C．过　D．得

21. 大卫是个旅游爱好者，他曾经去 _____ 很多地方。
    A．着　B．了　C．过　D．得

22. 顺着一条向南的小路走去，不多远，就进 _____ 沟。
    A．着　B．了　C．过　D．得

23. 我早就听说新疆的烤全羊很有名，就是没尝 _____ 。
    A．着　B．了　C．过　D．没

24. 大卫发高烧了，39.8℃，打了一针，迷迷糊糊 _____ 睡着了。
    A．的　B．地　C．得　D．着

25. 根据有关部门所做 _____ 统计，今年参加中考的人数比去年少了 20000 人。
    A．的　B．地　C．得　D．着

26. 五岁的孩子口才这么好，是你从小训练 _____ 吗？
    A．的　B．地　C．了　D．过

27. 你能接受他的邀请，他会高兴 _____ 。
    A．过　B．地　C．的　D．得

28. 到中国后，我都没出 _____ 北京，不知道上海是什么样子。
    A．着　B．了　C．过　D．得

29. 老年活动室里，看报 _____ 看报，下象棋 _____ 下象棋，老人们各得其乐。
    A．的　B．得　C．地　D．过

30. 英语歌我不是不会唱，只不过不想唱 _____ 。
    A．着　B．了　C．过　D．罢了

31. 女儿在全国作文比赛中得了一等奖，全家人高兴 _____ 不得了。
    A．的　B．地　C．得　D．着

32. 卢沟桥是公元 1189—1192 年间修建 _____ 。
    A．的　B．得　C．地　D．了

33. 他 _____ 反映的情况很有价值。
    A．的　B．地　C．所　D．得

34. 别生孩子 _____ 气了，气坏了身体不值得。
    A．的　B．地　C．得　D．着

35. 大冬天 _____ ，怎么只穿两件单衣，连件毛衣都不穿？
    A．地　B．的　C．得　D．罢了

答疑解惑 Answers and Explanations

1. 选择 C。"了"的用法之一是表示动作完成。在动词"毕"的后边加"了",与"就考研究生"构成连续的两个动作,表示前一动作完成后再发生后一动作,所以 C 是正确答案。

The answer is C. One of the usages of "le" is to indicate the finish of an action. Therefore, "le" is put after the verb "bì" and forms two continual actions together with "jiù kǎo yánjiūshēng". So C is the correct answer.

2. 选择 B。"曾+动词+过"表示"有过出访十几个国家的经历","曾"只能放在动词"出访"的前边。

The answer is B. "Céng + verb + guo" indicates "yǒuguo chūfǎng shí jǐ gè guójiā de jīnglì"; "céng" can only be used before the verb "chūfǎng".

3. 选择 D。"的"字一般用在名词前连接它的定语。在汉语语法的规则中,动词谓语前后都不能用"的",所以选 A,B,C 都不对,D 才是正确答案。

The answer is D. "De" is usually used before nouns to link with their attribute. In Chinese grammar, "de" cannot be used before verb predicate, neither can it be used after verb predicate, so A, B, C are all incorrect, and D is the correct answer.

4. 选择 A。本句中的多音节形容词"成双成对"做"鸳鸯和一些野鸭"的定语,"成双成对"和中心语之间需要用"的"连接,因此 A 是正确答案。

The answer is A. In this sentence, the multisyllabic adjective "chéng shuāng chéng duì" serves as the attribute of "yuānyāng hé yìxiē yěyā", so "de" is necessary to link the adjective with the keyword. Therefore, A is the correct answer.

5. 选择 C。 表示动作的结束,此时"了"一般用在动词的后边,动词常常有宾语,即"动词+了+宾语",表明句子结束, 因此选 C 是正确的。

The answer is C. When "le" indicates the finish of an action, it is usually used after the verb. While the verb is usually followed by an object, the pattern "verb + le + object" indicates a complete sentence, so C is the correct answer.

6. 选择 A。"着"用在动词后,表示动作正在进行,选择 A 表明"看"这一动作正在进行中。

The answer is A. When "zhe" is used after verbs, it indicates an action is going on. Choice A means the action "kàn" is going on.

7. 选择 C。在本句中"朋友"有两个定语,一是"我留学时期",另一是"最知心"。当中心语前有两个或多个定语时,如果定语都是双音节或多音节的词或短语,"的"一般在中心语的前面,多项定语的后面,因此选 C 是正确的。

The answer is C. In this sentence, "péngyou" has two attributes; one is "wǒ liúxué shíqī" and the other is "zuì zhīxīn". When there are two or more disyllabic or multisyllabic attributes before the word modified, "de" is usually used before the key word and after the attributes, so C is the correct answer.

8. 选择 D。"了"用在句末,只肯定已经出现的情况。在"把"字句中单独动词不能成句,动词后必须有其他成分,所以选择 D 是正确的。

The answer is D. "Le" can be used at the end of the sentence to affirm the situation appeared. In "bǎ" sentence, the verb must be followed by a component, so D is the correct answer.

9. 选择 B。谓语动词加"着"用在其它动词的前边,表示后一个动作的状态,"抱"是"说"的方式,因此选择 B 是唯一正确的。

The answer is B. When the predicate together with "zhe" is used before another verb, it indicates the state of the latter action. In this sentence, "bào" is the state of "shuō", so B is the correct answer.

10. 选择 D。动态助词"过"用在动词之后,表示行为或状态已经成为过去。

The answer is D. When the aspectual particle "guo" is used after a verb, it indicates an action or a state has passed.

11. 选择 B。"动词+了……马上"是一个固定的形式,表示前后两个动作紧密相连,A 前是形容词,一般情况下形容词后不加"了"(表示变化时除外),C、D 都不能加"了",所以唯一正确的答案是 B。

The answer is B. "Verb + le... mǎshàng" is a fixed pattern, which indicates two actions are closely linked together. Before A it is an adjective, which cannot be followed by "le" (except when indicating a change). C and D cannot match with "le", so B is the correct answer.

12. 选择 A。"了"的用法之一是表示动作的完成。这个"了"一般用在动词的后边,动词常常跟有宾语,而且宾语前应该有数量词做定语。A 用在动词"进"后边,宾语"书"前有数量词"一批",所以 A 是唯一正确答案。

The answer is A. When "le" indicates the finish of an action, it is usually used after the verb. And the verb is usually followed by an object, and the object should be preceded by a numeral attribute. In this sentence, A is after the verb "jìn", and the numeral attribute "yì pī" is before the object "shū", so A is the correct answer.

13. 选择 A。"着"的用法之一是用于动词后,表示动作正在进行,前面可以加"正"。本句"着"用在动词"看"的后边,表明动作"看"正在进行,选 A 是正确的。

The answer is A. "Zhe" can be used after a verb to indicate an action is going on, and can be preceded by "zhèng". In this sentence, "zhe" is used after the verb "kàn" and indicates "he is reading", so A is the correct answer.

14. 选择 D。"着"用在动词"摆弄"的后边,强调动作在进行,因此选择 D。

The answer is D. "Zhe" is used after the verb "bǎinòng" to indicate the action is going on. So D is the correct answer.

15. 选择 B。动态助词"过"用在动词后,表示行为或状态已经成为过去,所以选择 B 是正确的。

The answer is B. When the aspectual particle "guo" is used after verbs, it indicates an action or a state has passed. So B is the correct answer.

16. 选择 C。"得"用在形容词后边连接程度补语。形容词"大"+得+短语"吓人",补充说明浪头大的程度,所以选择 C。

The answer is C. "De" is used after an adjective to connect the degree complement. In answer C, the adjective "dà" + de + phrase "xiàrén" indicates the scale of the wave, so C is the correct answer.

17. 选择 A。本句中的双音节形容词"美丽"前边加指代词"那"做"景色"的定语,"美丽"和中心语"景色"之间需要用"的"连接,因此 A 是正确答案。

The answer is A. In this sentence, the disyllabic adjective "měilì" serves as the attribute of "jǐngsè", and "de" is needed to link "měilì" with the modified word "jǐngsè", so A is the correct answer.

18. 选择 C。"动词+得+了"是一个固定结构,表示有能力做某事。本题中"胜任"是动词,它的后面需要用"得"连接补语,因此 C 是正确答案。

The answer is C. "Verb + de + le" is a fixed structure, which indicates to have the ability to do something. In this sentence, "shèngrèn" is a verb, and it needs a "de" to link the complement, so C is the correct answer.

19. 选择 B。"地"用在某些词语的后面,构成"地"字短语,在句子中做状语。本句中的形容词重叠形式"轻轻"做"吹"的状语,所以选择 B。

The answer is B. "De" can be used after some words to form "de" phrase, which serves as an adverbial modifier in the sentence. In this sentence, the reduplicated adjective "qīngqīng" is the adverbial modifier of "chuī", so B is the correct answer.

20. 选择 A。"着"用于动词之后，表示动作或状态持续。本句"着"用于动词"流"的后面，表明"流"这一状态的持续，因此选择 A 是正确的。

The answer is A. When "zhe" is used after a verb, it indicates an action or a state is continuing. In this sentence, "zhe" is used after the verb "liú" to indicate the continuing of the state, so A is the correct answer.

21. 选择 C。"动词+过"的前面常有表示时间的词语，如"曾(经)""已经""从来""以前"等，表示行为或状态已经成为过去。本句动词"去"后面加"过"，前面加"曾经"表示大卫旅游的行为已经成为过去，因此 C 是正确答案。

The answer is C. In sentences with the pattern "verb + guo", there are usually time phrases such as "céng(jīng)", "yǐjīng", "cónglái", "yǐqián" before the verb, which indicates an action or a state has passed. In this sentence, "guo" follows the verb "qù" indicating the action of David's traveling has passed, so C is the correct answer.

22. 选择 B。"动词+ 了+宾语"表示动作行为的完成，动词"进"+"了"肯定了"进沟"的这一变化，B 是正确答案。

The answer is B. "Verb + le + object" affirms an action being finished. Verb "jìn" + "le" affirms the change of "jìn gōu", so B is the correct answer.

23. 选择 C。"过"用在动词后，表示行为或状态已经成为过去。无论在肯定句和否定句中，都应该在动词后加"过"。

The answer is C. When "guo" is used after verbs, it indicates the action or state has passed. "Guo" should be added after the verb either in positive or negative sentences. So C is the correct answer.

24. 选择 B。"地"用在某些词语的后面，构成"地"字短语，在句子中做状语。本句中的形容词重叠形式"迷迷糊糊"做"睡"的状语，所以 B 是正确答案。

The answer is B. "De" can be used after some words to form "de" phrase, which serves as an adverbial modifier. In this sentence, the reduplication of adjective "mímí–hūhū" is the adverbial modifier of "shuì", so B is the correct answer.

25. 选择 A。"所+动词+的"修饰名词"统计"。

The answer is A. "Suǒ + verb + de" modifies the noun "tǒngjì".

26. 选择 A。"的"用在句尾，加强肯定的语气。当用于已经发生的事情时，表示强调，常与"是"搭配使用。

The answer is A. "De" is used at the end of a sentence to reinforce the positive tone. When it is used to modify things passed, it indicates an emphasis, and often matches with "shì".

27. 选择C。"的"用在句尾,加强肯定的语气。当用于还没有发生的事情时,表示一种推测或判断。

The answer is C. "De" is used at the end of a sentence to reinforce the positive tone. When it is used to modify future events, it indicates a prediction or judgment.

28. 选择C。"过"用在动词后,表示行为或状态已经成为过去。无论在肯定句和否定句中,都应该在动词后加"过"。

The answer is C. When "guo" is used after verbs, it indicates an action or a state has passed. "Guo" should be added after the verb either in positive or negative sentences. So C is the correct answer.

29. 选择A。"的"用在两个相同的动词性成分之间,表示对某种情况的概括。

The answer is A. When "de" is used between two same verbal components, it indicates a generalization of a certain situation.

30. 选择D。"罢了"用于陈述句尾,表示仅此而已,有把事情往小里说的意味。常和"只不过""只是""无非"等词语搭配使用。

The answer is D. "Bàle" is used at the end of declarative sentences, indicating no more than what should have been done, containing a sense of underestimation. It often matches with "zhǐbúguò", "zhǐshì" and "wúfēi".

31. 选择C。"得"用在形容词后,连接程度补语。

The answer is C. "De" is used after an adjective to connect degree complements.

32. 选择A。"的"用在句尾,加强肯定的语气。当用于已经发生的事情时,表示强调,常与"是"搭配使用。

The answer is A. "De" is used at the end of a sentence to reinforce the positive tone. When it is used to modify things passed, it indicates an emphasis, and often matches with "shì".

33. 选择C。"代词+所+动词+的"修饰名词,被修饰的名词是前面动词的受事。

The answer is C. When "pronoun + suǒ +verb + de" modifies a noun, the modified noun in the structure is the recipient of the verb.

34. 选择A。"的"在某些动宾短语的中间,插入"指人的名词/代词",表示动作的对象。

The answer is A. When "noun/pronoun concerning people + de" is used within "verb + object" phrase, it indicates the object of an action.

35. 选择 B。"的"用在"大+时间词语+的"的格式中，强调原因、条件、情况等，隐含有另一种与此不相称的情况存在。

The answer is B. The pattern "dà + time phrase + de" emphasizes the reason, condition or situation, implying it's inappropriate for a certain situation.

6 能愿动词 Optative Verb

● 能愿动词是动词的一个小类。它能用在动词或形容词的前面,表示意愿、可能或必要等意义。

Optative verb is a sub-class of verbs; it can be used before verbs and adjectives, indicating intention, possibility and necessity.

考点精讲 Examination Points

一、能愿动词 Optative verbs

1. 分类 Classification of optative verbs

① 表示意愿的:要、想、愿、愿意、情愿、敢、肯

Indicating intention: yào, xiǎng, yuàn, yuànyì, qíngyuàn, gǎn, kěn.

② 表示可能的:可能、能、能够、可、可以、会

Indicating possibility: kěnéng, néng, nénggòu, kě, kěyǐ, huì.

③ 表示情理上需要的:应、该、应该、应当、得、要

Indicating necessity: yīng, gāi, yīnggāi, yīngdāng, děi, yào.

2. 语法特征 Grammatical features of optative verbs

① 能愿动词的后边只能与动词、形容词及其短语组合,不能与名词组合。

Optative verbs can only be followed by verbs, adjectives and their phrases, but not nouns.

例:他要去留学。　　　　　　(√)

你再不回去,妈妈会着急的。(√)

今天下午你应该写作业。　　(√)

今天下午你应该作业。　　　(×)

特别提示 Special Tips

☆ "会汉语""要钱"中的"会"和"要"是一般动词,不是能愿动词。

"Huì" in "Huì hànyǔ" and "yào" in "yào qián" are ordinary verbs, not optative verbs.

② 能愿动词不能重叠,但能愿动词后的动词仍然可以重叠。

Optative verbs cannot be used in reduplicated forms, verbs after optative verbs can still be reduplicated.

例:朋友之间应该互相帮助。　　　(√)

朋友之间应该应该互相帮助。(×)

朋友之间应该互相帮助帮助。(√)

③ 能愿动词的后边不能带"了""着""过"。

Optative verbs cannot be followed by "le", "zhe" and "guo".

例:你得休息了。　　　　　(√)

你得了休息。　　　　　(×)

④ 能愿动词的肯定形式、否定形式一起用时表示疑问。有能愿动词的句子不能用动词或形容词的肯定形式和否定形式并用的方法表示疑问。

When the positive and negative form of optative verbs are used together, the sentence indicates an interrogative tone. Sentences with optative verbs cannot indicate an interrogative tone by using both the positive and negative form of the verbs or adjectives.

例:他会不会来?　　　　　(√)

他会来不来?　　　　　(×)

⑤ 可以只用能愿动词回答问题,但不能只用动词部分。

We can use the optative verb only to answer a question, but not the verb only.

例:我可以打开窗子吗? ——可以。(√)

——打开。(×)

⑥ 能愿动词要用在介词短语和描写性的状语前。

Optative verbs should be used before prepositional phrases and descriptive adverbial modifiers.

例:你应该把作业写完再去玩。　　(√)

你把作业应该写完再去玩。　　(×)

咱们得好好地谈一谈了。　　(√)

咱们好好地得谈一谈了。　　(×)

二、几个能愿动词的用法 Usages of several optative verbs

1. 能、会 néng, huì

① 表示"有可能"时,用"能"或"会"都可以,常常表示对某种情况的估计或推测。用"会"时,句尾常加"的"。

Both "néng" and "huì" can mean "possible", indicating estimates or predictions of some circumstances. When "huì" is used, "de" is aften added at the end of the sentence.

例：外面雪那么大,他能/会来吗？

他已经答应了我们,就一定能来。 （√）

他已经答应了我们,就一定会来的。（√）

② 表示主观上具备某种技能、客观上具备某种条件,用"能";表示知道怎么做、具有某种技能或本能,用"会"。

"Néng" indicates having some skills subjectively or having some conditions objectively; "huì" indicates knowing how to do and having some skills or instincts.

例：你能用中文写信吗？（主观上具备某种技能）

我明天要加班,不能和你们一起去郊游了。（客观上具备某种条件）

我会做中国菜。（具有某种技能）

青蛙会游泳。（本能）

③ 表示初次学会某种动作或技能,用"能"或"会"都可以,但多用"会";表示某种技能得到恢复,只能用"能"。

Both "néng" and "huì" can indicate that someone learns some actions or skills for the first time, but "huì" is more often used; when indicating a certain skill is recovered, only "néng" can be used.

例：我女儿六个月的时候就能/会叫"爸爸"了。 （√）

他的伤已经恢复得差不多了,能自己下地走路了。（√）

他的伤已经恢复得差不多了,会自己下地走路了。（×）

④ 表示具备的某种技能已经达到某种程度,只能用"能"。

When indicating the skill has reached a certain degree, only "néng" can be used.

例：他一口气能吃几十个热狗。 （√）

他一口气会吃几十个热狗。 （×）

⑤ 表示善于做某事时,用"能"或"会"都可以,前面都可以用"很""最""真"等程度副词修饰。但"会"侧重于"技巧","能"侧重于"能力"。

Both "néng" and "huì" can be used to indicate being good at doing something, and degree adverbs such as "hěn", "zuì" and "zhēn" can be used before them as modifiers. "Huì" emphasizes "skill" and "néng" emphasizes "ability".

例：他很能干。（能力强）

他很会干。（有技巧）

2. 能、可以 néng, kěyǐ

① "能"侧重于"能力","可以"侧重于"可能"。"能"可以表示善于做某事,"可以"没有此用法。

"Néng" emphasizes "ability" and "kěyǐ" emphasizes "possibility". "Néng" can indicate being good at doing something while "kěyǐ" cannot.

例:他很能说,一说起来就没完没了。 (√)

他很可以说,一说起来就没完没了。(×)

② "能"可以对某种客观的可能性表示推测、估计,"可以"没有此用法。

"Néng" can indicate there is some objective possibility, and can indicate an estimate or a prediction; "kěyǐ" doesn't have this kind of usage.

例:车堵得这么厉害,我们不能按时到达了。 (√)

车堵得这么厉害,我们不可以按时到达了。(×)

③ "能"或"可以"都可以表示情理上、环境上的"允许",否定、疑问形式多用"能"。

Both "néng" and "kěyǐ" can indicate a possibility provided by circumstances, while "néng" is more often used in negative and interrogative forms.

例:遇到这样的事,我能袖手旁观吗? (√)

遇到这样的事,我可以袖手旁观吗? (×)

④ "可以"能单独做谓语,"能"不可以。

"Kěyǐ" alone can serve as an predicate while "néng" can not.

例:这个问题这样回答也可以。 (√)

这个问题这样回答也能。 (×)

3. 要 yào

① 表示某种意愿。其否定形式是"不想"。

"Yào" may indicate an intention, its negative form is "bùxiǎng".

例:我要学习文学,不想学习医学。

② 表示客观上需要。

"Yào" may indicate an objective need.

例:时间很紧,要抓紧啊!

③ 表示将要。

"Yào" may indicate "going to".

例:我们要放假了。

④ "不要"常放在动词的前边,表示禁止、劝阻,相当于口语里的"别"。

"Búyào" is often used before verbs to indicate prohibition or dissuasion and equals to "bié" in spoken language.

例:别人在上课,不要在楼道里大声说话。(别大声说话)

强化练习 Exercises

■ 1—15 题，在每一个句子下面都有一个指定的词语，句中 ABCD 是供选择的四个不同位置，请判断这一词语放在句中哪个位置上恰当。

Please find the proper position out of the four choices of A, B, C, and D for the word below each sentence.

1. 京津城际铁路客运专线 A 建成 B 以后，C 半个小时就 D 从北京到达天津。
　　　　　　　　　　　　　　　能

2. 我家住在深山区，A 下了汽车 B 走快点儿还 C 走 D 三个多小时的山路。
　　　　　　　　　　　　　　　要

3. 你看，A 西边的天阴得 B 多沉，那边 C 下雨了 D。
　　　　　　　　　可能

4. 不管你 A 提什么要求，B 我 C 都 D 答应你。
　　　　　　　　　能

5. 要想 A 有个好身体，B 坚持 C 天天 D 锻炼身体。
　　　　　　　　必须

6. A 像他 B 这么脸皮厚的人，C 咱们班 D 有几个？
　　　　　　　　　能

7. 橘子 A 不仅 B 好吃，它的皮 C 还 D 做药。
　　　　　　　　能

8. 每个人 A 遵守 B 交通规则，C 不能横穿乱跑，更 D 不能闯红灯。
　　　　　　　　　必须

9. 女儿 A 想 B 跟我一起 C 到书店 D 买书。
　　　　　　　　要

10. 与安娜接触了一 A 段时间后，我发现她除了 B 母语外，还 C 说 D 三国语言。
　　　　　　　　会

11. 现在刘老师不是在阅览室看书，就是在图书馆查资料，A 她是 B 在 C 其他地方 D 的。
　　　　　　　　不会

12. A 连自己父母 B 都 C 不爱的人，D 爱别人吗？
　　　　　　　　可能

13. 她 A 这个病 B 开刀 C 动手术 D 了。
　　　　　　　　得

14. 由于 A 害怕,B 他 C 始终不 D 开口讲话。

                                肯

15. 这个问题 A 并不算 B 很难,每个学生 C 都 D 会回答。

                             应该

■ 16—30 题,每个句子中有一个或两个空,请在 ABCD 四个答案中选择唯一恰当的一个。
Please choose the correct answer for each blank from the four choices of A, B, C, and D.

16. 明天有一个学术报告,你 _____ 参加?
    A. 能不能　　B. 能没能
    C. 不能能　　D. 能吗

17. 出国考察的名单都定下来了,你怎么还在考虑 _____ 。
    A. 应该去不去　　B. 不应该去应该去
    C. 应不应该去　　D. 应该不应该去不去

18. 阅览室里的报刊杂志不外借,只 _____ 在那儿看。
    A. 会　B. 要　C. 应该　D. 能

19. 你已经工作了,也 _____ 给父母买点儿东西,孝敬孝敬他们了。
    A. 应该　B. 会　C. 必须　D. 可能

20. 你别只顾工作,也 _____ 注意休息。
    A. 可能　B. 能　C. 得　D. 会

21. 你毕业以后 _____ 回国发展?
    A. 不愿意愿意　　B. 愿意不愿意
    C. 愿意不愿　　　D. 愿意不

22. 这个问题太简单了,我们认为 _____ 讨论了。
    A. 没有需要　B. 不是要　C. 没要　D. 不用

23. 运动完以后,你就 _____ 去洗个澡,消除一下疲劳。
    A. 可能　B. 能　C. 该　D. 可以

24. 作任何决定之前,都应该好好考虑考虑 _____ 这样做。
    A. 应该　B. 该　C. 该不该　D. 应该不应

25. 对不起,有什么问题明天再谈,我 _____ 开会去了。
    A. 可以　B. 能　C. 得　D. 会

26. 春天的天气乍暖还寒,外出时 _____ 多带几件衣服。
    A. 可能　B. 能　C. 得　D. 会

27. 孩子从小就 _____ 学会礼貌待人。
    A. 会　B. 应该　C. 可以　D. 能

28. 老师,端午节那天,您 _____ 带我们一起去划龙舟?
    A. 不可以可以　　B. 可不可以
    C. 可以不可　　　D. 可不可

29. 动物是我们人类的朋友,我们 _____ 爱护它们。
    A. 能够　B. 可能　C. 应该　D. 可以

30. 老总一再强调明天的会很重要,要求大家 _____ 准时出席。
    A. 可能　B. 必须　C. 能　D. 可以

答疑解惑 Answers and Explanations

1. 选择 D。当我们表示具备的某种技能已经达到某种效率时,只能用"能"。此时的"能"应放在时间后,结果前。

The answer is D. To indicate a certain skill has reached a certain degree of efficiency, only "néng" can be used. In this case, "néng" should be used before the result but after the time.

2. 选择 C。"要"可表示客观上需要。本题表达的意思是"下汽车"后,在"走快点儿"的前提下,还需要"走三个多小时"。因此,"要"应在 C 的位置上。

The answer is C. "Yào" is to indicate objective needs. In this sentence, it means there is more than three hours' walk after getting off the bus even if you walk fast. Therefore, "yào" should be in the position of C.

3. 选择 C。"可能"表示根据某种事实对一种情况的估计,用在动词或形容词前。"西边的天阴得多沉"是事实,"下雨"是估计出的情况。

The answer is C. "Kěnéng" indicates the estimate of a situation based on some facts; it is usually used before verbs or adjectives. In this sentence, "xībiān de tiān yīn de duō chén" is the fact, and "xià yǔ" is an estimate.

4. 选择 D。"能"可以表示有能力或有条件做某事,用在动词或形容词前。

The answer is D. "Néng" indicates having the ability or conditions to do something; it is used before verbs or adjectives.

5. 选择 B。"必须"表示在事实上、情理上必要,一定要。"坚持天天锻炼身体"是"有个好身体"的必要条件,所以"必须"应在 B 的位置上。

The answer is B. "Bìxū" indicates a practical and sensible necessity. In this sentence, "jiānchí tiān tiān duànliàn shēntǐ" is a necessary condition of "yǒu ge hǎo shēntǐ", so "bìxū" should be in the position of B.

6. 选择 D。"能"可以表示环境上的许可,而且多用于疑问句或否定句中。
The answer is D. When "néng" indicates a possibility provided by circumstances, it is usually used in interrogative or negative sentences.

7. 选择 D。"能"可以表示某物具有某种用途,用在动词前。本题中,"做药"是"橘子皮"的一个用途。
The answer is D. "Néng" indicates something has a kind of function or usage, and is used before verbs. In this sentence, "zuò yào" is one of the usages of "júzipí".

8. 选择 A。"必须"表示在事实上、情理上必要,一定要。本题中,"不能横穿乱跑"和"不能闯红灯"都是"遵守交通规则"的具体表现。
The answer is A. "Bìxū" indicates a practical and sensible necessity. In this sentence, "bù néng héngchuān luànpǎo" and "bù néng chuǎng hóngdēng" are all necessities of "zūnshǒu jiāotōng guīzé".

9. 选择 B。"要"可以表示某人做某事的意愿,前面常会出现"想"一词。本题中,"跟我一起到书店买书"是"女儿"想做的事。
The answer is B. "Yào" may indicate one's intention to do something, and usually comes after "xiǎng". In this sentence, "gēn wǒ yìqǐ dào shūdiàn mǎi shū" is the intention of "nǚ'ér".

10. 选择 C。"会"可以表示懂得怎样做,具有某种技能。本题的意思是安娜除了母语外,还懂得三个国家的语言怎么说。
The answer is C. "Huì" means knowing how to do something, which is used before verbs. This sentence means besides her native language, Anna knows how to speak three other languages.

11. 选择 B。"会"可以表示有可能,否定时用"不会",表示没有可能,用在动词前。"她是不会在其他地方的"是一个强调句,表示"她"不可能在其他地方。
The answer is B. "Huì" means there is a possibility, and the negative form is "bú huì", which means there is no possibility; they are used before verbs. In this sentence, "tā shì bú huì zài qítā dìfāng de" is an emphatic sentence, indicating it is not possible that she is in some other places.

12. 选择 D。"可能"表示根据某种事实对一种情况的估计,用在动词前。本题中,根据"不爱自己的父母"做出判断。"可能爱别人吗?"是一个反问句,表示不可能爱别人。

The answer is D. "Kěnéng" indicates an estimate of some situation based on some fact. It's used before verbs in this sentence, the second clause is a rhetorical question, indicating "they cannot love other people".

13. 选择 B。"得"表示情理上、事实上或意志上需要、应该、必须,用在动词前。本题中,"开刀"和"做手术"同义,"得"放在第一个动词"开"的前面。

The answer is B. "děi" means there is a sensible, practical, or intentional need; it is used before the verb. In this sentence, "kāi dāo" and "zuò shǒushù" are similar in meaning, so "děi" is used before the first verbal phrase.

14. 选择 D。"肯"表示愿意、乐意,否定用"不肯",表示不愿意、不乐意。

The answer is D. "Kěn" means willing to, glad to, and its negative form is "bù kěn", which means not willing to or unhappy to.

15. 选择 D。"应该"可以表示估计情况必然如此,用在动词或形容词前。本题中,"每个学生都会回答"是根据"这个问题并不算很难"估计出的情况。

The answer is D. "Yīnggāi" means something will surely be as estimated, and is used before verbs or adjectives. In this sentence, "měi gè xuéshēng dōu huì huídá" is an estimate based on the condition that "zhè gè wèntí bìng bú suàn hěn nán".

16. 选择 A。能愿动词的肯定、否定形式连用表示疑问。在本题中,因为问的是"明天"的事情,所以只能选择 A。

The answer is A. When the positive and negative forms of optative verbs are used together, it means a question. In this sentence, as the question is about something in the next day, so only A is the right choice.

17. 选择 C。能愿动词的肯定、否定形式连用表示疑问。双音节能愿动词肯定、否定形式连用表示疑问时,有两种形式:①AB 不 AB ②A 不 AB。

The answer is C. When the positive and negative forms of optative verbs are used together, it means a question. When it comes to disyllabic optative verbs, they can take on two forms: ①AB bù AB ②A bù AB.

18. 选择 D。"能"可以表示环境上的许可,用在动词前。本题的意思是:阅览室里的报刊杂志只允许在阅览室里看,不允许外借。

The answer is D. "Néng" can mean a permission under certain circumstances, and is used before verbs. The meaning of this sentence is "the periodicals and magazines in the reading room can only be read in the room but cannot be borrowed."

19. 选择 A。"应该"可以表示在情理上必须如此,用在动词结构的前面。
The answer is A. "Yīnggāi" can mean a sensible necessity, and is used before verbal structure.

20. 选择 C。"得"表示情理上、事实上或意志上需要、应该、必须,用在动词前。用于口语。
The answer is C. "Děi" means there is a sensible, practical or intentional need; it is used before verbs in spoken language.

21. 选择 B。能愿动词的肯定、否定形式连用表示疑问。双音节能愿动词的疑问形式有两种:①AB 不 AB;②A 不 AB。
The answer is B. When the positive and negative forms of optative verbs are used together, it means a question. When it comes to disyllabic optative verbs, they can take on two forms: ①AB bù AB ②A bù AB.

22. 选择 D。本题实际上是对"需要"的否定。能愿动词"需要"的否定形式有两个,一是"不需要",另一个是"不用"。"不用"多用于口语中。
The answer is D. This sentence actually indicates the negation of "xūyào". There are two negative forms of "xūyào", one is "bù xūyào", and the other is "bú yòng", which is more often used in spoken language.

23. 选择 C。"该"可以表示理应如此,应该,用在动词或形容词前。
The answer is C. "Gāi" means "should"; it is used before verbs or adjectives.

24. 选择 C。能愿动词的肯定、否定形式连用表示疑问。单音节能愿动词的疑问形式是:A 不 A;双音节能愿动词的疑问形式是:①AB 不 AB;②A 不 AB。
The answer is C. When the positive and negative forms of optative verbs are used together, it means a question. The interrogative form of monosyllabic verbs is A bù A. When it comes to disyllabic optative verbs, they can take on two forms: ①AB bù AB ②A bù AB.

25. 选择 C。"得"表示情理上、事实上或意志上需要、应该、必须,用在动词前。用于口语。
The answer is C. "Děi" means there is a sensible, practical or intentional need; it is used before verbs in spoken language.

26. 选择 C。"得"表示情理上、事实上或意志上需要、应该、必须,用在动词前。用于口语。
The answer is C. "Děi" means there is sensible, practical or intentional need; it is used before verbs and in spoken language.

27. 选择 B。"应该"表示在情理上必须如此,用在动词前。
The answer is B. "Yīnggāi" means there is sensible necessity.

28. 选择 B。能愿动词的肯定、否定形式连用表示疑问。双音节能愿动词的疑问形式有两种:①
AB 不 AB;②A 不 AB。
The answer is B. When the positive and negative forms of optative verbs are used together, it means a question. When it comes to disyllabic optative verbs, they can take on two forms: AB bù AB or A bù AB.

29. 选择 C。"应该"可以表示在情理上必须如此,用在动词前。
The answer is C. "Yīnggāi" means there is sensible necessity, and is used before verbs.

30. 选择 B。"必须"表示在事实上、情理上必要,一定要。常用在表示命令、要求的句子中。
The answer is B. "Bìxū" indicates a practical and sensible need, and is often used in sentences with orders and requirements.

7 重叠 Reduplication

一、动词的重叠 Reduplication of Verbs

考点精讲 Examination Points

	格式 Pattern		举例 Examples	说明 Explanation
动词的重叠 Reduplication of Verbs	单音节 Monosyllabic Verbs	AA 或 A 一 A	听听 / 听一听 tīngting/ tīng yī tīng	1.动词重叠一般表示短时的意义。 It indicates a short time. 2.表示尝试的意义,动词后常可加"看"。 It indicates trying, and "kàn" often follows the verb. 3. 用在祈使句中,有缓和语气的作用。 It can be used in the imperative sentence to soften the tone. 4. 可用以举例,含有轻松、随便的意味。 When used to raise examples, it conveys a sense of casualness.
		A 了 A（完成式)	听了听 tīng le tīng	
	双音节 Disyllabic Verbs	ABAB	讨论讨论 tǎolùn tǎolùn	
		AB 了 AB（完成式)	讨论了讨论 tǎolùn le tǎolùn	

1. 双音节动词不能用中间加"一"的方式进行重叠。

   Disyllabic verbs can't be reduplicated by putting "yī" in between. For example:

   例:讨论一讨论 (×)　　打扫一打扫 (×)

   　　讨论讨论 (√)　　　打扫打扫 (√)

2. 当表示正在进行或同时进行两个以上的动作、或者动词后有"了""着""过"的句子时,动词不能重叠。如:

   Verbs can't be reduplicated when they indicate something is being done or two or more actions are being done at the same time, or if verbs are followed by "zhe", "le", "guo".

   例:我正在看看电视,电话铃响了。(×)

3. 在句中起修饰限制作用的动词不能重叠。

Those verbs with the function of modifying and restricting can't be reduplicated. For example:

例：刚才试试的那双鞋不大不小，正合适。（×）

刚才试的那双鞋不大不小，正合适。（√）

4. 动词有补语时，动词不能重叠。如：

Verbs can't be reduplicated when they have complements. For example:

例：我听听懂了。（×）

我听懂了。（√）

强化练习 Exercises

■ 每个句子中有一个或两个空，请在 ABCD 四个答案中选择唯一恰当的一个。

Please choose the correct answer for each blank from the four choices of A, B, C, and D.

1. 夏季的夜晚，人们总喜欢出来走走，四处 _____ ，好乘凉消暑。
   A．看   B．看看   C．看见   D．看了看

2. 这件衣服是我为你买的，你 _____ 看。
   A．试试   B．试   C．尝试   D．试了试

3. 她总是喜欢看着电视 _____ 饭。
   A．吃一吃   B．吃了吃   C．吃   D．吃吃

4. 你给我们介绍一下你 _____ 的情况吧。
   A．了解一了解   B．了了解解   C．了解   D．了解了了解

5. 你在北京的时候，_____ 过京剧吗？
   A．欣赏欣赏   B．欣赏   C．欣赏了欣赏   D．欣欣赏赏

6. 等你 _____ 明白了以后，再来找我吧。
   A．弄一弄   B．弄弄   C．弄了弄   D．弄

7. 我还是不太明白，您再给我 _____ 吧。
   A．解释解释   B．解释一解释   C．解释了解释   D．解释

8. 你在这儿坐一会儿，我 _____ 就来。
   A．去   B．去了去   C．去去   D．去那里

9. 她 _____ ,还是走了。
   A．想　B．想想　C．想了想　D．想一想

10. 大家在 _____ 问题呢。
   A．研究研究　B．研究了研究　C．研究　D．研究一研究

答疑解惑 Answers and Explanations

1. 选择 B。用以举例,表示轻松、随便的语气;又因是表示人们习惯性的行为,应选用一般时态。
The answer is B. The verb here gives an example, representing a tone of relaxation and casualness; and it stands for people's routine behavior, so the present tense is chosen.

2. 选择 A。表示尝试的意思,且动作尚未进行。
The answer is A. The verb here represents trying to do something, and it has not been done.

3. 选择 C。表示同时进行的两个动作时,不能用动词的重叠形式。
The answer is C. The verb can't be reduplicated when two actions are being done at the same time.

4. 选择 C。在句中起修饰限制作用的动词不能重叠。
The answer is C. The verb can't be reduplicated when it takes the function of modifying and restricting.

5. 选择 B。因动词后有助词"过",不能选用动词的重叠形式。
The answer is B. The verb can't be reduplicated when it is followed by the auxiliary verb "guo".

6. 选择 D。因动词后有补语"明白",不能选用动词的重叠形式。
The answer is D. The verb can't be reduplicated when it is followed by the complement "míngbái".

7. 选择 A。在祈使句中,如想缓和语气,应选用动词的重叠形式。在此句中,动作尚未进行,不能选择完成式。B 为干扰项,不符合双音节动词的重叠格式。
The answer is A. The verb should be reduplicated in imperative sentences for a milder tone. In this example, the action is not taken, so the perfect tense can't be used. B is a choice to

confuse the students, it does not fit with the pattern of verb reduplication.

8. 选择C。动词"去"重叠表示时间很短。此句表示说话时尚未"去",将要"去"。

The answer is C. The verb "qù" indicates a short period of time, and it hasn't taken place.

9. 选择C。句中想表达的意思是"想"以后"走了"。动词重叠的完成式表示时间短暂。

The answer is C. The sentence is to express "zǒu le" after "xiǎng". The perfect form of verb reduplication indicates a short period.

10. 选择C。正在进行的动作不能用动词的重叠形式。

The answer is C. The verb can't be reduplicated when it represents something continuing.

二、形容词的重叠 Reduplication of adjectives

考点精讲 Examination Points

		格式 Pattern	举例 Examples	说明 Explanation
形容词 的重叠 Reduplication of Adjectives	单音节 Monosyllabic Adjectives	AA (的)	好好 (的)	表示程度加深和加强描写的作用,不能接受程度副词的修饰。 Indicating a higher degree or empha-sizing, they cannot be modified by de-gree adverbs.
	双音节 Disyllabic Adjectives	AABB (的)	大大方方 (的)	
		ABAB (的) (像 A 一样 B)	雪白雪白 (的)	
		A 里 AB (的) (贬义)	糊里糊涂 (的)	

1. 不是所有的形容词都可以重叠,形容词能否重叠主要是习惯问题。

   Not all the adjectives can be reduplicated. Whether they can be reduplicated is conventional.

   例:整洁——整洁整洁 (×)   美丽——美美丽丽 (×)

   整齐——整整齐齐 (√)   漂亮——漂漂亮亮 (√)

2. ABAB 式只限于状中结构的双音节形容词,含义为像 A 一样 B。

   Format ABAB is only restricted to disyllabic adjectives in the structure of "adverbial + a modified word", and the meaning is being B just like A.

Reduplication

例：笔直——笔直笔直(像笔一样直) (✓)

冰凉——冰凉冰凉(像冰一样凉) (✓)

3. A 里 AB 式的重叠方式有厌恶的意味，只限于含有贬义的形容词。在句中起修饰限制作用的形容词不能重叠。

The pattern "A li AB" implies something unsatisfying and can only be applied to those adjectives with a derogatory sense. Those adjectives functioning as modifiers can't be reduplicated. For example:

例：啰嗦——啰里啰嗦 (✓)

小气——小里小气 (✓)

4. 有些形容词兼有动词性，在使用时要区别词性选择不同的重叠形式。

Some adjectives take the function of verbs, in such cases, choices should be made according to their parts of speech.

例：屋里开着空调，凉凉快快的，真舒服！(形容词性，AABB 式)

外面太热了，赶快进屋凉快凉快吧。(动词性，ABAB 式)

特别提示 Special Tips

☆ 动词性形容词并不多，常见的有：安静、安心、干净、高兴、客气、精神、快活、宽敞、宽绰、乐和、冷淡、冷静、利索、凉快、啰嗦、明白、暖和、漂亮、平静、亲热、勤快、清楚、轻松、舒服、舒坦、舒心、痛快、新鲜、辛苦、大方、规矩、老实、认真、热心、害羞、满意、着急。

There are not too many verbal adjectives. The commonly seen ones are: ānjìng, ānxīn, gānjìng, gāoxìng, kèqi, jīngshen, kuàihuo, kuānchǎng, kuānchuò, lèhe, lěngdàn, lěngjìng, lìsuo, liángkuài, luōsuo, míngbai, nuǎnhuo, piàoliang, píngjìng, qīnrè, qínkuai, qīngchu, qīngsōng, shūfu, shūtan, shūxīn, tòngkuai, xīnxian, xīnkǔ, dàfang, guīju, lǎoshi, rènzhēn, rèxīn, hàixiū, mǎnyì, zháojí.

5. 有一类形容词是由"形容词+词缀"构成的，表示"很+形容词"的意思，同样不能接受程度副词的修饰。

There is one type of adjectives that is comprised of "adjective + suffix" to indicate "very much + adjectives". And they can't be modified by adverbs of degree. For example:

例：暖洋洋、香喷喷

强化练习 Exercises

■ **每个句子中有一个或两个空,请在 ABCD 四个答案中选择唯一恰当的一个。**

Please choose the correct answer for each blank from the four choices of A, B, C, and D.

1. 他的眼睛 _____ 的,真漂亮!
   A．大　B．大大　C．很大大　D．大一大

2. 咱们几个难得聚一次,哪儿能不去 _____ !
   A．痛痛快快　B．痛快　C．痛快痛快　D．痛快了

3. 电影院里正 _____ 地上演着《满城尽带黄金甲》,该片吸引了很多观众。
   A．热闹闹　B．热闹热闹　C．热闹了热闹　D．热热闹闹

4. 那条裙子 _____ 的,她穿上像个白雪公主。
   A．雪白　B．雪白白　C．雪雪白白　D．雪白雪白

5. 森林里 _____ 的,什么声音都听不到。
   A．静悄静悄　B．静悄悄　C．静静悄悄　D．悄悄静

答疑解惑 Answers and Explanations

1. 选择 B。单音节形容词重叠式为 AA,表示加强描写,含有"可爱、喜爱"的感情。
The answer is B. The reduplication for monosyllabic adjectives is AA, and indicates a higher degree description and implies being lovely and adorable.

2. 选择 C。在句中"痛快"为动词性,重叠式应为 ABAB。
The answer is C. In this sentence "tòngkuai" functions as a verb, so the reduplication is ABAB.

3. 选择 D。双音节形容词重叠式为 AABB。
The answer is D. The reduplication of disyllabic adjectives is AABB。

4. 选择 D。形容词"雪白"是状中结构,重叠式为 ABAB。
The answer is D. The structure of the adjective "xuěbái" is "adverbial + a modified word", therefore the pattern is ABAB。

5. 选择 B。是"形容词+词缀"的生动形式。
The answer is B. It is in a form of "adjective + suffix", which is vivid in language style.

Reduplication

三、名词和量词的重叠 Reduplication of nouns and quantifiers

考点精讲 Examination Points

名词 / 量词 Nouns/Quantifiers	格式 Pattern	举例 Examples	说明 Explanation
单音节名词 Monosyllabic Nouns	AA	人人	一般的单音节量词和少数单音节名词可以重叠，表示全部、每个。后常和"都"配合使用。
单音节量词 Monosyllabic Quantifiers	AA	家家	The common monosyllabic qualifiers and a few monosyllabic nouns can be reduplicated and indicate "all", or "each one of ", "dōu" usually follows.

1. 数词"一"也可以重叠，表示"逐一"的意思，在句中做状语。

The numeral "yī" can also be reduplicated, indicating "one by one" and serving as an adverbial in the sentence.

　　　例：他和大家一一握手告别。

　　　　我要把那里的情况一一讲给你听。

2. 数量短语也可以重叠，表示"多"或"一个接一个地"。

Quantity phrases can also be reduplicated to indicate "many" or "one after another".

　　　例：一支支的队伍出发了。（表示很多支队伍）

　　　　她一遍遍地嘱咐着我。　或：她一遍又一遍地嘱咐着我。（表示一遍接一遍地）

强化练习 Exercises

■ 1题下面有一个指定的词语，句中 ABCD 是供选择的四个不同位置，请判断这一词语放在句中哪个位置上恰当。2—5 题的句子中有一个或两个空，请在 ABCD 四个答案中选择唯一恰当的一个。

Please find the proper position out of the four choices of A, B, C, and D for the word below Sentence 1. And choose a correct answer for each blank in the sentences 2-5 from the four choices of A, B, C, and D.

1. 他 A 跳了 B 一遍 C 一遍，D 始终不能达到原来的高度。
　　　　　　　　　　又

2. 这些孩子真可爱，那一＿＿＿＿＿笑脸就像盛开的鲜花那样美丽。
　　A. 一张　B. 张　C. 张一张　D. 张张

3. 有句话叫"_____ 大路通罗马",意思是使用不同的方法可以达到同一个目标。
   A．条条　B．一条一条　C．一条　D．一条儿

4. _____ 放暑假他都要去附近的工厂干两个月活儿,来挣自己的学费。
   A．时时　B．天天　C．年年　D．月月

5. 春节的时候,_____ 都团聚在一起吃年夜饭。
   A．天天　B．家家　C．桌桌　D．每每

答疑解惑 Answers and Explanations

1. 选择 C。数量短语的重叠式为 AB（又）AB,本题中"一遍又一遍",表示一遍接一遍地跳。
The answer is C. The reduplication pattern of quantity phrases is AB (yòu) AB. "Yíbiàn yòu yíbiàn" indicates to jump one time after another.

2. 选择 D。"张张"表示很多张笑脸。
The answer is D. "Zhāngzhāng" represents many smiling faces.

3. 选择 A。"条条"表示每一条。
The answer is A. "Tiáotiáo" represents every road.

4. 选择 C。"年年"表示每一年。
The answer is C. "Niánnián" represents every year.

5. 选择 B。"家家"表示每一家人。
The answer is B. "Jiājiā" represents every family.

8 常见句式 Common Sentence Patterns

一、"把"字句 The "bǎ" sentence

1. 基本格式：名词/代词（施事）+把+名词/代词（受事）+动词+其他成分。

   Basic pattern: noun/pronoun (agent) + bǎ + noun/pronoun (object) + verb + other components

   例：玛丽把那件事告诉她了。

2. 语法特征 Grammatical features of the "bǎ" sentence

   ① 有些"把"字句能够变换成"主–述–宾"的句式，有些不能。一般能够进行变换的"把"字句中的动词结构都比较简单，有的只包含一个动词和其后的动态助词；有的只包含一个动词和它的结果补语。

   Some "bǎ" sentences can be changed into the pattern of "subject + predicate + object", while some cannot. Usually, the "bǎ" sentences that can be changed have simple verbal structures, such as, a verb and the following aspectual particle, or a verb and its result complement.

   例：他把那本书买了。→他买了那本书。

   他把茶杯打破了。→他打破了茶杯。

   如果动词后加上介词短语或情态补语，这一类的"把"字句就不能进行变换。

   If the verb of the sentence is followed by a preposition phrase or modal complement, the "bǎ" sentence cannot be changed.

   例：我已经把汽车开到楼下了。

   她把衣服洗得干干净净。

   ② 不是所有的动词都能用于"把"字句中，只有含有"处置"义（表示产生结果、发生变化）的动词才可以。

   Not all verbs can be used in "bǎ" sentences, only those with the meaning of "disposition" can be used in this structure.

   例：我是学生。

   桌子上有一本书。

   我知道了一个消息。

我把作业写完了。

他把老师气哭了。

特别提示 Special Tips

☆ 不能用于"把"字句的动词主要有:

Verbs that cannot be used in "bǎ" sentences mainly include:

表示感觉、认知的:看见、听见、闻见、感到、感觉、觉得、以为、认为、知道、懂……

Those indicating perception or cognition: kànjiàn, tīngjiàn, wénjiàn, gǎndào, gǎnjué, juéde, yǐwéi, rènwéi, zhīdào, dǒng...

表示存在、等同的:有、在、是、不如、等于、像……

Those indicating existence or equivalence: yǒu, zài, shì, bùrú, děngyú, xiàng...

表示心理的:同意、讨厌、生气、关心、怕、愿意……

Those indicating mentality: tóngyì, tǎoyàn, shēngqì, guānxīn, pà, yuànyì...

表示身体状态的:站、坐、躺、蹲、趴、跪……

Those indicating posture: zhàn, zuò, tǎng, dūn, pā, guì...

表示趋向的:来、去、上、下、起来、过去……

Those indicating tendency: lái, qù, shàng, xià, qǐlái, guòqù...

③ 动词后一定要有其他一些成分,一定不能只用一个动词结尾。

Verbs must be followed by some other components and the "bǎ" sentence shouldn't be ended with only a verb.

例:你把衣服洗了。 (√)

你把衣服洗完了。 (√)

你把衣服洗干净。 (√)

你把衣服洗一下。 (√)

你把衣服洗洗。 (√)

你把衣服递给我。 (√)

你把衣服洗/递。 (×)

④ "把"后出现的名词一般是确指的,不能是泛指的。如果名词前没有任何修饰词语,那么说明对话双方都知道指的是什么。

The nouns following "bǎ" are usually those definitely referred instead of generally referred. If there is no modifier before the noun, that means both the speakers know what they are talking about.

例：你把汉语书拿过来。（√）

你把那本书拿过来。（√）

你把书拿过来。（√）

你把一本书拿过来。（×）

⑤ 否定副词、能愿动词和时间词应在"把"字前。

Negative adverbs, optative verbs and time words should precede "bǎ".

例：我没把这件事告诉他。

你必须把作业写完。

我明天把那本书给你带来。

特别提示 Special Tips

☆ 有时"将"可代替"把"，一般出现在书面语中。"将"除了有"把"的意思外，还有"将要"的意思。请注意区别：做"把"字讲的"将"后加名词性短语；做"将要"讲的"将"后只能加动词性短语。

Sometimes "jiāng" can take the place of "bǎ", which often appears in written language. Besides "bǎ", "jiāng" can also mean "jiāngyào". The difference needs to be minded. "jiāng" with the meaning of "bǎ" is followed by a noun phrase, while "jiāng" with the meaning of "jiāngyào" can only be followed by a verbal phrase.

例：她们将电视打开了。（将＝把）

她们将回国。（将＝将要）

二、"被"字句 The "bèi" sentence

1. 基本格式：名词/代词（受事）+被/叫/让+名词/代词（施事）+动词+其他成分

Basic pattern: noun/pronoun(object)+ bèi/jiào/ràng + noun/pronoun(agent) + verb + other components.

例：那本书被她借走了。（她借走了那本书。）

2. 语法特征 Grammatical features of the "bèi" sentence

① "被"书面语色彩较浓，"叫、让"更口语化一些。"被"后的名词或代词有时可以不出现，而"叫"、"让"后必须出现名词或代词。

"Bèi" bears stronger coloring of written language, "jiào" and "ràng" are more oral. Sometimes nouns or pronouns after "bèi" can be omitted, while "jiào" and "ràng" must be followed by nouns or pronouns.

例：问题终于被/叫/让大家解决了。（√）

问题终于被解决了。　　　　（√）

问题终于叫／让解决了。　（×）

特别提示 Special Tips

☆"被"字句和"把"字句的动词都是具有处置意义的动词。能用于"被"字句中的动词比能用于"把"字句中的动词范围稍大一些,如"看见"、"听见"等感觉动词,"知道"、"认为"等认知动词。但是,表示人体自身部位动作的动词一般不用于"被"字句,如"举（手）"、"抬（头）"、"踢（腿）"、"睁（眼）"等,而这些词均可用于"把"字句。

Same as "bǎ" sentences, the verbs in "bèi" sentences are those with the meaning of "disposition". The range of verbs that can appear in "bèi" sentences is wider than that in "bǎ" sentences. Verbs indicating the meaning of feeling such as "kànjiàn" and "tīngjiàn" and verbs indicating cognition such as "zhīdào" and "rènwéi" can be used in "bèi" sentences. However, verbs concerning the action of human body cannot be used in "bèi" sentences, although they can be used in "bǎ" sentences, such as "jǔ(shǒu)", "tái(tóu)", "tī(tuǐ)" or "zhēng(yǎn)", etc.

例:那张照片被她看见了。　（√）

她把那张照片看见了。　（×）

她们的话叫玛丽知道了。（√）

玛丽把她们的话知道了。（×）

大家把头抬起来。　　　（√）

头被大家抬起来。　　　（×）

②"被"字句的主语是确指的。

The subject of "bèi" sentences should be definite and specific.

例:最后一本书被大卫买走了。　（√）

一本书被大卫买走了。　　　（×）

③"被"字句的谓语不能是单独一个动词,动词后要有其他成分。

The predicate of "bèi" sentences cannot be a single verb, it must be followed by other components.

例:夏天我去了一趟海边,被晒黑了。　（√）

夏天我去了一趟海边,被晒。　　　（×）

④"被"字句以前在口语中多用于不如意、不愉快的事情;现在也用于如意、愉快的事情,也时常出现在书面语中。

Previously, "bèi" sentences are often used for unwanted or unpleasant things. Now it can also be used for happy and pleasant things, more often in written language.

例:他被妈妈批评了一顿。

她被公司开除了。

他被选为我们的代表。

⑤ 否定副词、能愿动词和时间词应在"被"字前。

Negative adverbs, optative verbs and time words should be used before "bèi".

例：大家没被困难吓倒。

她们出去的时候没带雨伞，现在下雨了，她们得被淋湿了。

他昨天被选为班长。

⑥ 其他一些常用格式的用法

The usage of other commonly used patterns.

A. "被……给+动词+补语……"常用于口语中。

"Bèi... gěi... + verb + complement" is often used in spoken language.

例：玩具被孩子给弄坏了。

B. "被……所+动词……"常用于书面语。动词不能再加其他成分，双音节动词前的"所"可以省略。

"Bèi... suǒ + verb..." is often used in written language. In this pattern, the verbs cannot be modified by other components, and "suǒ" before disyllabic verbs can be omitted.

例：我们被这个故事（所）感动。

C. "A 被称为/称做 B"，表示 A 和 B 一样。

"A bèi chēngwéi/chēngzuò B" means A and B are the same.

例：在古代，月亮被中国人称为"月宫"。

三、兼语句 Pivotal sentence

1. 基本格式：主语 + 动词₁ + 宾语₁ + 动词₂ + 宾语₂

Basic pattern: subject + verb₁ + object₁ + verb₂ + object₂

例：老师叫你去办公室。

2. 语法特征 Grammatical features of pivotal sentences

① 宾语₁既是动词₁的宾语，又是动词₂的主语。

The object₁ is the object of verb₁ as well as the subject of verb₂.

② 动词₁有四个特点：

Verb₁ bears four features:

A. 具有使令意义。常见的这一类动词有：使、让、叫、派、请、令、逼、命令、强迫、吩咐、打发、促使、要求、发动。

Meaning to order, verbs in this category include: shǐ, ràng, jiào, pài, qǐng, lìng, bī, mínglìng, qiángpò, fēnfù, dǎfā, cùshǐ, yāoqiú, fādòng.

例：经理派你去上海。

B. 具有称谓、认定意义。常见的这一类动词有：叫、称、认、拜、选、推选。

Meaning to call or recognize, verbs in this category include: jiào, chēng, rèn, bài, xuǎn, tuīxuǎn.

例：我拜您为老师吧。

C. "有"也可做兼语句中的动词$_1$。

"Yǒu" sometimes can serve as verb$_1$ in the pivotal sentence.

例：他有一个朋友叫大卫。

③ 动词$_1$后一般不能带"了""着""过"。

Usually verb$_1$ can not be followed by "le", "zhe" or "guo".

例：老师让我们谈了各自的看法。（√）

老师让了我们谈各自的看法。（×）

④ 否定副词、能愿动词一般在动词$_1$前。

Negative adverbs and optative verbs are usually used before verb$_1$.

例：妈妈不请他来家里。　　（√）

这件事会让她感到为难的。　（√）

这件事让她会感到为难的。　（×）

四、连动句 Sentences with consecutive verbs

1. 基本格式：主语 + 动词$_1$ + 宾语$_1$ + 动词$_2$ +（宾语$_2$）

Basic pattern: subject + verb$_1$ + object$_1$ + verb$_2$ + subject$_2$

例：她穿好衣服去学校了。

李老师拿了书出去了。

2. 语法特征 Grammatical features of sentences with consecutive verbs

① 连动句中的动作具有先后顺序，不能颠倒，而且句子中间不能停顿。动词$_1$后可用"了""过"。

The verbs in this type of sentences are in order and their positions cannot be changed. There cannot be a pause in the middle of the sentence. Verb$_1$ can be followed by "le" or "guo".

例：我拿起书走了。　　（√）

我走拿起书了。　　（×）

我们下了课去你家。　（√）

② 动词₁后如有动态助词"着",动词₁则表示动词₂的方式状态。

　　If verb$_1$ is followed by the aspectual particle "zhe", then verb$_1$ indicates the way or state of verb$_2$.

　　　　例：他每天骑着车去学校。

　　　　　　他笑着走了。

③ 动词₁是"来""去"时,表示后一个动作是前一个动作的目的。宾语₁可省略。

　　When verb$_1$ is "lái" or "qù", it indicates the latter action is the aim of the first one, and object$_1$ can be omitted.

　　　　例：大家来这里参观。　　（√）

　　　　　　大家来参观。　　　　（√）

　　　　　　我去书店买书。　　　（√）

　　　　　　我去买书。　　　　　（√）

④ 动词₁是"到"时,句子不像"来""去"那样明确强调动作的方向,但却兼有"来""去"的意思,宾语₁不能省略。

　　When verb$_1$ is "dào", the sentence doesn't emphasize much on the direction of the action as "lái" and "qù" do, but it indicates the meanings of both, and object$_1$ cannot be omitted.

　　　　例：我到北京学习汉语。（√）

　　　　　　我到学习汉语。　（×）

⑤ 动词₁是"来""去""到"等动词时,动态助词"了""过"只能放在第二个动词之后。

　　When verb$_1$ is "lái", "qù" or "dào", the aspectual particle such as "le" and "guo" can only be used after verb$_2$.

　　　　例：我到北京学习过一段时间。　（√）

　　　　　　我到过北京学习一段时间。　（×）

⑥ 口语中,"来""去"可放在句子后边,句子的意思不变。

　　In spoken language, "lái" and "qù" can be used at the end of the sentence without changing the meaning of it.

　　　　例：我们看你来了。（我们来看你了。）

　　　　　　他吃饭去了。（他去吃饭了。）

⑦ 动词₁是"有"时,宾语一般是抽象名词。动词₂和宾语₂通常可以看做宾语₁的定语。

　　When verb$_1$ is "yǒu", the object usually is an abstract noun, and verb$_2$ and object$_2$ can be seen as the attribute of object$_1$.

　　　　例：我们有能力解决这个问题。（我们有解决这个问题的能力。）

五、存现句 Existential sentence

1. ① 表示存在的基本格式
   Basic patterns indicating existence

   A. "处所词语+是+名词"。
      location word + shì + noun

      例：教学楼旁边是图书馆。

   B. "处所词语+有+数量词语+名词"。
      location word + yǒu + numeral phrase + noun

      例：讲台上有几本书。

   C. "名词+在+处所词语"。
      noun + zài + location word

      例：可乐在冰箱里。

   D. "处所词语+动词+着+名词"。
      location word + verb + zhe + noun

      例：墙上挂着一张地图。

   ② 表示出现或消失的基本格式："处所词语/时间词语+动词+名词"。

   Basic pattern indicating appearance or disappearance: location word/time phrase + verb + noun

      例：前边走过来一个人。

      1919年发生了著名的"五·四"运动。

2. 语法特征 Grammatical features of existential sentences

   ① 动词是"在"时，处所词语在后边。除此以外，句首一定要有表示处所或时间的词语，否则句子是错误的。

   When the verb is "zài", the location words must be after it. In other cases, there must be location or time words at the beginning of the sentence, otherwise the sentence is wrong.

      例：桌上放着一些书。　　　（√）

      　　放着一些书。　　　　　（×）

      　　老师在前边，同学们在后边。（√）

      　　前边在老师，后边在同学们。（×）

   ② 动词表示持续意义或安放物体的意义时，动词后的动态助词"着"表示静止的状态。

   When the verbs contain the meaning of continuation or the placement of objects, the aspectual article "zhe"after the verb indicates a static state.

      例：花园里种着一些牡丹花。

      　　门外围着一群人。

③ 动词表示具体动作时,动词后的动态助词"着"表示动作在进行,是正在运动的状态。

When the verbs indicate a specific action, the aspectual particle "zhe" after the verb indicates the ongoing state of the action.

例:天上飞着一队大雁。

④ 动词如果表示物体移动时,动词后一般带趋向动词或动态助词"了"。

When the verb indicates the movement of objects, it is usually followed by tendency verbs or the aspectual particle "le".

例:门外走进来一个人。

书包里少了一串钥匙。

⑤ 存现句的宾语一般是不确指的,宾语前往往会出现数量或描写性的定语。

Usually the object of existential sentence is not definite, and it is often preceded by a numeral or descriptive attribute.

例:海面上升起一轮红日。

石碑上刻着几个醒目的大字。

六、比较句 Comparative sentence

1. ① 用"比"字表示比较的格式

Basic patterns of sentences with "bǐ" indicating a comparison

A. "A 比 B+(更/还)+形容词"。副词"更、还"表示强度更大。

A bǐ B + (gèng/hái) + adjective. The adverb "gèng" or "hái" shows a higher degree.

例:妹妹比姐姐还漂亮。

B. "A 比 B+形容词+差别"。

A bǐ B + adjective + the difference

例:哥哥比弟弟大四岁。

C. "A 比 B+动词+宾语/补语"。

A bǐ B + verb + object/complement

例:我比你爱她。

他比你骑得快。

D. "A 比 B+形容词+动词+差别"。

A bǐ B + adjective + verb + the difference

例:我比你早来了一个小时。

② 用"(没)有"表示比较的格式:"A (没)有 B+(这么/那么)+形容词"。

"(Méi)Yǒu" can also indicate a comparison: A (méi)yǒu B + (zhème/nàme) + adjective

例：妹妹已经有桌子这么高了。

上海的历史没有北京悠久。

③ 用"不如"表示比较的格式："A 不如 B+（形容词）"。

Pattern with "bùrú" for a comparison: A bùrú + B + (adjective)

例：姐姐不如妹妹。（学习上、工作上、智力、容貌……，要根据上下文理解）

昨天不如今天冷。

④ 用"和、跟、与、同"表示比较的格式："A 和/跟/与/同 B 一样/相同/相似/类似/差不多+（形容词/动词）"。

Pattern with "hé, gēn, yǔ and tóng" for a comparison: A hé/gēn/yǔ/tóng B yíyàng/xiāngtóng/xiāngsì/lèisì/chàbuduō + (adjective/verb)

例：我和你一样想家。

这里的空气跟乡间的一样新鲜。

这里的房价跟北京差不多。

⑤ A."越来越+谓词性词语+（了）"指程度随时间的推移而加深。

Yuèláiyuè + predicate words + (le)indicates the degree becomes intensified with the pass of time.

例：天气越来越热了。

B."越+谓词性词语，越+谓词性词语"指程度随情况的发展而变化。

Yuè + predicate words, yuè + predicate words indicates the degree changes with the development of a certain status.

例：我们越紧张，越说不出话来。

2. 语法特征 Grammatical features of comparative sentence

① "比"字句的否定形式是在"比"前加"不"，它的意义并不是肯定句的简单否定。

The negative form of "bǐ" sentence is to add "bù" before "bǐ", which is not a simple negation of the positive sentence.

例：我不比你高。（"我跟你一样高"或"我比你矮"）

② 比较的结果之前不能出现"很""最""非常""十分""特别"等程度副词。

There cannot be degree adverbs such as "hěn", "zuì", "fēicháng", "shífēn", "tèbié" before the result of comparison.

例：玛丽比大卫努力。　（√）

玛丽比大卫特别努力。（×）

③ 用"没有""不如"表示比较时，句中的形容词一定是带有积极色彩的。

When "méiyǒu", "bùrú" are used in comparison, the adjectives in the sentence must be of positive coloring.

例：我的房间没有你的大。　（√）

　　我的房间没有你的小。　（×）

　　他跑得不如我快。　　　（√）

　　他跑得不如我慢。　　　（×）

七、反问句 Rhetorical question

1. 基本格式 Basic patterns

① "难道/岂……吗？"进一步肯定已知的情况。

　　"Nándào/qǐ...ma?" further confirms a known fact.

　　例：你难道不知道这件事情吗？（你知道这件事）

　　　　这样做岂不浪费吗？（这样做太浪费）

② "不是……吗？"用以进一步肯定已知的情况。

　　"Búshì...ma?" further confirms a known fact.

　　例：你不是病了吗？你应该在家多休息几天。（你病了）

③ "没有……吗？"用以进一步肯定已知的情况。

　　"Méiyǒu...ma?" further confirms a known fact.

　　例：大卫没有回国吗？（大卫回国了）

④ "还……（吗）？"强调应该。

　　"Hái...(ma)" emphasizes "should do".

　　例：快考试了，你还玩儿？（不应该玩儿）

　　　　这么晚了，你还不回家？（应该回家）

⑤ "为什么/怎么……呢？"强调应该。

　　"Wèishénme/zěnme...ne?" emphasizes "should do".

　　例：你怎么 / 为什么不说话呢？（应该说话）

⑥ "何必……呢？"强调没有必要。

　　"Hébì...ne?" emphasizes "not necessary".

　　例：她不愿意去，你何必强迫她去呢？（没有必要强迫她去）

⑦ "哪儿（里）/怎么+形容词/动词"。表示对某种判断的否定，带有不同意或反驳的语气。

　　"Nǎr (li)/zěnme + adjective/verb" indicates negation of a judgment, with a sense of disagreement or retort.

　　例：这本小说哪儿难啊！一年级的学生都能看懂。（这本小说不难）

　　　　我刚才还看见她了，她怎么会不在呢？（她应该在）

⑧"形容词/可加"很"的动词+什么"。表示对某种判断的否定,带有不同意或反驳的语气。

"Adjective/verbs match with "hěn" + shénme" indicates negation of a judgment, with a sense of disagreement or retort.

> 例:这个词难什么? 一点儿也不难。（这个词不难）
>
> ——你一定很喜欢这部电影。
>
> ——喜欢什么? 一点儿意思也没有。（不喜欢这部电影）

⑨"动词+什么?"表示"没有必要""不应该"或"不能实现"。带有不满意或不赞同的语气。

"Verb + shénme" indicates "not necessary", "should not" or "can't be realized", with a sense of dissatisfaction or disapproval.

> 例:这件衬衫那么干净,还洗什么?（没必要洗）

2. 语法特征 Grammatical features of rhetorical question

① 反问句具有问句的形式,实际上句中已经有明确的表述,不需要回答。

Rhetorical question bears the form of a question, and the answer is contained in the sentence already. No answer is needed for a rhetorical question.

② 在反问句中,肯定形式表达否定意义,否定形式表达肯定意义。

In a rhetorical question, the positive form expresses a negative meaning, while the negative form indicates a positive meaning.

③ 反问句的作用主要是加强语气。由于反问句语气强烈，使用时要特别注意场合和谈话对象。

The function of a rhetorical question is to enhance the tone. As the tone of a rhetorical question is quite strong, special attention should be paid to the occasions and listeners when it is to be used.

八、强调句 Emphatic sentence

1. 基本格式 Basic patterns

① "主语+是+谓语"。

subject + shì + predicate

> 例:这条项链是漂亮。

② "(是)……的"。

(shì)... de

> 例:我是在学校里看见他的。

③ "连……也/都+动词+(……)"。

lián... yě/dōu + verb + (...)

例：这样的事，我连听都没听说过。

④ "一点儿也/都+动词/形容词+(……)"。

yìdiǎnr yě/dōu + verb/adjective + (...)

例：我一点儿也不喜欢这个电影。

⑤ "非……不可"。

fēi... bùkě

例：你们不好好训练，明天非输球不可。

2. 语法特征 Grammatical features of emphatic sentence

① "是……的"句中如果去掉"是"，句子仍然是正确的；而普通"是"字句中如果没有了"是"，则是一个错误的句子。

If "shì" in the pattern "shì... de" is omitted, it is still a correct sentence, but if "shì" in ordinary "shì" sentence is omitted, it is a wrong sentence.

例：你是什么时候来的？　　(√)

你什么时候来的？　　(√)

我们是留学生。　　　　(√)

我们留学生。　　　　　(×)

② 强调时间、地点和方式时，"的"一般在句末，但也可以放在动词与宾语之间。

When time, location and way are emphasized, "de" is usually put at the end of the sentence, but can also be put between the verb and the object.

例：我们是上星期去故宫的。　(√)

我们是上星期去的故宫。　(√)

③ 强调目的、用途、归类时，"的"一般只能放在句末。

When aim, usage and classification are emphasized, "de" is usually put at the end of the sentence.

例：我们是来参观展览的。　(√)

我们是来参观的展览。　(×)

④ "也/都"的后面常是否定形式。

"Yě/dōu" is usually followed by the negative form.

例：他连上网都不会。

我一点儿也不想家。

⑤ "非……不可"可以表示三种意义：

"Fēi... bùkě" indicates three meanings:

A. 表示很强的决心或愿望，是"一定要"的意思。

It may indicate a strong determination or hope, meaning "yídìng yào".

例：我非学好汉语不可。

B. 强调必要性,表示"必须"的意思。一般句子前面常会出现必须这样做的理由。

It may emphasize the necessity, meaning "bìxū". Usually the reason to do so will appear in the first part of the sentence.

例：只有大卫最了解情况,处理这个问题非他去不可。

C. 强调必然性,表示"一定会"的意思。

It may emphasize the certainty, meaning "yídìng huì".

例：现在天阴得这么沉,一会儿非下雨不可。

强化练习 Exercises

1—34 题,在每一个句子下面都有一个指定的词语,句中 ABCD 是供选择的四个不同位置,请判断这一词语放在句中哪个位置上恰当。

Please find the proper position out of the four choices of A, B, C, and D for the word below each sentence.

1. A 弟弟 B 还 C 没有 D 背下来。
　　　　把英语单词

2. A 大岛说汉语 B 说 C 得 D 好。
　　　　比我

3. 夏季,A 北京 B 很多家庭 C 到北戴河、青岛等海滨城市 D 去消夏。
　　　　有

4. 小林英语 A 说得 B 很好,他女儿 C 比他说得 D 好。
　　　　还

5. 小杨家中有事走得很急,临走时 A 她让 B 我 C 交给 D 李教授。
　　　　把毕业论文

6. 上课时 A,李老师 B 叫学生 C 都关上 D。
　　　　把手机

7. 我们已经 A 商量好,B 一放暑假 C 就 D 旅游。
　　　　去西藏

8. 幼儿园的老师既要教学又要照顾孩子们的吃喝拉撒,A 她们 B 不 C 轻松 D。
　　　　比中小学的老师

9. 云飞 A 比昊天 B 在北京 C 待了 D 一个月。
　　　　多

10. A 李教授 B 把论文 C 再修改 D 一下。
    让小杨

11. 张导演强调 A，这段表演 B 在感情上要 C 比上一段的感情 D。
    强烈一些

12. 人证物证都在，A 你 B 有 C 什么 D 辩解的吗?
    还

13. 刘老师连着 A 上了四堂课，B 累极了，下课后，C 一句话都 D 不想说了。
    连

14. A 妈妈 B 叫我 C 打开 D。
    把洗衣机

15. 妈妈做饭的水平 A 不 B 爸爸 C 高 D 多少。
    比

16. 小张告诉 A 明天 B 去 C 参观 D 故宫博物院。
    我

17. 王晶晶 A 的身材 B 比李娜娜的身材 C 略微 D。
    苗条一些

18. 安娜总是谦虚地说 A 她的汉字写得不好，B 其实她 C 写得好得 D 多。
    比我

19. 吴阿姨比妈妈大十岁，A 看上去 B 她 C 比妈妈 D 还年轻。
    倒

20. 颐和园的昆明湖水域历史超过 3500 年，A 比北京城 B 的历史 C 早 D400 多年。
    还

21. 你 A 这样 B 和父母 C 说话 D 呢?
    怎么

22. 请你 A 这些旧书 B 包上 C 书皮 D 放在书柜里。
    把

23. 孙石是我的好朋友，A 都 B 不支持我 C，D 何况其他人呢?
    连他

24. 妈妈 A，您辛苦了，B 来给您 C 揉揉肩膀 D 吧!
    让我

25. 爸爸要去看望爷爷，妈妈 A 让 B 爸爸 C 给爷爷带去 D。
    把这些北京特产

26. 到张家界旅游的人 A 无不 B 那里美丽的自然景色 C 吸引住 D 了。
　　　　　　　被

27. 索玛的中国民歌唱得很好，A 还是 B 为我们 C 唱一首"南泥湾"D 吧。
　　　　　　　请她

28. 吴茜今年 A 毕业于 B 中国传媒大学，C 留在学校 D 当老师了。
　　　　　　被

29. 美玲是个内向的姑娘，平时少言寡语，联欢会上 A 你们 B 让她 C 唱一首歌不可，
　　D 她一定很为难。
　　　　非

30. 老师 A 明天 B 穿得漂亮点儿，C 一起照一张 D 合影。
　　　　　让我们

31. A 大家 B 一致同意 C 坐飞机 D 旅游。
　　　　去西双版纳

32. 弟弟 A 今年 B 明显 C 长高了，懂事了，成熟多了 D。
　　　　比去年

33. A 下山本来 B 就比上山难，更 C 遇到 D 突然降下的大雨呢？
　　　　何况

34. 保罗 A 大汗淋漓地跑进家，B 半个西瓜 C 一口气 D 全吃光了。
　　　　　把冰箱里的

■ 35—50 题，每个句子中有一个或两个空，请在 ABCD 四个答案中选择唯一恰当的一个。
Please choose a correct answer for each blank from the four choices of A, B, C, and D.

35. 桌子 _____ 有做好的饭，如果凉了你热热再吃吧。
　　A. 里　B. 中　C. 上　D. 内

36. 景山的对面 _____ 故宫博物院。
　　A. 是　B. 在　C. 坐落　D. 坐

37. 这个书包 _____ 那个书包看起来差不多，可是价钱却如此悬殊。
　　A. 比　B. 把　C. 和　D. 对

38. 大卫是去年秋天结婚 _____。
　　A. 了　B. 着　C. 的　D. 过

39. 滨田 _____ 八木长得高。
　　A. 没有　B. 不是　C. 比不　D. 不一样

40. 钢琴上 _____ 着几本琴谱。
    A. 站立　B. 站　C. 放　D. 停留

41. 晾衣杆儿上 _____ 挂着衣服,却挂着几个鸟笼子。
    A. 不　B. 非　C. 未　D. 没

42. 跑了好几个书店, _____ 全买齐了。
    A. 几本书被我　B. 我把一本书
    C. 我把几本书　D. 我把那本书

43. 客厅的一面墙上 _____ 一张全家福。
    A. 挂　B. 挂着　C. 挂在　D. 挂住

44. 张力 _____ 稿费全捐给了希望工程。
    A. 让　B. 把　C. 叫　D. 使

45. 中国的石拱桥有悠久的历史,卢沟桥就 _____ 是世界著名的古代石拱桥。
    A. 被认为　B. 被以为　C. 被成为　D. 被想

46. 十五岁的女儿长得 _____ 妈妈一样高了。
    A. 跟　B. 对　C. 比　D. 从

47. 儿子开车的技术 _____ 老爸的技术还高。
    A. 比较　B. 跟　C. 不如　D. 比

48. 这部电视剧构思奇特,大家都 _____ 它的曲折情节吸引住了。
    A. 把　B. 被　C. 由　D. 为

49. 公司 _____ 她去洽谈这笔业务。
    A. 给　B. 对　C. 从　D. 派

50. 同学们说坐火车去天津玩儿,可是亮亮 _____ 要坐飞机 _____ 。
    A. 除了……以外　　B. 够……的
    C. 非……不可　　　D. 越……越

答疑解惑 Answers and Explanations

1. 选择 D。在"把"字句中,副词要在"把"的前面。本题中,"还"和"没有"都是副词,因此"把英语单词"应在 D 的位置上。
The answer is D. In "bǎ" sentences, adverbs should precede "bǎ". In this sentence, "hái" and "méiyǒu" are adverbs, so "bǎ yīngyǔ dāncí" should be in the position of D.

2. 选择 D。这也是比较句的一个基本格式:A+动词+宾语+动词+得+比+B+差别。本题中,A

是"大岛"，B 是"我"，"说"是动词，"汉语"是宾语，"好"是比较的差别。因此"比我"应在 D 的位置上。

The answer is D. One basic pattern of comparative sentences is "A + verb + object + verb + de + bǐ + B + difference". In this sentence, A is "Dàdǎo", B is "wǒ", "shuō" is the verb, "Hànyǔ" is the object, "hǎo" is the difference, so "bǐ wǒ" should be in the position of D.

3. 选择 B。这是一个存现句，它的基本格式是：某地+有+某人/某物+……。本题中，"北京"是某地，"很多家庭"是某人，因此"有"应在 B 的位置上。

The answer is B. This is an existential sentence and its basic pattern is: "somewhere + yǒu + someone/something". In this sentence, "Beijīng" is somewhere, "hěnduō jiātíng" is someone, so "yǒu" should be in the position of B.

4. 选择 D。这是一个比较句，它的基本格式是：A 比 B+动词+得+更/还+形容词。本题中，"他女儿"是 A，"他"是 B，因此"还"应在 D 的位置上。

The answer is D. This is a comparative sentence, and its basic pattern is: "A bǐ B + verb + de + gèng/hái + adjective". In this sentence, "tā nǔ'ér" is A, and "tā" is B, so "hái" should be in the position of D.

5. 选择 C。这是一个兼语句，它的基本格式是：主语+动词₁ + 宾语₁ + 动词₂ + 宾语₂。本题中，"她"是主语，"让"是兼语动词，"我"是宾语₁，同时又是后面"把毕业论文交给李教授"的主语。因此"把毕业论文"应在 C 的位置上。

The answer is C. This is a pivotal sentence, and its basic pattern is: "subject + verb₁ + object₁ + verb₂ + object₂". In this sentence, "tā" is the subject, "ràng" is the pivotal verb, "wǒ" is the object₁ as well as the subject of "bǎ bìyè lùnwén jiāogěi Lǐ jiàoshòu", so "bǎ bìyè lùnwén" should be in the position of C.

6. 选择 C。这是一个兼语句，它的基本格式是：主语+动词₁+宾语₁+动词₂+宾语₂。本题中，"李老师"是主语，"叫"是兼语动词，"学生"是宾语₁，同时又是后面"把手机关上"的主语。因此"把手机"应在 C 的位置上。

The answer is C. This is a pivotal sentence, and its basic pattern is: "subject + verb₁ + object₁ + verb₂+ object₂". In this sentence, "Lǐ lǎoshī" is the subject, "jiào" is the pivotal verb, "xuéshēng" is object₁ as well as the subject of "bǎ shǒujī guānshàng". So "bǎ shǒujī" should be in the position of C.

7. 选择 D。这是一个连动结构"去某地做某事"。因此"去西藏"应在 D 的位置上。

The answer is D. This is a consecutive verbal pattern of "going somewhere to do something", so "qù Xīzàng" should be in the position of D.

8. 选择 C。这是一个比较句。在"比"字句中,否定副词应该在"比"的前面。因此"比中小学的老师"应在 C 的位置上。

The answer is C. This is a comparative sentence. In "bǐ" sentence, the negative adverb should precede "bǐ", so "bǐ zhōng–xiǎoxué de lǎoshī" should be in the position of C.

9. 选择 C。这是一个比较句,它的基本格式是:A 比 B+形容词+动词+差别。本题中,"云飞"是 A,"昊天"是 B,"待"是动词,"一个月"是比较的差别,因此"多"应在 C 的位置上。

The answer is C. This is a comparative sentence, and its basic pattern is: "A bǐ B + adjective + verb+ difference", In this sentence, "Yúnfēi" is A, "Hàotiān" is B, "dāi" is the verb, and "yí gè yuè" is the difference, so "duō" should be in the position of C.

10. 选择 B。这是一个兼语句,它的基本格式是:主语+动词₁+宾语₁+动词₂+宾语₂。本题中,"李教授"是主语,"让"是兼语动词,"小杨"是宾语₁,同时又是后面"把论文再修改一下"的主语。因此"让小杨"应在 B 的位置上。

The answer is B. This is a pivotal sentence, and its basic pattern is: "subject + verb$_1$ + object$_1$ + verb$_2$ + object$_2$". In this sentence, "Lǐ jiàoshòu" is the subject, and "ràng" is the pivotal verb. "Xiǎo Yáng" is the object$_1$ as well as the subject of "bǎ lùnwén zài xiūgǎi yí xià", so "ràng Xiǎo Yáng" should be in the position of B.

11. 选择 D。这是一个比较句,它的基本格式是:A 比 B+形容词+差别。本题中,"这段表演"是 A,"上一段"是 B,"强烈"是形容词,"一些"是差别。因此"强烈一些"应在 D 的位置上。

The answer is D. This is a comparative sentence, and its basic pattern is: "A bǐ B + adjective + difference". In this sentence, "zhè duàn biǎoyǎn" is A, and "shàng yí duàn" is B, "qiángliè" is the adjective and "yìxiē" is the difference, so "qiángliè yìxiē" should be in the position of D.

12. 选择 B。这是一个反问句,它的基本格式是:还……吗?"还"用在动词前,如果动词是肯定形式,就表示不应该做某事;如果动词是否定形式,就表示应该做某事。因此"还"应在 B 的位置上。

The answer is B. This is a rhetorical question, and its basic pattern is: "hái...mɑ?". "Hái" is used before the verb. And if the verb is a positive verb, it means "shouldn't do something", If the verb is negative, it means "should do something". Therefore, "hái" should be in the position of B.

13. 选择 C。这是一个强调句,它的基本格式是:连……也/都+动词+(……)。因此"连"应在 C 的位置上。

The answer is C. This is an emphatic sentence, and its basic pattern is: "lián...yě/dōu...+ verb + (...)". So "lián" should be in the position of C.

14. 选择 C。这是一个兼语句,它的基本格式是:主语+动词₁+ 宾语₁ + 动词₂ + 宾语₂。本题中,"妈妈"是主语,"叫"是兼语动词,"我"是宾语₁,同时又是后面"把洗衣机打开"的主语。因此"把洗衣机"应在 C 的位置上。

The answer is C. This is a pivotal sentence, and its basic pattern is: "subject + $verb_1$ + $object_1$ + $verb_2$ + $object_2$". In this sentence, "māma" is the subject, "jiào" is the pivotal verb, "wǒ" is the $object_1$ as well as the subject of "bǎ xǐyījī dǎkāi". Therefore, "bǎ xǐyījī" should be in the position of C.

15. 选择 B。这是一个比较句。在"比"字句中,否定副词应该在"比"的前面。

The answer is B. This is a comparative sentence. In "bǐ" sentence, the negative adverb should be used before "bǐ".

16. 选择 A。这是一个兼语句,它的基本格式是:主语+动词₁+宾语₁+动词₂+宾语₂。本题中,"小张"是主语,"告诉"是兼语动词,"我"是宾语₁,同时又是后面"明天去参观故宫博物院"的主语。因此"我"应在 A 的位置上。

The answer is A. This is a pivotal sentence, and its basic pattern is: "subject + $verb_1$ + $object_1$ + $verb_2$ + $object_2$". In this sentence, "Xiǎo Zhāng" is the subject, and "gàosù" is the pivotal verb, "wǒ" is the $object_1$ as well as the subject of "míngtiān qù cānguān Gùgōng Bówùyuàn", so "wǒ" should be in the position of A.

17. 选择 D。这是一个比较句,它的基本格式是:A 比 B+形容词+差别。本题中,"王晶晶的身材"是 A,"李娜娜的身材"是 B,"苗条"是形容词,"一些"是差别。因此"苗条一些"应在 D 的位置上。

The answer is D. This is a comparative sentence, and its basic pattern is: "A bǐ B + adjective + difference". In this sentence, "Wáng Jīngjīng de shēncái" is A, and "Lǐ Nànà de shēncái" is B, "miáotiáo" is the adjective, and "yìxiē" is the difference, so "miáotiáo yìxiē" should be in the position of D.

18. 选择 C。这是比较句的扩展格式:A 比 B+动词+得+形容词+得+差别。本题中,"她"是 A,"我"是 B,"写"是动词,"好"是形容词,"多"是差别。因此"比我"应在 C 的位置上。

The answer is C. This is a comparative sentence, and its basic pattern is: "A bǐ B + verb + de + adjective + de + difference". In this sentence, "tā" is A, "wǒ" is B, "xiě" is the verb, "hǎo" is the adjective, and "duō" is the difference. So "bǐ wǒ" should be in the position of C.

19. 选择 C。在比较句中,副词要放在"比"的前面。因此"倒"应在 C 的位置上。

The answer is C. In comparative sentence, the adverb should be put before "bǐ", so "dào" should be in the position of C.

20. 选择 C。这是一个比较句，它的基本格式是：A 比 B+还+形容词+差别。本题中，"颐和园的昆明湖水域历史"是 A，"北京城的历史"是 B，"早"是形容词，"400 多年"是差别。因此"还"应在 C 的位置上。

The answer is C. This is a comparative sentence, and its basic pattern is "A bǐ B + hái + adjective + difference". In this sentence, "Yíhéyuán de Kūnmíng Hú shuǐyù lìshǐ" is A, and "Běijīng chéng de lìshǐ" is B, "zǎo" is the adjective, and "sìbǎi duō nián" is the difference. So "hái" should be in the position of C.

21. 选择 A。这是一个反问句，它的基本格式是：怎么……呢？"怎么"用在动词前，如果动词是肯定形式，就表示不应该做某事；如果动词是否定形式，就表示应该做某事。因此"怎么"应在 A 的位置上。

The answer is A. This is a rhetorical question, and its basic pattern is "zěnme... ne?" "Zěnme" is used before the verb. If the verb is a positive verb, it means "shouldn't do something". If the verb is negative, it means "should do something". Therefore, "zěnme" should be in the position of A.

22. 选择 A。这是一个"把"字句，它的基本格式是：名词/代词（施事）+把+名词/代词（受事）+动词+其他成分。本题中，"你"是施事主语，"这些旧书"是受事宾语，"包"和"放"是动词，"上书皮"和"在书柜里"是动词后的其他成分。因此"把"应在 A 的位置上。

The answer is A. This is a "bǎ" sentence, and its basic pattern is: "noun/pronoun (agent) + bǎ + noun/pronoun (object) + verb + other components". In this sentence, "nǐ" is the agent subject, and "zhèxiē jiùshū" is the object, "bāo" and "fàng" are verbs, and "shàng shūpí" and "zài shūguì li" are the other components after the verb, therefore, "bǎ" should be in the position of A.

23. 选择 A。这是一个强调句，它的基本格式是：连……也/都+动词+（……）。因此"连他"应在 A 的位置上。

The answer is A. This is an emphatic sentence, and its basic sentence is: "lián...yě/dōu + verb + (...)", therefore, "lián tā" should be in the position of A.

24. 选择 B。这是一个兼语句，它的基本格式是：主语+动词₁+ 宾语₁ + 动词₂ + 宾语₂。本题中，"您"是主语，"让"是兼语动词，"我"是宾语₁，同时又是后面"给您揉揉肩膀"的主语。因此"让我"应在 B 的位置上。

The answer is B. This is a pivotal sentence, and its basic sentence is: "subject + verb₁ + object₁ + verb₂ + object₂". In this sentence, "nín" is the subject, "ràng" is the pivotal verb, "wǒ" is object₁ as well as the subject of "gěi nín róuróu jiānbǎng". Therefore, "ràng wǒ" should be in the position of B.

25. 选择 C。这是一个兼语句,它的基本格式是:主语 + 动词₁ + 宾语₁ + 动词₂ + 宾语₂。本题中,"妈妈"是主语,"让"是兼语动词,"爸爸"是宾语₁,同时又是后面"把这些北京特产给爷爷带去"的主语。因此"把这些北京特产"应在 C 的位置上。

The answer is C. This is a pivotal sentence, and its basic sentence is: "subject + verb₁ + object₁ + verb₂ + object₂". In this sentence, "māma" is the subject, and "ràng" is the pivotal verb, "bàba" is object₁ as well as the subject of "bǎ zhèxiē Běijīng tèchǎn gěi yéye dàiqù". Therefore, "bǎ zhèxiē bēijīng tèchǎn" should be in the position of C.

26. 选择 B。这是一个"被"字句,它的基本格式是:名词/代词(受事)+被+名词/代词(施事)+动词+其他成分。本题中,"到张家界旅游的人"是受事主语,"那里美丽的自然景色"是施事宾语,"无不"表示"每一个、都",用在"被"的前面。因此"被"应在 B 的位置上。

The answer is B. This is a "bèi" sentence, and its basic pattern is "noun/pronoun (object) + bèi + noun/pronoun (agent) + verb + other components". In this sentence, "dào Zhāngjiājiè lǚyóu de rén" is the object subject, and "nàli měilì de zìrán jǐngsè" is the agent object, "wú bù" indicates "everyone, all", and is used before "bèi". Therefore, "bèi" should be in the position of B.

27. 选择 B。这是一个兼语句,它的基本格式是:主语+动词₁+宾语₁+动词₂+宾语₂。本题中,"我们"是主语,但在句中被省略掉了;"请"是兼语动词;"她"是宾语₁,同时又是后面"为我们唱一首'南泥湾'"的主语。因此"请她"应在 B 的位置上。

The answer is B. This is a pivotal sentence, and its basic pattern is: "subject + verb₁ + object₁ + verb₂ + object₂". In this sentence, "wǒmēn" is the subject but is omitted. "Qǐng" is the pivotal verb and "tā" is object₁ as well as the subject of "wèi wǒmen chàng yì shǒu 'Nánníwān'". So "qǐng tā" should be in the position of B.

28. 选择 C。这是一个"被"字句,它的基本格式是:名词/代词(受事)+被+名词/代词(施事)+动词+其他成分。本题中,"吴茜"是受事主语;施事宾语在句中省略,没有出现。因此"被"应在 C 的位置上。

The answer is C. This is a "bèi" sentence, and its basic structure is: "noun/pronoun (object) + bèi + noun/pronoun (agent) + verb + other components". In this sentence, "Wú Xī" is the object subject and the object is omitted, so "bèi" should be in the position of C.

29. 选择 B。这是一个强调句,它的基本格式是:非……不可。"非"要用在动词结构前。因此"非"应在 B 的位置上。

The answer is B. This is an emphatic sentence, and its basic pattern is: "fēi... bùkě". "fēi" should be used before the verb structure, so it should be in the position of B.

30. 选择 A。这是一个兼语句,它的基本格式是:主语 + 动词₁ + 宾语₁ + 动词₂ + 宾语₂。本题中,"老师"是主语,"让"是兼语动词,"我们"是宾语₁,同时又是后面"穿得漂亮点儿"的主语。因此"让我们"应在 A 的位置上。

The answer is A. This is a pivotal sentence, and its basic pattern is: "subject + verb₁ + object₁ + verb₂ + object₂". In this sentence, "lǎoshī" is the subject, "ràng" is the pivotal verb, "wǒmen" is object₁ as well as the subject of "chuān de piàoliang diǎnr". So "ràng wǒmen" should be in the position of A.

31. 选择 D。这是一个连动句,它的基本格式是:主语 + 动词₁ + 宾语₁ + 动词₂ + 宾语₂……。动词性结构"坐飞机"表示去的方式,应在"去"的前面。因此"去西双版纳"应在 D 的位置上。

The answer is D. This is a sentence with consecutive verbs, and its basic pattern is: "subject + verb₁ + object₁ + verb₂ + object₂". The verb phrase "zuò fēijī" is the way of going, and should be put before "qù". So "qù Xīshuāngbǎnnà" should be in the position of D.

32. 选择 C。这是一个比较句,它的基本格式是:A 比 B+形容词。本题中,"今年"是 A,"去年"是 B,"明显"是形容词,要用在"比"的前面。因此"比去年"应在 C 的位置上。

The answer is C. This is a comparative sentence, and its basic pattern is: "A bǐ B + adjective". In this sentence, "jīn nián" is A, "qù nián" is B, "míngxiǎn" is the adjective, and should be used before "bǐ". Therefore, "bǐ qù nián" should be used in the position of C.

33. 选择 C。这是一个反问句,它的基本格式是:(更)何况……呢?"何况"用在动词结构前。因此"何况"应在 C 的位置上。

The answer is C. It's a rhetorical question, and its basic pattern is: "(gèng) hékuàng... ne?" "hékuàng" should be used before the verb structure. Therefore, C is the right answer.

34. 选择 B。这是一个"把"字句,它的基本格式是:名词/代词(施事)+把+名词/代词(受事)+动词+其他成分。本题中,"保罗"是施事主语,"冰箱里的半个西瓜"是受事宾语,"吃"是动词。因此"把冰箱里的"应在 B 的位置上。

The answer is B. This is a "bǎ" sentence, and its basic pattern is: "noun/pronoun (agent) + bǎ + noun/pronoun (object) + verb + other components". In this sentence, "Bǎoluó" is the agent subject, "bīngxiāng li de bàn gè xīguā" is the object, and "chī" is the verb, so "bǎ bīngxiāng li de" should be in the position of B.

35. 选择 C。这是一个存现句,它的基本格式是:处所词语+有+修饰成分+名词。"饭"应该是放在桌子上的,而不是放在桌子里的,所以选择 C 是正确的。

The answer is C. This is an existential sentence, and its basic pattern is: "location words +

yǒu + modifier + noun." "Fàn" should be put on the table instead of in it. Therefore C is the right answer.

36. 选择 A。这是一个存现句,它的基本格式是:处所词语+是+名词(具体的地点)。本题中,"景山的对面"是表示处所的词语,"故宫博物院"是具体的地点。因此选择 A 是正确的。
The answer is A. This is an existential sentence, and its basic pattern is: "location words + shì + noun (definite location)". In this sentence, "JǐngShān de duìmiàn" is the location word, and "Gùgōng Bówùyuàn" is the definite location, so A is the right answer.

37. 选择 C。这是一个比较句,它的基本格式是:A 和/跟/与/同 B 一样/相同/相似/类似/差不多。本题中,"这个书包"是 A,"那个书包"是 B。因此选择 C 是正确的。
The answer is C. This is a comparative sentence, and its basic pattern is "A hé/gēn/yǔ/tóng B yíyàng/xiāngtóng/xiāngsì/lèisì/chàbùduō". In this sentence, "zhè gè shūbāo" is A and "nà gè shūbāo" is B, so C is the right answer.

38. 选择 C。这是一个强调句,它的基本格式是:(是)……的。"是"用在需要强调的词语的前面,"的"用在句尾。因此选择 C 是正确的。
The answer is C. This is an emphatic sentence, and its basic pattern is "(shì)... de". "Shì" is used before the emphatic words and "de" is used at the end of the sentence, so C is the correct answer.

39. 选择 A。这是一个比较句,它的基本格式是:A(没)有 B+动词+得+形容词。本题中,"滨田"是 A,"八木"是 B。因此选择 A 是正确的。
The answer is A. This is a comparative sentence, and its basic pattern is: "A (méi) yǒu B + verb + de + adjective". In this sentence, "Bīntián" is A, and "Bāmù" is B, so A is the right answer.

40. 选择 C。这是一个存现句,它的基本格式是:处所词语(钢琴上)+动词+着+名词(琴谱)。
The answer is C. This is an existential sentence, and its basic pattern is: "location word (gāngqín shàng) + verb + zhe + noun(qínpǔ)".

41. 选择 D。这是一个存现句的否定形式,要用否定副词"没(有)"。
The answer is D. This is the negation form of an existential sentence, so the negative adverb "méi(yǒu)" should be used.

42. 选择 C。这是一个"把"字句,它的基本格式是:名词/代词(施事)+把+名词/代词(受事)+动词+其他成分。"把"后出现的名词一般是确指的,不能是泛指的。所以,答案 B 不对。句中"全买齐了"告诉我们买的书不是一本,因此选择 C 是正确的。

The answer is C. This is a "bǎ" sentence, and its basic pattern is: "noun/pronoun (agent) + bǎ + noun/pronoun(object) + verb + other components". The nouns following "bǎ" are usually definitely referred instead of generally referred, so B is not the right answer. In this sentence, "quán mǎiqí le" tells us more than one book were bought, so C is the right answer.

43. 选择 B。这是一个存现句,它的基本格式是:处所词语+动词+着+名词。

The answer is B. This is an existential sentence, and its basic pattern is: "location words + verbs + zhe + noun".

44. 选择 B。这是一个"把"字句,它的基本格式是:名词/代词(施事)+把+名词/代词(受事)+动词+其他成分。本题中,"张力"是施事主语,"稿费"是受事宾语,"捐"是动词。因此选择 B 是正确的。

The answer is B. This is a "bǎ" sentence, and its basic pattern is: "noun/pronoun (agent) + bǎ + noun/pronoun(object) + verb + other components". In this sentence, "Zhāng Lì" is the agent subject, and "gǎofèi" is the object, and "juān" is the verb, so B is the correct answer.

45. 选择 A。这是一个"被"字句,它的基本格式是:名词/代词(受事)+被+名词/代词(施事)+动词+其他成分。本题中,"卢沟桥"是受事主语;施事宾语在句中省略,没有出现。"以为"常表示想法和实际不符;"成为"不能用于"被"字句中;"想"用在"被"字句中,可以说"被想成是",而不能说"被想是"。

The answer is A. This is a "bèi" sentence, and its basic pattern is: "noun/pronoun (object) + bèi + noun/pronoun (agent) + verb + other components". In this sentence, "Lúgōu qiáo" is the object subject, and the object is omitted. "Yǐwéi" usually means the fact is different from what is originally thought; "chéngwéi" can not be used in the "bèi" sentence; "xiǎng" in "bèi" sentence should be "bèi xiǎngchéng shì" instead of "bèi xiǎngshì".

46. 选择 A。这是一个比较句,它的基本格式是:A 和/跟/与/同 B 一样/相同/相似/类似/差不多。本题中,"女儿"是 A,"妈妈"是 B。

The answer is A. This is a comparative sentence, and its basic pattern is: "A hé/gēn/yǔ/tóng B yíyàng/xiāngtóng/xiāngsì/lèisì/chàbùduō". In this sentence, "nǔ'ér" is A and "māma" is B.

47. 选择 D。这是一个比较句,它的基本格式是:A 比 B+还+形容词。本题中,"儿子开车的技术"是 A,"老爸的技术"是 B。

The answer is D. This is a comparative sentence, and its basic pattern is: "A bǐ B + hái + adjective". In this sentence, "érzi kāichē de jìshù" is A, and "lǎobà de jìshù" is B.

48. 选择 B。这是一个"被"字句，它的基本格式是：名词/代词 (受事) +被+名词/代词 (施事) +动词+其他成分。本题中，"大家"是受事主语；"它的曲折情节"是施事宾语。

The answer is B. This is a "bèi" sentence, and its basic pattern is: "noun/pronoun(object) + bèi + noun/pronoun (agent) + verb + other components". In this sentence, "dàjiā" is the object subject, "tā de qūzhé qíngjié" is the object.

49. 选择 D。这是一个兼语句，它的基本格式是：主语 + 动词₁ + 宾语₁ + 动词₂ + 宾语₂。本题中，"公司"是主语，"派"是兼语动词，"她"是宾语₁，同时又是后面"去洽谈这笔业务"的主语。因此选择 D 是正确的。

The answer is D. This is a pivotal sentence, and its basic pattern is: "subject + verb₁ + object₁ +verb₂ + object₂". In this sentence, "gōngsī" is the subject, and "pài" is the pivotal verb. "Tā" is object₁ as well as the subject of "qù qiàtán zhè bǐ yèwù", so D is the right answer.

50. 选择 C。这是一个强调句，它的基本格式是：非……不可。"非"要用在动词结构前。

The answer is C. This is an emphatic sentence, and its basic pattern is: "fēi... bùkě". "Fēi" should be used before the verb structure.

9 补语 Complement

考点精讲 Examination Points

一、结果补语 Result Complement

结果补语一般由动词、形容词充当,表示动作、变化的结果。

Result complement is comprised of verbs or adjectives and indicates the result of an action or change.

1. 基本格式 Basic pattern

① 动词+形容词

verb + adjective

例:吃饱、擦干净

② 动词+动词

verb + verb

例:救活、写完

2. 语法特征 Grammatical feature of result complement

① 结果补语紧跟在动词、形容词后,动词和补语之间不能加进别的词语,动态助词"了"也只能放在补语之后。

Result complement follows verbs or adjectives. There are no other words that can be inserted between the complement and verbs. The dynamic auxiliary "le" can only be put after the complement.

例:写完了　(√)

写了完　(×)

预习好了生词　(√)

预习了好生词　(×)

② 有结果补语的句子表示现在以前的动作是否完成或实现某个结果,因此,结果补语的否定形式是在动词前加"没"。只有在假设某种情况下才能用"不"。

The sentence with the result complement indicates whether an action done before has completed or shown some effect. Therefore, the negative form of result complement is adding "méi" before the verb. "Bù" will only be used when something is hypothesized.

例：我复习好了。

我没复习好。　　　（√）

我不复习好。　　　（×）

明天就要考试了，不复习好可不行呀。　（√）

③ 结果补语一般会有"得到""附上""离开""分离""固定不变"等意义，要注意与动词的搭配。

Result complement often has the meaning of "dédào", "fùshàng", "líkāi", "fēnlí" and "gùdìng–búbiàn", etc. Please pay attention to the allocation with verbs.

例：看到、听见、写完、买着、挂上、拿走、脱下、记住……

3. 常见结果补语 Common result complement

① "动词+见/到/着/完"。表示动作达到目的或完成。

"Verb + jiàn/dào/zháo/wán" shows that an action reaches its goal or is finished.

例：听见、看到、买着、读完

② "动词+上"。表示动作达到目的、完成或开始并继续。

"Verb + shàng"shows that an action gains its goal, finishes, begins or continues.

例：考上了大学、关上了窗户、迷上了京剧

③ "动词+下"。表示动作由高到低、分离或固定不变。

"Verb + xià" shows that an action is done from high to low, or separated or fixed.

例：坐下、摘下帽子、写下日记

④ "动词+住"。表示通过动作使某事物固定不动。

"Verb + zhù" indicates to make something fixed through an action.

例：停住脚步、记住这个句子

⑤ "动词+会"。表示通过学习掌握了某种技能。

"Verb + huì" indicates to master a skill through learning.

例：学会了写汉字

⑥ "动词+懂"。表示通过动作理解、明白了某种含义。

"Verb + dǒng" indicates to understand the meaning through an action

例：听懂了中国话

⑦ "动词+成"。表示成功。

"Verb + chéng" indicates to succeed in doing something.

例：做成了这件事

⑧ "动词+走"。表示离开。

"Verb + zǒu" indicates to leave.

例：开走了汽车

⑨ "动词+形容词"。形容词本身一般已经告诉了动作的结果。

"Verb + adjective" indicates the adjective itself can tell the result of the action.

Complement

☆ 特别需要注意的是，"忘干净"中"干净"的意思不同于"洗干净"中"干净"的意思，是"全部忘记、一点儿也没记住"的意思。

Special attention should be paid that the meaning of "gānjìng in "wàng gānjìng" is different from that of "gānjìng in "xǐ gānjìng". The former means "totally".

二、趋向补语 Tendency complement

趋向补语由趋向动词充当，表示动作的趋向，包括简单趋向补语和复合趋向补语两种。

Tendency complement is comprised of tendency verbs to show the tendency of an action. It includes simple tendency complement and complex tendency complement.

1. 基本格式 Basic pattern

① 简单趋向补语：动词+来/去。

Simple tendency complement of "verb + lái/qù".

例：买来、拿去

② 复合趋向补语：动词+起来/上来/上去/下来/下去/进来/进去/出来/出去/回来/回去/过来/过去。

Complex tendency complement of "verb + qǐlái, shànglái, shàngqù, xiàlái, xiàqù, jìnlái, jìnqù, chūlái, chūqù, huílái, huíqù, guòlái, guòqù".

例：站起来、走下去

2. 语法特点 Grammatical feature of tendency complement

① 简单趋向补语一般跟在动词后、宾语前。宾语表示抽象事物或是存现宾语，趋向动词"来、去"只位于宾语前；命令句或宾语表示处所时，"来、去"只位于宾语后。

Simple tendency complement is usually put after the verb and before the object. The object represents abstract things or is an existential object, and the tendency verb "lái" or "qù" can only be put before the object. In imperative sentences or when the object shows a location, the complement is only after the object.

例：打来电话　（一般情况）

传来歌声 (宾语表示抽象事物)

跑来一个人 (存现宾语)

下楼去　 (宾语表示处所)

端饭来！　(命令句)

② 复合趋向补语有三种情况

There are three kinds of complex tendency complement：

A. 宾语是表示一般事物或人的名词，位于补语中间或补语之后都可以。

The object is a noun for common things or people, and it can be put between or after the complement.

例：买回来一张票　（√）

买回一张票来　（√）

B. 宾语是处所名词，只能位于补语中间。

The object is a noun for location, and can be put only between the complement.

例：走上山来　　（√）

走上来山　　（×）

C. 离合动词后宾语位于补语中间。

The object in the verb–object construction is put between the complement.

例：唱起歌来　　（√）

唱歌起来　　（×）

3. 趋向补语的主要引申用法

Extended usages of tendency complement

① 上 shàng

A. 表示靠近、合拢或关闭。

Showing approaching, closing or turning off.

例：我紧走几步追上了汽车。（靠近）

大家合上书。（合拢）

请你关上电视。（关闭）

B. 表示使某物存在于某处。

Showing to put something somewhere.

例：在这里摆上一盆花吧。

C. 表示达到了不太容易达到的目的。

Showing a goal has been realized which is not easily done.

例：我终于考上了大学。

D. 表示动作开始并继续下去。

Showing an action begins and continues.

例：大卫迷上京剧了。

② 下 xià

A. 表示固定下来。

Showing something is fixed or done.

例：我们记下了这句话。

B. 表示使某物脱离或离开某处。

Showing to make an object separate from somewhere.

例：他摘下帽子，擦了擦汗。

C. 表示容纳一定的数量。

Showing the number contained.

例：这间教室能坐下五十个学生。

③ 起来 qǐlái

A. 表示动作开始并继续。

Showing an action begins and continues.

例：大家高兴地唱起来。

B. 表示由分散到集中。

Showing something changing from discrete to centralized.

例：快把桌子上的书收拾起来。

C. 表示从某方面进行估计或评价。

Showing an estimation or appraisal from a certain angle.

例：看起来，他今天不太舒服。

D. 表示动作有了结果并达到了目的。

Showing an action has a result and reaches its goal.

例：我想起来了，这部电影我以前看过。

④ 上来 shànglái

表示成功地完成一个动作。

Showing an action has been finished successfully.

例：这个问题我回答上来了。

⑤ 上去 shàngqù

A. 表示添加或附着在某个地方。

Showing adding or attaching something to somewhere.

例：请把这张照片贴上去。

B. 表示从某个方面进行估计或评价。

Showing an estimation or appraisal from a certain angle.

例：看上去，她恢复得不错。

这条毛巾摸上去很柔软。

⑥ 下来 xiàlái

A. 表示动作使事物分离。

Showing an action that separates things.

例：屋里热，快把大衣脱下来吧。

B. 表示使事物固定在某处。

Showing something is fixed somewhere.

例：汽车在我身边停了下来。

C. 表示从过去继续到最后。

Showing an action continues to the end.

例：在马拉松比赛中，玛丽终于跑下来了。

D. 表示开始出现并继续发展。（强度、亮度等由强到弱）

Showing the beginning and development of something. (The intensity or brightness turning from strong to weak)

例：他慢慢放松下来了。

天逐渐黑下来了。

⑦ 下去 xiàqù

表示动作或情况的继续，之前的形容词在句中一般含有不如意的感情色彩。

Showing the continuation of an action or a situation. The adjective before it usually has a negative meaning.

例：我们一定要坚持下去，总会成功的。

你再胖下去可不行了。

⑧ 过来 guòlái

A. 表示状态从不正常到正常、从不正确到正确。

Showing something changing from abnormal to normal, or from wrong to right.

例：他终于苏醒过来了。

请把作业中的错字改过来。

B. 表示能够完成，常跟能力、时间、数量等有关。

Showing something can be finished, and is usually related to ability, time and quantity, etc.

例：要做的事情太多了，我都忙不过来了

橱窗里摆放着各种各样的工艺品，我都看不过来了。

⑨ 过去 guòqù

表示状态从正常到不正常。

Showing something changing from normal to abnormal.

例：奶奶晕过去了。

⑩ 出来 chūlái

A. 表示从某个方面分辨或识别某人或某物。

Showing to distinguish or identify somebody or something from a certain perspective.

例：我拿起电话一听就听出来了，是王老师打来的。

B. 表示从无到有。

Showing something develops from scratch.

例：大家想出来一个好办法。

三、可能补语 Possibility complement

可能补语表示动作可能或不可能达到的某种结果。

Possibility complement indicates the possibility or impossibility of an action reaching certain result.

1. 基本格式 Basic pattern

① 动词+得/不+结果补语/趋向补语

verb + de/bù + result complement/tendency complement

例：吃得饱、想不起来

② 动词/形容词+得/不+了

verb/adjective + de/bù + liǎo

例：去得了、热不了

③ 动词+得/不得

verb + de/bùde

例：过期的药吃不得。

2. 语法特征 Grammatical feature of possibility complement

① 如果动词有宾语，宾语可以有两个位置：补语后或提前做主语。

If a verb takes an object, the object can be in two positions: after the complement or to be the subject before the main verb.

例：我看得懂这篇课文。　　（√）

这篇课文我看得懂。　　（√）

② 可能补语的句子表现的是主客观条件是否允许实现某动作、变化、结果等，因此一般用于未完成的动作或临时变化的情况，动词或补语后不能用表示完成意义的"了"。

A sentence with possibility complement shows whether the subjective and objective conditions help realize some actions, changes and results, so it is mainly used for unfinished actions or temporary changes. "Le" meaning finished can't be used after the verb or complement.

例：这些文件你一个人能处理得完吗？——处理得完。

昨天的文件你处理完了吗？——处理完了。

③ 当表示"不应该""不允许"的意义时，要用"不能"否定，不能用表示不可能的补语。

When "shouldn't" or "mustn't" is expressed, "bù néng" should be used for negation, and the complement with impossibility can't be used.

例：他们正在上课，你不能进去。（√）

他们正在上课，你进不去。（×）

④ 表示不可能的程度差别时，可在补语中间加上"太""大"一类的程度副词。

When indicating different degrees of impossibility, degree adverbs like "tài" and "dà" can be put between the complement.

例：年纪大了，听不大清楚了。

他什么时候回来，我说不太准。

⑤ 有一部分结构形式和"动词+得/不得"形式相同的短语，已形成一种固定结构，相当于一个词了。

Some structures same as "verb + dé/bùdé" have become fixed ones and are used as one word.

例：怪不得、顾不得、巴不得、恨不得、值得/值不得、舍得/舍不得、记得/记不得

四、情态补语 Modal complement

情态补语主要是对动作或动作的结果加以描写性的说明。

Modal complement mainly describes an action or the result of an action.

1. 基本格式：动词+得+怎么样：

Basic pattern: verb + de + zěnmeyàng:

例：起得很早、走得太急了

2. 语法特征 Grammatical feature of modal complement

① 情态补语有的是说明动作的，有的是说明主语的。

Modal complement explains an action or a subject.

例：这场雨来得很及时。 （说明动作）

这个姑娘长得很漂亮。 （说明主语）

② 情态补语除了用"得"引进之外，还有用"个""得个"引进的。这样的表达，更具口语色彩。

Modal complement can also be introduced by "gè" and "degè" in addition to "de". These expressions are more colloquial.

例：今天我们要玩个痛快。

他们的球队被我们打得个落花流水。

③ 用"得"引进的补语一般都表示已经实现的情况；用"个"引进的补语表示未实现的情况，要表达已实现的情况就要在"个"前加上"了"。

Complement with "de" usually indicates something finished. And "gè" indicates something unfinished, if one wants to show something is finished, then "le" should be put before "gè".

例：我们今天又唱歌又跳舞，玩得很痛快。（已经实现）

我们今天一定要玩个痛快。（未实现）

我们今天又唱歌又跳舞，玩了个痛快。（已经实现）

Complement

五、程度补语 Degree complement

程度补语由在形容词或表示心理活动的动词与补语之间加上"得"构成,表示动作达到的某种性状程度。

Degree complement is comprised of "de" between adjectives or verbs indicating mental activities and the complement to indicate the state or degree of an action.

1. 基本格式 Basic pattern

① 动词/形容词+得+很/慌/多/要命/要死/不行/不得了/像……似的

verb/adjective + de + hěn/huāng/duō/yàomìng/yàosǐ/bùxíng/bùdéliǎo/xiàng... shìde

例:急得很、美得像朵花似的

② 动词/形容词+极了/透了/死了/坏了/一点儿/一些

verb/adjective + jí le/tòu le/sǐ le/huài le/yìdiānr/yìxiē

例:热极了、舒服一些

2. 语法特征 Grammatical feature of degree complement

① 如果动词带宾语,可以在宾语后重复动词再加"得"和补语;也可以在宾语前加"对",然后提到动词前。补语不能直接跟在宾语之后。

If a verb takes an object, the verb can be repeated after the object, then "de" and the complement would follow. Or the object can be put before the verb while adding "duì" before the object. The complement can't be put directly after the object.

例:妈妈爱女儿爱得要命。 (√)

妈妈对女儿爱得要命。 (√)

妈妈爱女儿要命。 (×)

② 在程度补语之前,可以用"很""十分""非常""不""不太"等表示程度或否定的副词加以修饰。

Before the degree complement, adverbs of degree or negation like "hěn", "shífēn" "fēicháng", "bù", "bútài", etc. can be used for modification.

例:你做得非常好。

你答得不太好。

六、数量补语 Quantity complement

数量补语表示动作和变化的数量,包括动量补语、时量补语、比较数量补语三种。

Quantity complement indicates the quantity of actions and changes. It includes dynamic complement, time complement, and comparative quantity complement.

1. 基本格式 Basic pattern

① 动词+(了/过)+时量补语+一般宾语

verb + le/guo +time complement + common object

　　例：等了十分钟汽车

② 动词+了/过+宾语(指人的宾语或处所名词)+时量补语

verb + le/guo + object (indicating person or location) + time complement

　　例：劝了他三个小时、来中国一年了

③ 动词+(了/过)+动量补语+一般宾语(包括人名)

verb + le/guo + dynamic complement + common object (including person's name)

　　例：去过两次故宫、打了一下孩子

④ 动词+了/过+宾语(人称代词或名词)+动量补语

verb + le/guo + object (personal pronoun or noun) + dynamic complement

　　例：看过他一次、打了孩子一下

⑤ A 比 B+形容词+数量短语

A bǐ B + adjective + quantity phrase

　　例：我比你大三岁。

2. 语法特征 Grammatical feature of quantity complement

① 某些形容词表示变化意义时,后边也可以用动量补语。

Some adjectives showing the meaning of change can be followed by the dynamic complement.

　　例：灯亮了一下,又灭了。

② 带动量补语的句子一般多为肯定式,很少见否定式。如用否定式,一般是在动词前加"没"。在疑问句中,也可以用"不"表示否定。

The sentence with the dynamic complement is usually affirmative, the negative one is rarely seen. If the negative form is used, "méi" should often be put before the verb. In interrogative sentences, "bù" can also be used for negation.

　　例：我没去过几次上海。

　　　　你不写一遍吗?

③ 比较数量补语用在形容词后,其中的量词是名量词。如果用在动词后,名量短语就成为宾语了。

Comparative quantity complement is used after adjectives and the quantifiers are the ones for substances or persons. If a quantifier phrase for substances or persons is used after a verb, it becomes an object.

　　例：这件衣服比那件衣服贵一百元。(比较数量补语)

　　　　这个工厂今年的产量比去年提高了两倍。(宾语)

Complement

七、介宾补语 Preposition-object complement

汉语中的一部分介宾短语可以用在动词或形容词后做补语,表示时间、处所、来源、对象、方向或比较等。介宾短语多用于书面语之中。

Part of preposition-object phrases in Chinese can be used after verbs or adjectives as the complement to indicate time, location, source, target, direction or comparison. This kind of complement is usually used in written language.

1. 基本格式 Basic pattern

① 动词+于/自/在/向/往/到+宾语

verb + yú/zì/zài/xiàng/wǎng/dào + object

例:开往上海、生于八十年代

② 形容词+于+宾语

adjective + yú + object

例:我们班的学生成绩高于他们班。

2. 语法特征 Grammatical feature of preposition-object complement

① 在汉语中,动词带介宾短语之后,一般不再带宾语或其他补语。

In Chinese, the verb taking a preposition-object phrase is usually not followed by an object or other complements.

② 介词短语做补语时,语音停顿在介词后。表示时态意义时,"了"要放在介词后。

When a prepositional phrase is used as a complement, phonetic pause should be put after the preposition. When indicating the tense, "le" should be put after the preposition.

例:狼扑向了正在吃草的小羊。

强化练习 Exercises

■ 1—11 题,在每一个句子下面都有一个指定的词语,句中 ABCD 是供选择的四个不同位置,请判断这一词语放在句中哪个位置上恰当。

Please find the proper position out of the four choices of A, B, C, and D for the word below each sentence.

1. 李老师又 A 给同学们 B 强调了 C 本课的 D 重点。
   　　　　　　　　　　　一遍

2. 这道题我已经 A 解 B 了 C 了,D 还是解不出来。
   　　　　　　　　　　一下午

3. 你们说 A 大卫现在能 B 胜任得 C 教练这项工作 D 吗?
                             了

4. 这个 A 来 B 非洲的小姑娘,她一时 C 还适应不了 D 哈尔滨的气候。
               自

5. 我们 A 一年内 B 爬过 C 长城了,目前不想再去 D 了。
                   五次

6. 等 A 爸爸借 B 了钱赶 C 码头的时候,儿子坐的船早已开 D 走了。
                   到

7. 说好八点在北海前门集合,都 A 过 B 了,安娜 C 怎么 D 还没来?
                 一个多小时

8. 爸爸妈妈退休 A 了,他们 B 决定 C 每个星期爬 D 香山。
                 两次

9. 对不起,请等 A,我 B 上楼 C 拿了钥匙咱们 D 就走。
               一下

10. 八木毕业 A 九十年代,B 先后 C 在北京、D 上海等地工作。
               于

11. 大卫,把你的摄像机 A 借 B 给我 C 用 D 可以吗?
                 一下

12—50 题,每个句子中有一个或两个空,请在 ABCD 四个答案中选择唯一恰当的一个。
Please choose the correct answer for each blank from the four choices of A, B, C, and D.

12. 刚才那个电话来 _____ 大洋彼岸。
    A. 从　B. 自　C. 在　D. 现

13. 这部电视剧真没意思,再看 _____ 我们都得睡着了。
    A. 上来　B. 下去　C. 出来　D. 起来

14. 我的背包要掉了,你能帮我扶 _____ 吗?
    A. 一会儿　B. 一下儿　C. 一阵儿　D. 一点儿

15. 节目单终于定 _____ 了,还有我的独唱呢。
    A. 下去　B. 下来　C. 出来　D. 起来

16. 安娜把地上的果皮捡 _____ 扔到了垃圾箱里。
    A. 过来　B. 起来　C. 进来　D. 出来

17. 今天运气不好,坐了大半天,也没钓 _____ 几条鱼。
    A. 上来　B. 下来　C. 起来　D. 出来

18. 这个电视剧太精彩了,我再困也要坚持看 _____ 。
    A. 起来　B. 过去　C. 下来　D. 下去

19. 这个孩子看 _____ 缺乏营养,面黄肌瘦的。
    A. 上来　B. 上去　C. 下来　D. 下去

20. 中国的古典小说没有标点,我的古文底子薄,往往看着看着就 _____ 了。
    A. 看不下去　　B. 看下不去
    C. 不看下去　　D. 下去不看

21. 妈妈做的饭菜别有风味儿,我一吃就吃 _____ 了,这桌菜不是妈妈做的。
    A. 出来　B. 起来　C. 下来　D. 过来

22. 这几个芭比娃娃太好看了,爸爸决定把它们都 _____ 送给女儿。
    A. 买来回家　　B. 买家回来
    C. 买回家来　　D. 买回来家

23. 大卫和安娜刚好了几天,怎么今天又 _____ 了?
    A. 吵起架来　　B. 吵了起来架
    C. 吵架起来　　D. 吵架起来了

24. 他终于从昏迷中苏醒 _____ ,慢慢地睁开了双眼。
    A. 上来　B. 过来　C. 起来　D. 过去

25. 爷爷常说他老了已经 _____ 时代的脚步了。
    A. 不跟上　B. 没跟得上
    C. 跟不上　D. 不跟得上

26. 小李正在气头儿上,连大家的好话都听不 _____ 。
    A. 起来　B. 下去　C. 进来　D. 进去

27. 邢台发生了地震,周总理亲自 _____ 到灾区 _____ 了解灾情,慰问灾民。
    A. 下……去　B. 过……来　C. 起……来　D. 回……去

28. 听到这个好消息,大家高兴得跳 _____ 舞 _____ 了。
    A. 下……去　B. 过……来　C. 起……来　D. 回……去

29. 火箭发射成功了,全体工作人员高兴得欢呼 _____ 。
    A. 下去　B. 上来　C. 过来　D. 起来

30. 餐馆的老板对门外避雨的人们说:"快 _____ ,别淋病了。"
    A. 过来　B. 进来　C. 进去　D. 起来

31. 飓风过后,波涛汹涌的海面渐渐地平静 _____ 了。
    A. 起来　B. 下来　C. 下去　D. 过去

32. 弟弟的书太多了,一个书柜装不 _____ 。

A．起来　B．下　C．上　D．进来

33．我的外语水平不高,你给我的书又这么厚,恐怕半年也 _____ 。
　　A．不翻译完　　B．译不完
　　C．翻不译完　　D．翻译完

34．这么多东西,我一个老太太可 _____ 。
　　A．拿得动　　B．拿不了
　　C．拿起来　　D．拿不起来

35．飞机就是比火车快,从北京到青岛 _____ 两小时就到了。
　　A．用得了　　B．用不了
　　C．用不完　　D．用完了

36．《西游记》一套共三册,恐怕我两天 _____ ,对不起,不能按时还你了。
　　A．看不完　　B．看完了
　　C．不看完　　D．没看完

37．我来中国已经学习一年汉语了,你听我这汉语 _____ ?
　　A．说得标准不标准　　B．说得标准和不标准
　　C．说得标准说不标准　　D．说得标准说得不标准

38．你总是事事拔尖儿,处处占便宜,同学们能和你 _____ 吗?
　　A．不好了　　B．好不了
　　C．好得了　　D．好了得

39．你儿子聪明又用功,一定 _____ 清华。
　　A．考得了　　B．考得去
　　C．考得上　　D．考上得

40．如今人们的生活越来越好了,越来越多的普通家庭都 _____ 私家车了。
　　A．买得来　　B．买不来
　　C．买得起　　D．买不起

41．他有自己的想法,谁的建议他也听不 _____ 。
　　A．起来　B．下来　C．进去　D．进来

42．他一走就是音信皆无,真让我们大家担心他 _____ 。
　　A．得要命　　B．担心得要命
　　C．不要命　　D．担心不要命

43．除了学校和家教留的作业,妈妈又给我留了十页的数学题,一夜不睡觉恐怕我也 _____ 。
　　A．不完成　　B．完不成
　　C．完没成　　D．没完成

44．妈妈下班回到家,把提包挂 _____ 衣架上,换上衣服就进厨房做饭去了。

A．过　B．在　C．好　D．给

45．因为想把这部小说看完，昨天我 _____ 。
　　A．只睡觉了两个小时　　B．只两个小时睡觉了
　　C．两个小时只睡觉了　　D．只睡了两个小时觉

46．明天就要论文答辩了，我闭门谢客在家里 _____ 。
　　A．看整一天书了　　B．看了一整天书
　　C．一整天看了书　　D．看书了一整天

47．加入世贸组织以后，中国市场上的进口商品更加丰富 _____ 。
　　A．出来　B．过来　C．起来　D．上来

48．龙井茶几百年前就已经闻名 _____ 世了。
　　A．于　B．跟　C．从　D．在

49．他话里的意思你听不 _____ 吗？
　　A．出来　B．过来　C．起来　D．进去

50．可以看出，老师的喜悦是发 _____ 内心的。
　　A．出　B．自　C．从　D．在

答疑解惑 Answers and Explanations

1.　选择 C。"一遍"是一个动量补语，它的基本格式是：动词+了/过+动量补语+一般宾语（包括人名）。所以，"一遍"应该在 C 的位置上。
The answer is C. "Yí biàn" is a dynamic complement. Its basic pattern is: "verb + le/guo + dynamic complement + general object (including person's name)". So "yí biàn" should be in the position of C.

2.　选择 C。"一下午"是一个数量补语，它的基本形式是：动词+了/过+时量补语+一般宾语。本题中的宾语"这道题"已提前到句首，所以"一下午"应该在 C 的位置上。
The answer is C. "Yí xiàwǔ" is a quantity complement. Its basic form is: verb + le/guo + time complement + general object. The object "zhè dào tí" in this sentence has been put to the beginning, so "yí xiàwǔ" should be in the position of C.

3.　选择 C。"了"在本题中应该读 liǎo，它与"得"构成可能补语，它的基本格式是：动词/形容词+得/不+了。所以"了"应该在 C 的位置上。
The answer is C. "了" should be read as "liǎo". It makes up the possibility complement

together with "de". Its basic pattern is: verb/adjective + de/bù + liǎo. So "liǎo" should be put in the position of C.

4. 选择 B。"自"引出介宾补语,它的基本形式是:动词+自+宾语。所以,"自"应该在 B 的位置上。

The answer is B. "Zì" introduces a preposition + object complement. Its basic pattern is: "verb + zì + object". So "zì" should be in the position of B.

5. 选择 C。"五次"是一个数量补语,它的基本形式是:动词+了/过+动量补语+一般宾语(包括人名)。所以,"五次"应该在 C 的位置上。

The answer is C. "Wǔ cì" is a quantity complement. Its basic pattern is: verb + le/guo + dynamic complement +general object (including person's name). So "wǔ cì" should be in the position of C.

6. 选择 C。"到"是一个结果补语,它的基本形式是:动词+动词,表示动作达到目的或完成。所以,"到"应该在 C 的位置上。

The answer is C. "Dào" is a result complement. Its basic pattern is: "verb + verb". It shows an action reaches its goal or is accomplished. So "dào" should be in the position of C.

7. 选择 B。"一个多小时"是一个数量补语,其形式是:动词+时量补语+了,表示动作已经进行得很长。所以,"一个多小时"应该在 B 的位置上。

The answer is B. "Yí gè duō xiǎoshí" is a quantity complement. Its basic pattern is: "verb + time complement + le" and it shows the long period of a progressing action. So "yí gè duō xiǎoshí" should be in the position of B.

8. 选择 D。"两次"是一个数量补语,它的基本形式是:动词+动量补语+一般宾语(包括人名)。所以,"两次"应该在 D 的位置上。

The answer is D. "Liǎng cì" is a quantity complement. Its basic pattern is: "verb + dynamic complement + general object (including person's name)". So "liǎng cì" should be put in the position of D.

9. 选择 A。"一下"是一个数量补语,它的基本形式是:动词+动量补语。所以"一下"应该在 A 的位置上。

The answer is A. "Yí xià" is a quantity complement. Its basic pattern is: "verb + dynamic complement". So "Yí xià" should be in the position of A.

10. 选择 A。"于"是引出介宾补语,它的基本形式是:动词+于+宾语。所以,"于"应该在 A 的位置上。

The answer is A. "Yú" introduces a preposition + object complement. Its basic pattern is: "verb + yú + object". So "yú" should be in the position of A.

11. 选择 D。"一下"是一个数量补语,它的基本形式是:动词+动量补语+一般宾语(包括人名)。本题中的宾语已被介词"把"提前到动词前,所以"一下"应该在 D 的位置上。

The answer is D. "Yí xià" is a quantitaty complement. Its basic pattern is: "verb + dynamic complement + general object (including person's name)". In this sentence, the object has been put before the verb by the preposition "bǎ". So "yí xià" should be in the position of D.

12. 选择 B。"自"和后面的名词性短语组成的介宾结构做补语,它的基本形式是:动词+自+宾语。

The answer is B. "Zì" makes up a preposition-object complement together with the nominal phrase after it. Its basic pattern is: "verb + zì + object".

13. 选择 B。"下去"表示动作的继续,而且该句含有不如意的感情色彩,符合题意。"上来"表示成功地完成一个动作。"出来"表示:①从某个方面分辨或识别某人或某物;②从无到有。"起来"表示:①动作开始并继续;②由分散到集中;③从某方面进行估计或评价;④动作有了结果并达到了目的。

The answer is B. "Xiàqù" shows the continuation of an action and there is a negative meaning, thus it is the correct answer. "Shànglái" shows accomplishing an action successfully. "Chūlái" shows: ① distinguishing or recognizing a person or something from a certain aspect; ② developing from scratch. "Qǐlái" shows: ① an action begins and continues; ② from discrete to centralized; ③ evaluation or appraisal from a certain aspect; ④ an action takes its effect and reaches its goal.

14. 选择 B。"一下儿"做补语时表示动作的次数,含有轻松随意的语气。"一会儿""一阵儿"表示动作或情况持续的一段时间。"一点儿"表示很小或很少或不确定的数量。

The answer is B. "Yíxiàr" shows the number of the times of an action with a casual tone. "Yíhuìr" and "yízhènr" shows a period of time of an action or event. "Yìdiǎnr" shows a very small, or very little or an uncertain amount.

15. 选择 B。"下来"可以表示:①动作使事物分离;②使事物固定在某处;③从过去继续到最后;④开始出现并继续发展(强度、亮度等由强到弱)。本题中"下来"是第二种含义。

The answer is B. "Xiàlái" can show: ① an action that separates things; ② making a thing fastened in some places; ③ continuing from the past to the end; ④ beginning to appear and develop continuously (intensity or brightness from strong to weak). In this question "xiàlái" takes the second meaning.

16. 选择 B。表示动作由下而上进行的选项,只有"起来"符合题意。

The answer is B. "Qǐlái" means an action goes on from downward to upward.

17. 选择 A。"上来"表示成功地完成一个自下而上的动作,符合题意。

The answer is A. "Shànglái" shows accomplishing an action from downward to upward successfully.

18. 选择 D。"下去"表示动作的继续。

The answer is D. "Xiàqù" shows the continuation of an action.

19. 选择 B。"上去"可以表示:①添加或附着在某个地方;②从某个方面进行估计或评价,符合题意。

The answer is B. "Shàngqù" may show: ① adding or attaching to a certain place; ② evaluation or appraisal from a certain aspect. In this sentence, "shàngqù" takes the second meaning.

20. 选择 A。"看不下去"是可能补语的否定形式,意思是不能继续看。所以,A 是正确的。

The answer is A. "Kàn bú xiàqù" is the negative form of a possibility complement meaning the action cannot go on. So A is correct.

21. 选择 A。"出来"可表示从某个方面分辨或识别某人或某物,符合题意。

The answer is A. "Chūlái" shows distinguishing or recognizing a person or something from a certain aspect.

22. 选择 C。"买"是谓语动词;"家"是表示处所的宾语;"回来"是复合趋向动词,做"买"的趋向补语。当宾语是处所名词时,它只能位于补语中间。所以,C 是正确的。

The answer is C. "Mǎi" is the predicate; "jiā" is the object of location; "huílái" is the complex tendency verb, used as the tendency complement of "mǎi". When the object is a noun of location, it can only be put between the complements. So C is correct.

23. 选择 A。"吵架"是一个离合词,它的宾语应该位于补语中间。所以,A 是正确的。

The answer is A. "Chǎo jià" is a verb–object word. Its object should be put between the complement. So A is correct.

24. 选择 B。"过来"可表示从不正常到正常、从不正确到正确,符合题意。

The answer is B. "Guòlái" shows changing from abnormal to normal, from incorrect to correct.

25. 选择 C。可能补语的形式是：动词+得/不+结果补语/趋向补语。所以，C 是正确的。
The answer is C. The format of a possibility complement is: "verb + de/bù + result complement/tendency complement". So C is correct.

26. 选择 D。"进去"表示动作由外向里进行，这里"听不进去"是表示不接受的意思。
The answer is D. "Jìnqù" shows an action goes on from outside to inside, and here "tíng bú jìnqù" means not accepting.

27. 选择 A。在本题中"下……去"表示上级领导到基层视察工作。
The answer is A. In this sentence, "xià... qù" shows a leader going to the grassroots to inspect work.

28. 选择 C。"起……来"可以表示：①动作开始并继续；②由分散到集中；③从某方面进行估计或评价；④动作有了结果并达到了目的。本题中"起来"是第一种含义。
The answer is C. "Qǐ... lái" shows: ① an action begins and continues; ② changing from discrete to centralized; ③ evaluation or appraisal from a certain aspect; ④ an action takes its effect and reaches its goal. In this sentence, "qǐlái" takes the first meaning.

29. 选择 D。"起来"可以表示：①动作开始并继续；②由分散到集中；③从某方面进行估计或评价；④动作有了结果并达到了目的。本题中"起来"是第一种含义。
The answer is D. "Qǐlái" shows: ① an action begins and continues; ② changing from discrete to centralized; ③ evaluation or appraisal from a certain aspect; ④ an action that takes its effect and reaches its goal. In this sentence, "qǐlái" takes the first meaning.

30. 选择 B。"进来"表示动作由外向里进行，说话人在里面，符合题意。
The answer is B. "Jìnlái" shows an action goes on from outside to inside, and the speaker is inside.

31. 选择 B。"下来"表示：①动作使事物分离；②使事物固定在某处；③从过去继续到最后；④开始出现并继续发展（强度、亮度等由强到弱），符合题意。
The answer is B. "Xiàlái" can show: ① an action that separates things; ② making a thing fixed in some place; ③ continuing from the past to the end; ④ beginning to appear and develop continuously (intensity or brightness from strong to weak).

32. 选择 B。"下"可以表示：①固定下来；②使某物脱离或离开某处；③容纳一定的数量，符合题意。
The answer is B. "Xià" can show: ① settling down; ② making something separate from or leave some place; ③ holding a certain amount. In this sentence, "xià" takes the third meaning.

33. 选择 B。因为水平不高、书又厚,所以半年的时间不可能翻译完。可能补语的否定形式是: 动词+不+结果补语。所以,B 是正确的。

The answer is B. Because of the caliber is low and there are too many pages, the person cannot finish translating the book in half a year. The negative possibility of result complement is: "verb + bù + result complement". So B is correct.

34. 选择 B。"拿得动"表示有足够的力气拿动某物。"拿不了"表示东西太多没有能力拿。"拿起来"表示"拿"的动作从下向上进行。"拿不起来"是"拿起来"的否定形式,含有"物品太重"的意思。根据句意,应该选择 B。

The answer is B. "Ná de dòng" shows one has enough strength to carry something. "Ná bù liǎo" shows the incapability to carry too many items. "Ná qǐlái" shows taking something from downward to upward. "Ná bù qǐlái" is the negative from of "ná qǐlái", which means "the thing is too heavy". According to the meaning of the sentence, B should be chosen.

35. 选择 B。"用不了"表示含有"不需要用……"的意思,句中强调所说的时间太多了。"用不完"虽然也含有"不需要用……"的意思,但是一般不用来表达有关时间的内容。

The answer is B. "Yòng bù liǎo" shows the implication of "needn't take...". In this sentence, it emphasizes the time mentioned is too much. Although "yòng bù wán" has the meaning of "no need to take", it's often not used to indicate time.

36. 选择 A。因为《西游记》共三册,所以两天的时间不可能看完。可能补语的否定形式是:动词+不+结果补语。所以,A 是正确的。

The answer is A. As *Journey to the West* contains three volumes, one can't finish reading them in two days. The negative format for possibility complement is: "verb + bù + result complement". So A is correct.

37. 选择 A。情态补语的正反疑问形式是:动词+得+怎么样+不+怎么样。所以应该选择 A。

The answer is A. The question format for modal complement is: "verb + de + zěnmeyàng + bù + zěnmeyàng". So A should be chosen.

38. 选择 C。"好得了"是"可能好"的意思。本题中最后是反问语气,所以根据句子的意思,应该选择 C,以表达否定的含义——不可能好。

The answer is C. The meaning of "hǎo de liǎo" is "possibly good". In this sentence, it has a rhetorical tone. According to the meaning of the sentence, C should be chosen to show the negative implication, that is, unlikely to be good.

Complement

39. 选择 C。"考得上"是能考上的意思,宾语常是学校;"考得了"后面的宾语常是具体的分数。
The answer is C. "Kǎo de shàng" has the meaning of "néng kǎoshàng". Its object is usually a school; while the object after "kǎo de liǎo" is often score.

40. 选择 C。"买得起"表示有足够的经济能力购买某物。"买不起"是它的否定形式。"买得来"和"买不来"表示有没有可能买到某物。根据句子的意思,应该选择 C。
The answer is C. "Mǎi de qǐ" shows having sufficient economic power to buy something. "Mǎi bù qǐ" is its negative form. "Mǎi de lái" and "mǎi bù lái" show whether it is possible to buy something. According to the meaning of the sentence, C should be chosen.

41. 选择 C。"进去"表示动作由外向里进行,这里"听进去"是表示接受的意思。
The answer is C. "Jìnqù" shows an action goes on from outside to inside, here "tīng jìnqù" means acception.

42. 选择 B。当句中有程度补语的时候,如果动词带宾语,可以在宾语后重复动词再加"得"和补语,所以,B 是正确的。
The answer is B. When there is a degree complement in the sentence and if the verb takes an object, the verb can be repeated after the object, then "de" and the complement are added; So B is correct.

43. 选择 B。因为作业很多,妈妈又给我留了十页数学题,所以一夜不睡觉也不能完成。可能补语的否定形式是:动词+不+结果补语。所以,B 是正确的。
The answer is B. As I have a lot of homework, and what's worse, my mother has assigned me ten pages of math problems, I can't finish them even I do not go to sleep. The negative format for possibility complement is: "verb + bù + result complement". So B is correct.

44. 选择 B。"衣架上"是一个表示处所的词语,在动词"挂"和"衣架上"之间需要一个介词。介词"在"的后面多是表示处所的词语。所以应该选择 B。
The answer is B. "Yījià shang" is a phrase of location. There should be a preposition between the verb "guà" and "yījià shang". The word after the preposition "zài" is often the one about location. So B should be chosen.

45. 选择 D。"睡觉"是一个离合词,当带有时量补语时,离合词必须分开使用,时量补语在离合词的中间。
The answer is D. "Shuìjiào" is a verb-object word. When it takes a time complement, the verb and the object must be separated, and the time complement is put in between.

46. 选择 B。"看"是动词；"书"是它的宾语。"一整天"是时量补语,应在动词"看"的后面,宾语"书"的前面。

The answer is B. "Kàn" is the verb; "shū" is its object. "Yì zhěng tiān" is the time complement, which should be put after the verb "kàn" and before the object "shū".

47. 选择 C。"起来"可以表示:①动作开始并继续;②由分散到集中;③从某方面进行估计或评价;④动作有了结果并达到了目的,本题中"起来"是第一种含义。

The answer is C. "Qǐlái" shows: ① an action begins and continues; ② from discrete to centralized; ③ evaluation or appraisal from a certain aspect; ④ an action that takes its effect and reaches its goal.

48. 选择 A。"于"和后面的名词性短语组成的介宾结构做补语,它的基本形式是:动词+于+宾语,多用于书面语。

The answer is A. "Yú" together with its followinig noun phrase forms a preposition–object complement. Its basic pattern is "verb + yú + object". It is often used in written language.

49. 选择 A。"出来"可表示从某个方面分辨或识别某人或某物,符合题意。

The answer is A. "Chūlái" shows distinguishing or recognizing a person or something from a certain aspect.

50. 选择 B。"自"和后面的名词性短语组成的介宾结构做补语,它的基本形式是:动词+自+宾语。

The answer is B. "Zì" makes up a preposition–obiect complement together with the nominal phrase after it. Its basic pattern is "verb + zì + object".

10 关联词语与复句 Relative Phrases and Complex Sentences

1. 因果关系 Causative relation

常见格式 Pattern	说明 Explanation	例句 Examples
因为 / 由于……，所以…… yīnwèi…, suǒyǐ…	前为原因，后为结果。 The former part is cause, the latter is effect.	因为天气不好，所以大家取消了外出的计划。
因为……，而…… yīnwèi…, ér…	前为原因，后为结果。 The former part is cause, the latter is effect.	他因为路上堵车而迟到了。
因为……的关系，…… yīnwèi… de guānxì, …	前为原因，后为结果。 The former part is cause, the latter is effect.	因为时间的关系，我们今天就学到这儿了。
由于……，(因此) …… yóuyú…, (yīncǐ)…	前为原因，后为结果。 The former part is cause, the latter is effect.	由于最近备考，(因此) 我常常开夜车。
……，以至于 / 以致…… …, yǐzhìyú/yǐzhì…	后多是不好的结果。 The effect is usually not good.	她太紧张了，以至于演出时忘记了台词。
既然……，就…… jìrán…, jiù…	前句已有事实，后句推断出结果。 The former is the fact, and the latter is what inferred.	既然天已经晚了，你就别走了。
之所以……，是因为 / 是由于…… zhīsuǒyǐ…, shì yīnwèi/ shì yóuyú…	前为结果，后为原因。 The former part is effect, the latter is cause.	她之所以没来上班，是因为孩子病了。

2. 递进关系 Progressive relation

常见格式 Pattern	说明 Explanation	例句 Examples
主语＋不但 / 不只 / 不仅……， 而且 / 还 / 也 / 甚至还…… subject + búdàn/bùzhǐ/bùjǐn…, érqiě/hái/yě/shènzhì hái…	全句只有一个主语，后一分句比前一分句更进一步。 There is only one subject in the sentence, the latter clause is furthering in meaning compared with the former clause.	小王不但字写得好，画儿画得也好。

不但 / 不只 / 不仅＋主语₁ ……，而且＋主语₂＋也…… búdàn/bùzhǐ/bùjǐn + subject₁…， érqiě + subject₂ + yě…	前后分句的主语不同，关联词语放在主语前。 The subjects in the two clauses are different, and the relative words are put before the subjects.	不但小王字写得好，而且小李字写得也好。
不仅不 / 不但不……，反而 / 甚至还…… bùjǐn bù/búdàn bù…，fǎn'ér/shènzhì hái…	前一分句多为否定形式。 The former clause is usually negative.	风不但不停，反而越刮越大。
连……都 / 也……，何况…… lián…dōu/yě…，hékuàng…	含有对比的意思，表示前者都这样，后者更应该如此。 There is a comparison between the two subjects implying that since the former is like this, the latter should be like this too.	这个道理连小孩都懂，何况大人呢?
……，更不用说…… …，gèng bú yòng shuō…	含有对比的意思，表示前者都这样，后者更应该如此。 There is a comparison between the two subjects implying that since the former is like this, the latter should be like this.	这个道理小孩都懂，更不用说大人了。
别说……，就是…… biéshuō…，jiùshì…	含有对比的意思，表示后者都这样，前者更应该如此。 There is a comparison between the two subjects implying that since the latter is like this, the former should be like this.	这个道理别说大人了，就是小孩都懂。

3. 转折关系 Transitional relation

常见格式 Pattern	说明 Explanation	例句 Examples
虽然……，但是 / 可是 / 却…… suīrán…，dànshì/kěshì/què…	前后分句所表达的意思相对或相反。 The meanings expressed in the two clauses are in contrast.	虽然我不聪明，但是我很用功。
尽管……，但 (是) / 也…… jǐnguǎn…，dàn (shì) /yě…	前一分句先承认某一事实，后一分句再提出说话人的看法。 The first clause states the fact, while the second gives the opinion of the speaker.	尽管他的错误很严重，你也不应该打他。
固然……，也…… gùrán…，yě…	前一分句先承认某一事实，后一分句再提出说话人的看法。 The first clause states the fact, while the second gives the opinion of the speaker.	他的错误固然很严重，你也不应该打他。
即使……，也…… jíshǐ…，yě…	前一分句先承认某一事实，后一分句再提出说话人的看法。 The first clause states the fact, while the second gives the opinion of the speaker.	即使他的错误很严重，你也不应该打他。

哪怕 / 就是……, 也…… nǎpà/jiùshì..., yě...	前一分句先承认某一事实，后一分句再提出说话人的看法。 The first clause states the fact, while the second gives the opinion of the speaker.	哪怕他的错误很严重，你也不应该打他。

4. 条件关系 Conditional relation

常见格式 Pattern	说明 Explanation	例句 Examples
只要……, 就…… zhǐyào..., jiù...	表示有了前面的条件，一定出现后面的结果。"就"在后一分句的主语后。 The condition in the first clause presupposes the result in the second clause. "Jiù" appears after the subject in the second clause.	只要坚持练习，你的语音就会越来越标准。
只有……, 才…… zhǐyǒu..., cái...	表示必须有前面的条件，才能出现后面的结果。后一分句如有主语出现，"才"在这个主语的后面。 This structure indicates the latter result is on the basis of the former condition. If there is a subject in the second clause, "cái" appears after the subject.	只有吃这种药，才能治好他的病。 只有吃这种药，他的病才能治好。
无论 / 不论 / 不管 / 任……, 都 / 也 / 反正…… wúlùn/búlùn/bùguǎn/rèn..., dōu/yě/fǎnzhèng...	表示在任何条件下，都会出现后面的结果。前一分句常有以下几种基本格式： 1. 动词或形容词的肯定否定形式连用； 2. 用疑问代词表示任何条件，如"什么""谁""怎么""哪儿"等； 3. 用"多（么）"表示任何条件； 4. 用"是 A 还是 B"表示任何条件，A、B 是名词或形容词。 The result is sure to appear on any condition. The first clause usually takes the following patterns: 1. The positive and negative forms of verbs or adjectives； 2. Interrogative pronouns for any conditions, such as "what", "who", "how", "where", etc.； 3. "Duō(me) + adjective" for any conditions； 4. "A or B" for any conditions, A and B are nouns or adjectives.	1.（1）无论你去不去，我都不去。 （2）不管天气好不好，我们都照常活动。 2. 不论是谁，都应该遵守国家的法律。 3. 任你说得多（么）好听，我都不会相信你。 4.（1）无论是老师还是学生，都非常高兴。 （2）你送我的礼物不管是便宜还是贵，我都喜欢。
凡是……, 都…… fánshì..., dōu...	表示在任何条件下，都会出现后面的结果。 The result is sure to appear on any conditions.	凡是你喜欢的，我都喜欢。
除非……, 才 / 否则 /（要）不然…… chúfēi..., cái/fǒuzé/(yào)bùrán	前一分句表示唯一条件。 The conditional clause indicates the only condition.	除非他先向我道歉，否则我不会原谅他。

5. 假设关系 Hypothetical relation

常见格式 Pattern	说明 Explanation	例句 Examples
如果 / 要是 / 假如 / 倘若 / 若……,就 / 则…… rúguǒ/yàoshi/jiǎrú/tǎngruò/ruò..., jiù/zé...	表示假设,前一分句是没有出现的事实。 This structure indicates a hypothesis, and the former clause doesn't happen.	如果有时间, 你就来找我 玩吧。
即使 / 哪怕 / 就是 / 就算 ……,也…… jíshǐ/nǎpà/jiùshì/jiùsuàn..., yě...	前一分句可以表示没有出现的事情, 也可以是跟既成事实相反的事情,后一分句表示结果不受上述情况的影响。 The first clause indicates something doesn't happen or something is the opposite of the fact, while the second shows the result is not influenced by the above.	即使明天下 雨,我也要去 颐和园。
没有……,就没有…… méiyǒu..., jiù méiyǒu...	前一分句表示与事实相反的情况, 后一分句表示与实际结果相反的情况。 The first clause is contrary to the fact, while the second indicates the contrary to the result.	没有大家的 帮助,就没有 我今天的进 步。
(要)不是 / 幸亏 / 多亏 / 亏 得 / 好在……,否则 / (要) 不然…… (yào) búshì/xìngkuī/duōkuī/kuīde/hǎozài..., fǒuzé/ (yào) bùrán...	"幸亏"等词一般用在前一分句的主语前,表示某种有利的条件,后一分句引出已经避免了的后果。 "Xìngkuī" and others are put before the subject of the first clause to indicate something favorable, while the second introduces the result avoided.	幸亏你提醒 我,要不然我 就迟到了。

6. 并列关系 Coordinate relation

常见格式 Patterns	说明 Explanation	例句 Examples
既 / 又 + 动词₁/ 形容词₁……,又 + 动词₂/ 形容词₂…… jì/yòu + verb₁ / adjective₁..., yòu + verb₂ / adjective₂...	表示两个动作或两种状态同时存在。复句只有一个主语。 Two actions or states exist at the same time. There is only one subject.	1. 大家又唱又跳,高兴 极了。 2. 这件衣服既美观,又 大方。
既 + 动词₁/ 形容词₁……,也 + 动词₂/ 形容词₂…… jì + verb₁ / adjective₁..., yě + verb₂ / adjective₂...	表示两个动作或两种状态同时存在。复句只有一个主语。 Two actions or states exist at the same time. There is only one subject.	1. 我既喜欢听京剧,也 喜欢唱京剧。 2. 这里的风景既优美, 也安静。
也 + 动词₁/ 形容词₁……, 也 + 动词₂/ 形容词₂…… yě + verb₁ / adjective₁..., yě + verb₂ / adjective₂...	表示两个动作或两种状态同时存在。 Two actions or states exist at the same time.	1. 你也拿,我也拿,很 快就没有了。 2. 你也忙,他也忙,谁 都帮不了我。

(一)边 / (一)面 + 动词₁……, (一)边 / (一)面 + 动词₂…… (yì)biān/(yí)miàn + verb₁..., (yì)biān/(yí)miàn + verb₂......	表示两个动作同时进行,复句只有一个主语。 Two actions exist at the same time. There is only one subject.	我们一边吃月饼,一边赏月。
一方面……,另一方面…… yì fāngmiàn..., lìng yì fāngmiàn...	表示一个事物的两个方面同时存在。 Two aspects of one thing exist at the same time.	我这次来,一方面是想看看老朋友,另一方面是想好好休息休息。

7. 承接关系 Successive relation

常见格式 Pattern	说明 Explanation	例句 Examples
先 + 动词₁……,再 + 动词₂…… xiān + verb₁..., zài + verb₂...	表示动作的先后顺序,一般用于还没有发生的事情。 The structure shows time sequence of actions and applies to things undone.	我们先学生词,再学课文。
先 + 动词₁……,又 + 动词₂…… xiān+verb₁..., yòu+verb₂...	表示动作的先后顺序,一般用于已经发生的事情。 The structure shows time sequence of actions and applies to things that already happened.	妈妈先洗了衣服,又做了饭。
先 + 动词₁……,然后 (再)+ 动词₂…… xiān + verb₁..., ránhòu(zài) + verb₂...	表示动作的先后顺序,一般用于还没有发生的事情。 The structure shows time sequence of actions and applies to things undone.	我先去超市买东西,然后再回家。
一 + 动词₁……,就 + 动词₂…… yī + verb₁..., jiù + verb₂...	表示两个动作紧接着发生。 The structure indicates two actions happen one following closely the other.	我一下课就去找你。

8. 选择关系 Alternative relation

常见格式 Pattern	说明 Explanation	例句 Examples
(是)……,还是…… (shì)..., háishi...	在前后两者间选择。 Making a choice from two.	你 (是) 喝茶还是咖啡?
不是……,就是…… búshì..., jiùshì...	答案一定是两者中的一个。 The answer must be one of the two.	他不是日本人,就是韩国人。
要么……,要么…… yàome..., yàome...	答案一定是两者中的一个。 The answer must be one of the two.	我们要么在家吃,要么出去吃。

或者……,或者…… huòzhě..., huòzhě...	答案一定是两者中的一个。 The answer must be one of the two.	明天的会,或者你去,或者他去。
不是……,而是…… búshì..., érshì...	否定前者,肯定后者。 Negating the former, and affirming the latter	这里不是北京,而是南京。
与其……,不如…… yǔqí..., bùrú...	否定前者,肯定后者。 Negating the former, and affirming the latter.	与其排队等车,不如走着回去。
宁可/宁愿……,也不…… nìngkě/nìngyuàn..., yě bù...	肯定前者,否定后者。 Affirming the former, and negating the latter.	我宁愿一个人在家,也不和他一起去。
宁可不/宁愿不……,也要…… nìngkě bù/nìngyuàn bù..., yě yào...	否定前者,肯定后者。 Negating the former, and affirming the latter.	我们宁可不休息,也要把今天的工作做完。

9. 目的关系 Purposive relation

常见格式 Pattern	说明 Explanation	例句 Examples
为了……,…… wèile..., ...	前一分句表示目的,后一分句表示行为。 The first clause states the purpose, while the second shows the action.	为了大家的安全,请走人行横道线。
……,以便/为的是…… ..., yǐbiàn/wèi de shì...	前一分句表示行为,后一分句表示目的。 The first clause states the action, while the second shows the purpose.	我来中国,为的是学习汉语。
……,以免/免得/省得…… ..., yǐmiǎn/miǎnde/shěngde...	前一分句表示行为,后一分句表示不希望出现的结果。 The first clause states the action, while the second shows the unwanted outcome.	大家外出的时候一定要注意安全,以免发生意外。

10. 让步关系 Concession relation

常见格式 Pattern	说明 Explanation	例句 Examples
即使/哪怕/就是/纵然……,也/还是…… jíshǐ/nǎpà/jiùshì/zòngrán..., yě/háishì…	表示让步,前一分句常常是没有出现的假设,后一分句是不变的结果。 The structure indicates a concession. The first clause is often a hypothesis, the second is the unchanged outcome.	即使明天下雨,我们也按时出发。

Relative Phrases and Complex Sentences

11. 紧缩复句 Contraction Complex Sentence

常见格式 Pattern	说明 Explanation	例句 Examples
一 / 刚……就…… yì/gāng... jiù...	表示两个动作紧接着发生。"一""刚"用在动词前。 The structure states two actions that happen one following closely the other. "Yī" "gāng" are put before verbs.	1. 我一下课就去找你。 2. 刚下课,她就回家了。
动词 + 了 / 完……就…… verb+le/wán... jiù...	表示两个动作紧接着发生。 The structure states two actions that happen one following closely the other.	1. 下了课,我就去找你。 2. 上完课,她就回家了。
越 + 动词 / 形容词 + 越 + 动词 / 形容词 yuè + verb/adjective + yuè + verb / adjective	表示程度随着情况的发展而变化。 The degree changes with the changing situation.	1. 她越吃越胖。 2. 房间不是越大越好。
越是 + 名词 / 动词 / 形容词 + 越是 + 名词 / 动词 / 形容词 yuè shì + noun/verb/adjective + yuè shì + noun/verb/adjective	表示程度随着情况的发展而变化。 The degree changes with the changing situation.	1. 现代人的压力很大,越是男人越是如此。 2. 天气越是炎热,去海边的人越是多。 3. 你越是想家,越是要坚持。
再……也…… zài... yě...	表示无论如何都会怎么样的意思。 The structure indicates something will be like this no matter what happens.	你再吃也胖不了。
非……不 / 才…… fēi... bù/cái...	表示一定的意思。 Showing something is a must.	1. 你非去不可。 2. 我非学好汉语才回国。
不 / 没有……不 / 没有…… bù/méiyǒu... bù/méiyǒu...	双重否定,表示特别强调、特别肯定的意思。 Double negation showing emphasis and affirmation.	1. 你不参加不行。 2. 你现在不说就没有机会了。 3. 没有调查研究就没有发言权。 4. 没有证件不能入场。

强化练习 Exercises

■ 每个句子中有一个或两个空,请在 ABCD 四个答案中选择唯一恰当的一个。
Please choose the correct answer for each blank from the four choices of A, B, C, and D.

1. 一位好老师 _____ 要教给孩子知识, _____ 要教给孩子怎样做人。
   A. 或者……或者……　　B. 不是……而是……
   C. 不但……而且……　　D. 无论……都……

- 214 -

2. ＿＿＿＿＿ 你说得再动听,我也不会改变主意。
   A. 即使　B. 假如　C. 既然　D. 尽管

3. 从天津回国,＿＿＿＿＿ 坐飞机,＿＿＿＿＿ 坐船,没有别的办法。
   A. 不是……就是……　　B. 不是……而是……
   C. 不如……那么……　　D. 不仅……而且……

4. 他 ＿＿＿＿＿ 有书本知识,＿＿＿＿＿ 有工作经验和能力。
   A. 因为……所以……　　B. 不仅……而且……
   C. 尽管……还是……　　D. 虽然……但是……

5. ＿＿＿＿＿ 不让你管这件事,＿＿＿＿＿ 你不了解年轻人的想法,管不了。
   A. 因为……所以……　　B. 不仅……而且……
   C. 不是……就是……　　D. 不是……而是……

6. ＿＿＿＿＿ 大家一起开动脑筋想办法,＿＿＿＿＿ 能攻克这个难题。
   A. 固然……也……　　B. 不管……都……
   C. 除非……才……　　D. 凡是……都……

7. ＿＿＿＿＿ 我怎么解释,他 ＿＿＿＿＿ 不相信。
   A. 除了……还……　　B. 不管……也……
   C. 如果……就……　　D. 尽管……但……

8. 我们约好在剧院门口见面,她 ＿＿＿＿＿ 开车来,＿＿＿＿＿ 坐出租车来。
   A. 不光……还要……　　B. 虽然……但是……
   C. 除非……否则……　　D. 不是……就是……

9. ＿＿＿＿＿ 修一座立交桥,＿＿＿＿＿ 能解决这个地区交通拥堵的问题。
   A. 尽管……也……　　B. 虽说……也……
   C. 除非……才……　　D. 固然……可……

10. 学好一门外语 ＿＿＿＿＿ 一件容易的事,＿＿＿＿＿ 需要经过艰苦的努力。
    A. 不是……而是……　　B. 因为……所以……
    C. 固然……可是……　　D. 如果……那么……

11. ＿＿＿＿＿ 是白痴,＿＿＿＿＿ 谁也不会那样做。
    A. 除非……才……　　B. 除非……否则……
    C. 由于……因此……　　D. 幸亏……不然……

12. 这样做,好 ＿＿＿＿＿ 好,＿＿＿＿＿ 太费时间了。
    A. 因为……所以……　　B. 固然……但是……
    C. 即使……也……　　D. 固然……也……

13. ＿＿＿＿＿ 看电影,＿＿＿＿＿ 听音乐,周末一定要轻松轻松。
    A. 不是……而是……　　B. 如果……那么……
    C. 或者……或者……　　D. 一会儿……一会儿……

14. 大运动量的锻炼 _____ 对身体有益,但唱歌、舞剑、做保健操对身体 _____ 是有好处的。
    A. 固然……也……　　B. 即使……也……
    C. 固然……但……　　D. 只要……就……

15. _____ 他不参加,我们 _____ 组织这次活动。
    A. 即使……也……　　B. 假如……就……
    C. 无论……都……　　D. 既然……就……

16. 这部小说 _____ 有不少缺点, _____ 仍有不少读者喜欢看。
    A. 不是……而是……　　B. 不仅……而且……
    C. 尽管……可是……　　D. 因为……所以……

17. 你 _____ 已经说过了,我 _____ 不再重复。
    A. 虽然……但是……　　B. 如果……就……
    C. 既然……就……　　D. 尽管……却……

18. _____ 明天下大雨,那我们的外出活动就得改期了。
    A. 虽然　　B. 假如　　C. 不管　　D. 尽管

19. 尽管他 _____ 精通英语, _____ 掌握电脑,可是现在还没找到一个理想的工作。
    A. 虽……但……　　B. 既……又……
    C. 一……就……　　D. 越……越……

20. _____ 我们和她谈了好半天,她却继续坚持自己的观点。
    A. 因为　　B. 尽管　　C. 既然　　D. 不管

21. _____ 你有事,你 _____ 先走吧!
    A. 如果……就……　　B. 如果……那么……
    C. 即使……也……　　D. 不仅……而且……

22. 王老师批改作文非常认真仔细,哪怕一个标点符号用错了,他 _____ 要改过来。
    A. 也　　B. 又　　C. 再　　D. 才

23. 来到北京,我准备 _____ 登长城, _____ 去游览颐和园。
    A. 先……再……　　B. 又……又……
    C. 既……又……　　D. 一……就……

24. _____ 什么样的困难,我们 _____ 不怕。
    A. 只要……就……　　B. 假如……那……
    C. 任凭……都……　　D. 因为……所以……

25. 早晨起床,她总是 _____ 喝一大杯凉开水, _____ 去操场跑步。
    A. 虽……可是……　　B. 于是……就……
    C. 先……然后……　　D. 不光……也……

26. _____ 居住环境比较拥挤, _____ 接触或者感染的机会就比较多。

A．如果……那么…… 　B．虽然……但是……
C．尽管……可是…… 　D．不仅……而且……

27. 他的病 _____ 很重，_____ 还是可以治好的。
 A．如果……就…… 　B．既然……就……
 C．假如……就…… 　D．虽然……不过……

28. 这些知识，_____ 对你，对我，都是很重要的。
 A．虽然　B．无论　C．因为　D．只要

29. 他 _____ 经受着长年的风吹日晒，_____ 无法改变他要成为一名优秀军人的信念。
 A．即使……也…… 　B．或者……或者……
 C．不仅……也…… 　D．不是……就是……

30. 他先去了景山公园，_____ 去了北海公园。
 A．又　B．再　C．仍　D．却

31. 小王 _____ 自己受累，_____ 麻烦别人。
 A．宁可……也不…… 　B．如果……那么……
 C．虽然……但是…… 　D．因为……所以……

32. _____ 去博物馆，_____ 去商场，同一个时间我只能去一个地方。
 A．要么……要么…… 　B．有时……有时……
 C．有的……有的…… 　D．不仅……而且……

33. 工程 _____ 出现质量问题，_____ 埋下了安全隐患。
 A．即使……也…… 　B．一旦……就……
 C．虽然……但…… 　D．尽管……但……

34. 小猴子 _____ 窜到树上，_____ 又扑到妈妈的怀里，玩得可开心了。
 A．虽然……但是…… 　B．之所以……是因为……
 C．一下子……一下子…… 　D．时而……时而……

35. 妈妈坐在沙发上，_____ 织毛衣，_____ 看电视。
 A．因为……所以…… 　B．与其……不如……
 C．一边……一边…… 　D．固然……不过……

36. 我们 _____ 到公园去玩，_____ 去郊游。
 A．因为……所以…… 　B．尽管……还是……
 C．固然……可是…… 　D．与其……不如……

37. 他的病很重，可是 _____ 痛苦，他 _____ 不肯哼一声。
 A．既……又…… 　B．再……也……
 C．连……也…… 　D．由于……才……

38. 她的字 _____ 写得这么好，_____ 他平时多看多练的缘故。
 A．因为……所以…… 　B．虽然……但是……

C. 固然……可是……   D. 之所以……是因为……

39. 他 _____ 有时间, _____ 去图书馆看书,查资料。
    A. 即使……也……   B. 哪怕……都……
    C. 只要……就……   D. 虽然……但是……

40. _____ 亲自到苏州杭州看一看,你 _____ 能真正理解"上有天堂,下有苏杭"。
    A. 只有……才……   B. 只要……就……
    C. 尽管……也……   D. 如果……就……

41. 这件事, _____ 你浑身是嘴,也说不清了。
    A. 不仅 B. 因为 C. 纵然 D. 由于

42. 激光 _____ 可以焊接不同种类的金属, _____ 能够将金属和陶瓷焊接起来。
    A. 不仅……而且……   B. 不是……而是……
    C. 因为……所以……   D. 不是……就是……

43. 他 _____ 牺牲生命, _____ 肯泄漏国家的机密。
    A. 哪怕……就……   B. 宁可……也不……
    C. 不是……就是……   D. 虽然……但是……

44. _____ 身后发生重大的事情, _____ 不准回头看。
    A. 即使……也……   B. 不仅……而且……
    C. 只有……才……   D. 不是……而是……

45. 大家都说黄山的景色美极了, _____ 再高,我 _____ 要登上去看看。
    A. 虽然……但是……   B. 就是……也……
    C. 不但……而且……   D. 不管……还……

46. 我住的房间是一室多用, _____ 是我的工作室, _____ 是我的餐厅兼卧室。
    A. 由于……所以……   B. 既……又……
    C. 如果……那么……   D. 无论……都……

47. 就这一张电影票, _____ 弟弟去, _____ 妹妹去,反正只能去一个人。
    A. 不是……而是……   B. 或者……或者……
    C. 与其……不如……   D. 宁可……也不……

48. 杨老 _____ 80多岁了, _____ 走起路来健步如飞,比我这50多岁的人走得还快。
    A. 不是……就是……   B. 如果……就……
    C. 虽然……但是……   D. 是……还是……

49. _____ 王莉突然生病,否则她一定会来的。
    A. 要 B. 除非 C. 除 D. 假如

50. 你 _____ 今天有时间,就应该回家看看父母。
    A. 虽然 B. 既然 C. 即使 D. 如果

51. _____ 他们从不同的地方出发, _____ 他们到北京的时间不一样。
    A. 因为……因而……　　　B. 因为……因此……
    C. 由于……所以……　　　D. 因此……所以……

52. _____ 我们喜欢大熊猫, 外国朋友 _____ 喜欢大熊猫。
    A. 不仅……也……　　　B. 不但……而且……
    C. 不仅……还……　　　D. 不但……反而……

53. 他们夫妻俩 _____ 有时间, _____ 到外地去旅游。
    A. 只要……就……　　　B. 只有……才……
    C. 不论……都……　　　D. 不论……也……

54. 这支老年秧歌队 _____ 天气如何, 他们 _____ 坚持锻炼身体。
    A. 不管……就……　　　B. 哪怕……也……
    C. 无论……都……　　　D. 既然……也……

55. _____ 我们餐馆的卫生环境不好, 顾客 _____ 不会到我们这儿来就餐。
    A. 只要……才……　　　B. 尽管……也……
    C. 如果……就……　　　D. 宁可……也……

56. 放暑假了, 咱们 _____ 去哈尔滨 _____ 去张家界?
    A. 是……还是……　　　B. 不是……而是……
    C. 无论……都……　　　D. 因为……所以……

57. _____ 我们取得了好成绩, _____ 还得继续努力, 争取取得更好的成绩。
    A. 不但……而且……　　　B. 虽然……但是……
    C. 是……还是……　　　D. 不是……就是……

58. 为了早日恢复健康, 再苦的药我 _____ 能喝下去。
    A. 也　　B. 就　　C. 却　　D. 仅

59. _____ 坐在这里空谈, _____ 抓紧时间实干。
    A. 不是……而是……　　　B. 既然……就……
    C. 不仅……而且……　　　D. 与其……不如……

60. 去上海 _____ 坐飞机, 我才去!
    A. 除了　　B. 除非　　C. 即使　　D. 而且

61. 王亮 _____ 经常外出采访, _____ 他接触面越来越广, 结交的朋友越来越多。
    A. 不是……就是……　　　B. 因为……所以……
    C. 尽管……可是……　　　D. 只要……就……

62. 行人和车辆 _____ 不遵守交通规则, 想怎么走就怎么走, 那马路上 _____ 乱了。
    A. 除非……就……　　　B. 如果……就……
    C. 即使……就……　　　D. 既然……就……

63. _____ 有毅力的人, _____ 能攀登上科学的高峰。

A. 只有……才……　　B. 无论……都……
C. 因为……所以……　D. 不但……而且……

64. _____ 在这儿等死，不如冲出去。
A. 与其　B. 即使　C. 宁可　D. 假如

65. _____ 遇到多大的困难，我们 _____ 不能灰心呀。
A. 既然……也……　　B. 无论……也……
C. 虽然……但是……　D. 不是……就是……

66. 张爷爷收养了几个孤儿，他深知没有文化的苦，下决心 _____ 多困难，_____ 要供他们读书。
A. 不管……都……　　B. 除非……才……
C. 只要……就……　　D. 即使……也……

67. 今年的冬天出奇地冷，_____ 穿着厚厚的防寒服，_____ 冷得受不了。
A. 如果……就……　　B. 即使……也……
C. 既然……就……　　D. 不但……而且……

68. 周恩来 _____ 受到中国人民乃至世界各国人民的尊敬和爱戴，_____ 他具有超人的智慧和高尚的道德风范。
A. 因为……所以……　B. 虽然……但是……
C. 既然……就……　　D. 之所以……是因为……

69. 天然食品 _____ 有营养，_____ 经济实惠。
A. 因为……所以……　B. 既……又……
C. 虽然……但是……　D. 只有……才……

70. 苏州园林 _____ 在布局、结构、风格上都各有自己的艺术特色，_____ 各有个性，各有自己的美。
A. 不是……而是……　B. 既然……就……
C. 不仅……而且……　D. 如果……就……

71. _____ 你有时间，_____ 你就先来接我一趟吧！
A. 如果……就……　　B. 如果……那么……
C. 即使……也……　　D. 不仅……而且……

72. 我到这里来可 _____ 来享受的，_____ 来工作的，请不要搞特殊化。
A. 不是……就是……　B. 不是……而是……
C. 不仅……而且……　D. 既……又……

73. _____ 大家有兴趣，双休日我们 _____ 去郊区吃农家饭。
A. 只要……就……　　B. 即使……也……
C. 不管……都……　　D. 不但……而且……

74. _____ 你有多大本事，这么狂妄，目中无人 _____ 是不对的。
A. 哪怕……都……　　B. 只要……都……

C. 不管……都……　　D. 除了……都……

75. 在这春光明媚、万物复苏的大好季节里，_____ 在家闲聊，_____ 出去散步。
　　A. 宁可……也不……　　B. 与其……不如……
　　C. 不是……而是……　　D. 不论……都……

76. _____ 心胸豁达的人，_____ 能和周围的人搞好关系。
　　A. 虽然……但是……　　B. 只有……才……
　　C. 只管……才……　　D. 既……也……

77. 学生 _____ 那么喜欢黄老师，_____ 黄老师的教学水平高，对学生一视同仁。
　　A. 之所以……是因为……　　B. 因为……所以……
　　C. 以至于……以至……　　D. 不仅……而且……

78. _____ 大家的支持与帮助，_____ 我今天的成功。
　　A. 哪怕……也……　　B. 别说……就是……
　　C. 不是……就是……　　D. 没有……就没有……

79. _____ 今天晚上熬夜，我 _____ 要把这篇论文写出来。
　　A. 要不是……就　　B. 无论……也
　　C. 是……不是　　D. 就算……也

80. _____ 取消了去四川的计划，我们现在早 _____ 在峨眉山上看日出了。
　　A. 幸亏……否则……　　B. 要不是……就……
　　C. 不是……还……　　D. 除非……否则……

81. 他儿子真有意思，_____ 听音乐，_____ 写作业。
　　A. 就是……也……　　B. 不但……而且……
　　C. 不光……也……　　D. 一边……一边……

82. 这枚戒指 _____ 做工精巧，样式新颖，_____ 它的价格太昂贵了。
　　A. 不但……而且……　　B. 先……然后……
　　C. 虽然……但是……　　D. 既……又……

83. 老北京炸酱面，北京人 _____ 爱吃，一些外国人 _____ 爱吃。
　　A. 又……又……　　B. 也……也……
　　C. 既……又……　　D. 即使……也……

84. _____ 工作多么紧张，她 _____ 要挤出时间给女儿和老公做点儿好吃的。
　　A. 只要……才……　　B. 只要……就……
　　C. 无论……都……　　D. 如果……就……

85. 黎明时分突然下起雨来，_____ 打闪，_____ 打雷，害得我早早就起床了。
　　A. 有时……有时……　　B. 一边……一边……
　　C. 或者……或者……　　D. 又是……又是……

86. 秦老师不是不想去旅游，_____ 有一个高考的女儿需要照顾，抽不出身。

A．就是　B．而是　C．也是　D．还是

87. 像长城、故宫这样的名胜古迹，_____ 中国人知道,外国人也知道。
    A．既然　B．不仅　C．虽然　D．由于

88. 我们先去海洋馆,_____ 再去动物园。
    A．以后　B．后　C．然后　D．后来

89. 他只有逢年过节 _____ 回家看看父母。
    A．会　B．才　C．就　D．刚

90. _____ 明天下多大雪,我都会准时到达集合地点。
    A．既然　B．不管　C．虽然　D．因为

91. 幸子虽然只学了一年中文,_____ 她的汉语说得非常流利。
    A．都　B．就　C．但是　D．而且

92. _____ 什么季节,一口气爬上香山都要出一身汗。
    A．尽管　B．或者　C．只有　D．不管

93. _____ 以前他只有小学的水平,但是经过这几年的学习,他已经拿到了大专文凭。
    A．可是　B．不管　C．因为　D．虽然

94. 她 _____ 是外国人,但是特别爱吃饺子。
    A．如果　B．无论　C．就算　D．虽然

95. _____ 修一条通往山外的路,山里的特产才能运出去。
    A．除了　B．除非　C．只要　D．就算

96. _____ 是名牌,价钱就贵。
    A．只有　B．只要　C．既然　D．即使

97. 我不仅去过韩国,_____ 还不止一次。
    A．而且　B．反而　C．何况　D．更

98. 我 _____ 喜欢北京,而且深深地爱上了这个地方。
    A．因为　B．即使　C．不但　D．只有

99. _____ 多听、多说、多读、多写,_____ 能学好一门外语。
    A．只是……就……　B．只有……才……
    C．如果……才……　D．只有……就……

100. 这件事,你 _____ 不说,我 _____ 知道。
     A．即使……还……　B．即便……就……
     C．不但……还……　D．就是……也……

答疑解惑 Answers and Explanations

1. 选择 C。"不但……而且……"是最常见的一组表示递进关系的关联词语。"不但"用来引出前边的内容，承认一层意思，但这并不是说话人的全部意思；"而且"引出后面的内容，表示比前面的意思更进一层。

The answer is C. "Búdàn... érqiě..." is the most commonly seen relative phrases for furthering relation. "Búdàn" introduces part of the meaning. "Érqiě" introduces the latter contents to show a furthering meaning.

2. 选择 A。"即使……也……"是一组表示假设的让步关系的关联词语。"即使"表示的条件可以是还没有实现的事情，也可以是跟既成事实相反的事情；"也"表示的结果或结论不受前面情况的影响。

The answer is A. "Jíshǐ... yě..." is a relative phrase showing supposed concession. The condition shown by "jíshǐ" can be either something unrealized, or something contrary to the fact. The result or conclusion shown by "yě" is not influenced by the condition stated before.

3. 选择 A。"不是……就是……"是一组表示选择关系的关联词语。有时表示两项之中必有一项是事实，有时是借用两个事例来概括某种情况。

The answer is A. "Búshì... jiùshì..." is a relative phrase for alternative relation. It sometimes shows one of the two choices must be the fact, sometimes shows a generalization of two employed examples.

4. 选择 B。"不仅……而且……"是一组表示递进关系的关联词语。"不仅"相当于"不但"；"而且"承接上文，表示更进一层的意思。

The answer is B. "Bùjǐn... érqiě..." is a relative phrase for progressive relation. "Bùjǐn" is similar to "búdàn"; "érqiě" connects the former content to show a furthering meaning.

5. 选择 D。"不是……而是……"是一组表示并列关系的关联词语。前半句用"不是"表示否定的一面，后半句用"而是"表示肯定的一面。前后正反相对，使肯定的意思更加突出。

The answer is D. "Búshì... érshì..." is a relative phrase for coordinate relation. The first half of the sentence shows negation by using "búshì", while the second half shows affirmation using "érshì". The contents are contrary, which highlight the affirmative meaning.

6. 选择 C。"除非……才……"是一组表示唯一条件关系的关联词语。"除非"从反面指出唯一的先决条件；"才"表示只有在这一唯一的特定条件下才会产生的结果。

The answer is C. "Chúfēi... cái..." is a relative phrase for the sole condition. "Chúfēi" points out the sole condition from the oppsite aspect; while "cái" refers to the result which will come out only under this condition.

7. 选择 B。"不管……也……"是一组表示无条件关系的关联词语。"不管"用在前半句中表示排除一切条件,常带有疑问代词、副词或并列项;"也"用在后半句中的谓语前,表示在任何条件下结果或结论都相同。

The answer is B. "Bùguǎn... yě..." is a relative phrase for unconditional relation. "Bùguǎn" is used in the first half of the sentence to show the elimination of all the conditions. It is often followed by an interrogative pronoun, interrogative adverb or juxtaposed items. "Yě" is used before the predicate in the second half of the sentence to show the result or conclusion keeps the same no matter under what circumstances.

8. 选择 D。"不是……就是……"是一组表示选择关系的关联词语。在本句中表示两项之中必有一项是事实。

The answer is D. "Búshì... jiùshì..." is a relative phrase for alternative relation. In this sentence, it shows one of the two must be the fact.

9. 选择 C。"除非……才……"是一组表示唯一条件关系的关联词语。"除非"从反面指出唯一的先决条件;"才"表示只有在这一唯一的特定条件下才会产生的结果。

The answer is C. "Chúfēi... cái..." is a relative phrase for the sole condition. "Chúfēi" points out the sole precondition from the opposite aspect; while "cái" refers to the result which will come out only under this condition.

10. 选择 A。"不是……而是……"是一组表示并列关系的关联词语。前半句用"不是"表示否定的一面,后半句用"而是"表示肯定的一面。前后正反相对,使肯定的意思更加突出。

The answer is A. "Búshì... érshì..." is a relative phrase for coordinate relation. The first half of the sentence shows negation by using "búshì", while the second half shows affirmation using "érshì". The contents are opposite, which highlights the affirmative meaning.

11. 选择 B。"除非……否则……"是一组表示条件关系的关联词语。这一格式表示一定要这样,如果不这样的话,就不可能得到某种结果。

The answer is B. "Chúfēi... fǒuzé..." is a relative phrase for conditional relation. This phrase shows something must be like this, otherwise, some result cannot be reached.

12. 选择 B。"固然……但是……"是一组表示转折关系的关联词语。"固然"用在前半句中,表示承认某一事实;"但是"用在后半句中,转入相反的情况。

The answer is B. "Gùrán... dànshì..." is a relative phrase for transitional relation. "Gùrán" is used in the first half of the sentence to show the acknowledgment of a fact; while "dànshì" is used in the second half to show an opposite condition.

13. 选择 C。"或者……或者……"是一组表示选择关系的关联词语,句中提出两种可能性,从中选择一个。选项 D "一会儿……一会儿……"表示两种情况交替出现,多用于过去时态。

The answer is C. "Huòzhě... huòzhě..." is a relative phrase for alternative relation. Two possbilities are raised and one of them is to be chosen. "Yíhuìr... yíhuìr..." in D indicates two things happen alternatively, more used in the past tense.

14. 选择 A。"固然……也……"格式中的"固然"用在前半句中,表示承认某一事实;"也"用在后半句中,表示也不否认另一事实。

The answer is A. "Gùrán" in "gùrán... yě..." is used in the first half of a sentence to show the acknowledgment of a fact; while "yě" is used in the second half to show another fact is not denied.

15. 选择 A。"即使……也……"是一组表示假设的让步关系的关联词语。"即使"表示的条件可以是还没有实现的事情,也可以是跟既成事实相反的事情;"也"表示的结果或结论不受前面情况的影响。

The answer is A. "Jíshǐ... yě..." is a relative phrase to show supposed concession relation. The condition shown by "jíshǐ" can be either something unrealized or something contrary to the fact. The result or conclusion shown by "yě" is not influenced by the condition as mentioned.

16. 选择 C。"尽管……可是……"是一组表示转折关系的关联词语。这一格式表示姑且承认某一事实,然后再说出跟前文相反或相对的事。

The answer is C. "Jǐnguǎn... kěshì..." is a relative phrase for transitional relation. This phrase shows to acknowledge a fact first, then propose another fact which is different or opposite.

17. 选择 C。"既然……就……"是一组表示推论性因果关系的关联词语。"既然"在前半句中提出原因、理由或事实;"就"在后半句中引出由此推得的结果或结论。前后半句的主语可以不同。

The answer is C. "Jìrán... jiù..." is a relative phrase for inferential causative relation. "Jìrán" is used in the first half of a sentence to show a reason or fact; "jiù" is in the second half to introduce an inferred result or conclusion. The subjects in the two sentences can be different.

18. 选择 B。"假如……就……"是一组表示假设关系的关联词语。"假如"相当于"如果";"就"承接上文,表示如果前面的假设实现后,就自然会产生后面的结果。

The answer is B. "Jiǎrú... jiù..." is a relative phrase for hypothetical relation. "Jiǎrú" is similar to "rúguǒ"; "jiù" connects the former content and shows if the hypothesis mentioned is realized, a result will surely come out.

19. 选择 B。"既……又……"是一组表示并列关系的关联词语。这一格式表示两种情况同时存在，可以连接动词或形容词，被连接的两部分的结构和音节数目常常相同。
The answer is B. "Jì... yòu..." is a relative phrase for coordinate relation. This phrase shows that two situations exist at the same time. It can connect verbs or adjectives. The structures and syllables of the two connected parts are usually the same.

20. 选择 B。"尽管……却……"是一组表示转折关系的关联词语。"尽管"用在前半句中，表示让步，承认某一事实；"却"在后半句中与之呼应，起转折作用，表示所说的情况与前面相对或相反，是出乎意料的。
The answer is B. "Jǐnguǎn... què..." is a relative phrase for transition relation. "Jǐnguǎn" is used in the first half of a sentence to show concession and acknowledgment of a fact; "què" echoes with it in the second half of the sentence and functions as a transition, which shows the situation mentioned is on the opposite and beyond one's expectation.

21. 选择 A。"如果……就……"是一组表示假设关系的关联词语。"如果"引出一种事实或判断，"就"引出相关的另一种事实或判断。前后对比，强调后者。
The answer is A. "Rúguǒ... jiù..." is a relative phrase for hypothetical relation. "Rúguǒ" introduces a fact or judgment, while "jiù" introduces another related fact or judgment. There is a comparison between the two, and the emphasis is on the latter.

22. 选择 A。"哪怕……也……"是一组表示让步关系的关联词语。"哪怕"先假设出一个条件，"也"强调即使在这样的条件下，也不会改变原来的计划或结论。多用于口语。
The answer is A. "Nǎpà... yě..." is a relative phrase for concession relation. "Nǎpà" hypothesizes a condition; "yě" emphasizes the original plan or conclusion will not be changed even under this condition. It's often used in spoken language.

23. 选择 A。"先……再……"是一组表示承接关系的关联词语。这一格式表示还没有实现的动作的先后承接顺序。
The answer is A. "Xiān... zài..." is a relative phrase for successive relation. This phrase shows the connection sequence of unrealized actions.

24. 选择 C。"任凭……都……"是一组表示无条件关系的关联词语。"任凭"后可以有疑问代词、副词或有选择的并列成分，表示任何条件都加以排除；"都"表示在上述任何条件下，结果完全相同。

The answer is C. "Rènpíng... dōu..." is a relative phrase for unconditional relation. "Rènpíng" can be followed by an interrogative pronoun, interrogative adverb or some selective juxtaposed elements to show any condition can be eliminated; "dōu" shows the result will be the same under any condition as mentioned.

25. 选择 C。"先……然后……"是一组表示承接关系的关联词语。这一格式表示两件以上的事情按照先后顺序发生。
The answer is C. "Xiān... ránhòu..." is a relative phrase for successive relation. This phrase shows that two or more things happen according to the time sequence.

26. 选择 A。"如果……那么……"是一组表示假设关系的关联词语。"如果"引出一种事实或判断,"那么"引出相关的另一种事实或判断。前后对比,强调后者。
The answer is A. "Rúguǒ... nàme..." is a relative phrase for hypothetical relation. "Rúguǒ" introduces a fact or judgment, while "nàme" introduces another related fact or judgment. There is a comparison between the two, and the emphasis is on the latter.

27. 选择 D。"虽然……不过……"是一组表示转折关系的关联词语。"虽然"先做让步,承认前一分句的事实;后半句由"不过"做转折,指出后一分句的成立不受前一分句的影响,前后两件事相反或不一致。
The answer is D. "Suīrán... búguò..." is a relative phrase for transition. "Suīrán" makes a concession first and acknowledges one thing; "búguò" makes a transition in the second half of the sentence, which points out the existence of another thing irrelevant to the first one. The two things are contrary or not unanimous.

28. 选择 B。"无论……都……"是一组表示无条件关系的关联词语。"无论"后可以有疑问代词,也可以有表示选择关系的并列成分,表示任何条件都加以排除;后有"都"呼应,表示在任何条件下,结果完全相同。
The answer is B. "Wúlùn... dōu..." is a relative phrase for unconditional relation. "Wúlùn" can be followed by the interrogative pronoun or juxtaposed elements for choosing, which shows any condition can be eliminated. "Dōu" echoes with it and indicates the result is the same under any condition.

29. 选择 A。"即使……也……"是一组表示无条件关系的关联词语。"即使"后可以有疑问代词、副词或有选择的并列成分,表示任何条件都加以排除;"也"表示在上述任何条件下,结果完全相同。
The answer is A. "Jíshǐ... yě..." is a relative phrase for unconditional relation. "jíshǐ" can be followed by the interrogative pronoun, adverb or selective juxtaposed elements for choosing,

which shows any condition can be eliminated. "Yě" indicates the result is the same under any condition.

30. 选择 A。"先……又……"是一组表示承接关系的关联词语。这一格式表示已经实现的动作的先后承接顺序。

The answer is A. "Xiān... yòu..." is a relative phrase for successive relation. This phrase shows the time sequence of things happened.

31. 选择 A。"宁可……也不……"是一组表示选择关系的关联词语。这一格式表示在比较两方面的利害得失以后选择前者,舍弃后者。

The answer is A. "Nìngkě... yě bù..." is a relative phrase for alternative relation. This phrase shows that after comparing the advantages and disadvantages of two aspects, one chooses the former and discards the latter.

32. 选择 A。"要么……要么……"是一组表示选择关系的关联词语。这一格式表示在前后对举、互相排斥的两种情况或事物之间进行选择,有"不是这个,就是那个"的意思。

The answer is A. "Yàome... yàome..." is a relative phrase for alternative relation. This phrase shows one chooses one from two contradictory things. It has the meaning of "if not this, then that".

33. 选择 B。"一旦……就……"是一组表示条件关系的关联词语。"一旦"表示有了某种条件,"就"表示一定会产生或出现某种结果。

The answer is B. "Yídàn... jiù..." is a relative phrase for condition. "Yídàn" shows if there is a condition, "jiù" shows a result will surely come out.

34. 选择 D。"时而……时而……"是一组表示并列关系的关联词语。这一格式表示不同的动作或事情在一定的时间内交替发生,多用于书面语。

The answer is D. "Shí'ér... shí'ér..." is a relative phrase for coordinate relation. This phrase shows different actions or things happen alternatively within a certain time. It's often used in written language.

35. 选择 C。"一边……一边……"是一组表示并列关系的关联词语。这一格式表示两个动作同时进行,分别用在两个动词或动词短语前,多用于书面语。

The answer is C. "Yìbiān... yìbiān..." is a relative phrase for coordinate relation. This phrase shows that two actions take place at the same time, which is used respectively before two verbs or verbal phrases. It's often used in written language.

36. 选择D。"与其……不如……"是一组表示选择关系的关联词语。用"与其"先指出舍弃的某事;"不如"后指出选择的某事。需要注意的是,在这一格式中,无论是选择的,还是舍弃的,都不是说话人特别愿意做的事。

The answer is D. "Yǔqí... bùrú..." is a relative phrase for alternative relation. The part with "yǔqí" points out a thing being given up; another thing to be chosen is pointed out after "bùrú". Please note that in this phrase, neither the thing being given up or the one chosen is what the speaker is willing to do.

37. 选择B。"再……也……"是一组表示让步的假设关系的关联词语。"再"表示假设让步,后面如果是形容词,则表示程度进一步加强;"也"表示无论情况怎样变化,结果都相同。

The answer is B. "Zài... yě..." is a relative phrase for concession hypothetical relation. "Zài" shows hypothesized concession. If it is followed by an adjective, it shows a stronger degree. "Yě" shows the result will be the same no matter how the condition changes.

38. 选择D。"之所以……是因为……"是一组表示因果关系的关联词语。先用"之所以"引出结果或结论,再用"是因为"说明原因或理由。这一格式更加强调突出了原因或理由。

The answer is D. "Zhīsuǒyǐ... shì yīnwèi..." is a relative phrase for causative relation. A result or conclusion is made by using "zhīsuǒyǐ", then a reason is stated by "shì yīnwèi". This phrase emphasizes and highlights the reason.

39. 选择C。"只要……就……"是一组表示条件关系的关联词语。"只要"引出充分条件;"就"引出结果。这一格式表示在所说的充分条件下,肯定会产生某种结果。

The answer is C. "Zhǐyào... jiù..." is a relative phrase for condition. "Zhǐyào" introduces a full condition; "jiù" introduces a result. This phrase shows there will be a certain result under the stated condition.

40. 选择A。"只有……才……"是一组表示条件关系的关联词语。"只有"引出唯一条件;"才"引出期望出现的结果或实现的目的。这一格式表示如果没有前面的唯一条件,就不会出现或实现后面的结果或目的。

The answer is A. "Zhǐyǒu... cái..." is a relative phrase for condition. "Zhǐyǒu" introduces a sole condition; "cái" introduces an expected result or purpose. This phrase shows there will be no result or purpose to be realized without the sole condition as mentioned.

41. 选择C,"纵然……也……"是一组表示让步的假设关系的关联词语。"纵然"相当于"即使",表示让步的假设,先承认某种情况是事实;"也"说出与之相反的情况,前后有转折之意。多用于书面语。

The answer is C. "Zòngrán... yě..." is a relative phrase to show supposed concession. "Zòngrán" is similar to "jíshǐ", which shows a conceded hypothesis and acknowledgment of a fact; "yě" shows an opposite situation. There is a transition between "zòngrán..." and "yě". It's often used in written language.

42. 选择 A。"不仅……而且……"是一组表示递进关系的关联词语。"不仅"相当于"不但";"而且"承接上文,表示更进一层的意思。

The answer is A. "Bùjǐn... érqiě..." is a relative phrase for progressive relation. "Bùjǐn" is similar to "búdàn"; "érqiě" connects the former content to show a furthering meaning.

43. 选择 B。"宁可……也不……"是一组表示选择关系的关联词语。这一格式表示在比较两方面的利害得失以后选择前者,舍弃后者。

The answer is B. "Nìngkě... yěbù..." is a relative phrase for alternative relation. This phrase shows after comparing the advantages and disadvantages of two aspects, one chooses the former and discards the latter.

44. 选择 A。"即使……也……"是一组表示假设的让步关系的关联词语。"即使"表示的条件可以是还没有实现的事情,也可以是跟既成事实相反的事情;"也"表示的结果或结论不受前面情况的影响。

The answer is A. "Jíshǐ... yě..." is a relative phrase to show supposed concession. The condition shown by "jíshǐ" can be either something unrealized, or something contrary to the fact. The result or conclusion shown by "yě" is not influenced by the formerly stated condition.

45. 选择 B。"就是……也……"是一组表示让步的假设关系的关联词语。"就是"表示让步的假设;"也"表示无论前面的情况怎样,结果或结论都相同。

The answer is B. "Jiùshì... yě..." is a relative phrase for conceded hypothesis. "Jiùshì" shows conceded hypothesis; "yě" shows a result or conclusion remain the same no matter what the former condition is.

46. 选择 B,"既……又……"是一组表示并列关系的关联词语。这一格式表示两种情况同时存在,可以连接动词或形容词,被连接的两部分的结构和音节数目常常相同。

The answer is B. "Jì... yòu..." is a relative phrase for coordinate relation. This phrase shows that two situations exist at the same time. It can connect verbs or adjectives. The structures and syllables of the two connected parts are usually the same.

47. 选择 B。"或者……或者……"是一组表示选择关系的关联词语,用在陈述句中。

The answer is B. "Huòzhě... huòzhě..." is a relative phrase for alternative relation and used in declarative sentences.

48. 选择 C。"虽然……但是……"是一组表示转折关系的关联词语。"虽然"先做让步,承认前一分句的事实;后一小句由"但是"做转折,指出后一事的成立不受前面一事的影响,两件事相反或不一致。

The answer is C. "Suīrán... dànshì..." is a relative phrase for transition. "Suīrán" makes a concession first and acknowledges one thing; "dànshì" makes a transition in the second half of the sentence, which points out the existence of another thing irrelevant to the first one. The two things are contrary or not unanimous.

49. 选择 B。"除非……否则……"是一组表示条件关系的关联词语。这一格式表示一定是这样,如果不这样的话,就不可能得出某种结果。

The answer is B. "Chúfēi... fǒuzé..." is a relative phrase for condition. This phrase shows something must be so, otherwise, some result cannot be achieved.

50. 选择 B。"既然……就……"是一组表示推论性因果关系的关联词语。"既然"在前半句中提出原因、理由或事实;"就"在后半句中引出由此推得的结果或结论。

The answer is B. "Jìrán... jiù..." is a relative phrase for inferential causative relation. "Jìrán" is used in the first half of a sentence to show a reason or fact; "jiù" is in the second half to introduce an inferred result or conclusion.

51. 选择 C。"由于……所以……"是一组表示因果关系的关联词语。"由于"说明原因;"所以"说明结果。这一格式用于书面语。

The answer is C. "Yóuyú... suǒyǐ..." is a relative phrase for causative relation. "Yóuyú" accounts for a reason, "suǒyǐ" for a result. This pattern is used in written language.

52. 选择 A。"不仅……也……"是一组表示递进关系的关联词语。"不仅"用来引出前边的内容,承认一层意思,但这并不是说话人的全部意思;"也"引出后面的内容,表示比前面的意思更进一层。特别需要注意的是,前后小句的主语不同。"不仅"应在第一个主语前,"也"应在第二个主语后。

The answer is A. "Bùjǐn... yě..." is a relative phrase for progressive relation. "Bùjǐn" is to introduce the former content and acknowledge one meaning, but it is not the full meaning of the speaker. "Yě" is to introduce the latter content to show a furthering meaning. Please note the subjects in the two halves of the sentence are different. "Bùjǐn" should be put before the first subject, "yě" should be after the second subject.

53. 选择A。"只要……就……"是一组表示条件关系的关联词语。"只要"引出充分条件;"就"引出结果。这一格式表示在所说的充分条件下,肯定会产生某种结果。

The answer is A. "Zhǐyào... jiù..." is a relative phrase for condition. "Zhǐyào" introduces a full condition; "jiù" introduces a result. This pattern shows under the stated condition, there will be a certain result.

54. 选择C。"无论……都……"是一组表示无条件关系的关联词语。"无论"后可以有疑问代词、副词或有选择的并列成分,表示任何条件都加以排除;"都"表示在上述任何条件下,结果完全相同。

The answer is C. "Wúlùn... dōu..." is a relative phrase for unconditional relation. "Wúlùn" can be followed by the interrogative pronoun or juxtaposed elements for choosing, which shows any condition can be eliminated. "Dōu" echoes with it and indicates the result is the same under any condition.

55. 选择C。"如果……就……"是一组表示假设关系的关联词语。"如果"引出一种事实或判断,"就"引出相关的另一种事实或判断。前后对比,强调后者。

The answer is C. "Rúguǒ... jiù..." is a relative phrase for hypothetical relation. "Rúguǒ" introduces a fact or judgment, while "jiù" introduces another related fact or judgment. There is a comparison between the two, and the emphasis is on the latter.

56. 选择A。"是……还是……"是一组表示选择关系的关联词语。常用在疑问句中,表示从两项之中选取一项。

The answer is A. "Shì... háishi..." is a relative phrase for alternative relation. It's often used in the interrogative sentences to show choosing one from two.

57. 选择B。"虽然……但是……"是一组表示转折关系的关联词语。"虽然"先做让步,承认甲事;后一小句由"但是"做转折,指出乙事的成立不受甲事的影响,甲乙两件事相反或不一致。

The answer is B. "Suīrán...dànshì..." is a relative phrase for transition. "Suīrán" makes a concession first and acknowledges one thing; "dànshì" makes a transition in the second half of the sentence, which points out the existence of another thing irrelevant to the first one. The two things are contrary or not unanimous.

58. 选择A。"再……也……"是一组表示让步的假设关系的关联词语。"再"表示假设让步,后面如果是形容词,则表示程度进一步加强;"也"表示无论情况怎样变化,结果都相同。

The answer is A. "Zài... yě..." is a relative phrase for conceded hypothesis. "Zài" shows hypothesized concession. If it is followed by an adjective, it shows a stronger degree. "Yě" shows the result will be the same no matter how the condition changes.

59. 选择 D。"与其……不如……"是一组表示选择关系的关联词语。用"与其"先指出舍弃的某事；"不如"后指出选择的某事。

The answer is D. "Yǔqí... bùrú..." is a relative phrase for alternative relation. The part with "yǔqí" points out the thing given up; the thing to be chosen is pointed out after "bùrú".

60. 选择 B。"除非……才……"是一组表示唯一条件关系的关联词语。"除非"从反面指出唯一的先决条件；"才"表示只有在这一唯一的特定条件下才会产生的结果。

The answer is B. "Chúfēi... cāi..." is a relative phrase for the sole condition. "Chúfēi" points out the sole condition from the opposite aspect; while "cái" refers to the result made only by this condition.

61. 选择 B。"因为……所以……"是一组表示因果关系的关联词语。"因为"说明原因；"所以"说明结果。

The answer is B. "Yīnwèi... suǒyǐ..." is a relative phrase for causative relation. "Yīnwèi" accounts for a reason, "suǒyǐ" for a result.

62. 选择 B。"如果……就……"是一组表示假设关系的关联词语。"如果"引出一种事实或判断，"就"引出相关的另一种事实或判断。前后对比，强调后者。

The answer is B. "Rúguǒ... jiù..." is a relative phrase for hypothetical relation. "Rúguǒ" introduces a fact or judgment, while "jiù" introduces another related fact or judgment. There is a comparison between the two, and the emphasis is on the latter.

63. 选择 A。"只有……才……"是一组表示条件关系的关联词语。"只有"引出唯一条件；"才"引出期望出现的结果或实现的目的。这一格式表示如果没有前面的唯一条件，就不会出现或实现后面的结果或目的。

The answer is A. "Zhǐyǒu... cái..." is a relative phrase for condition. "Zhǐyǒu" introduces the sole condition; "cái" introduces an expected result or realized purpose. This pattern shows if the sole condition is not mentioned, there will be no result or purpose to be realized.

64. 选择 A。"与其……不如……"是一组表示选择关系的关联词语。用"与其"先指出舍弃的某事；"不如"后指出选择的某事。需要注意的是，在这一格式中，无论是选择的，还是舍弃的，都不是说话人特别愿意做的事。

The answer is A. "Yǔqí... bùrú..." is a relative phrase for alternative relation. The part with "yǔqí" points out the thing given up; the thing to be chosen is pointed out after "bùrú". Please note that in this pattern, neither the thing given up or the one chosen is what the speaker is willing to do.

65. 选择 B。"无论……也……"是一组表示无条件关系的关联词语。"无论"后可以有疑问代词、副词或有选择的并列成分,表示任何条件都加以排除;"也"表示在上述任何条件下,结果完全相同。

The answer is B. "Wúlùn... yě..." is a relative phrase for unconditional relation. "Wúlùn" can be followed by the interrogative pronoun or juxtaposed elements for choosing, which shows any condition can be eliminated. "Yě" echoes with it and indicates the result is the same under any condition.

66. 选择 A。"不管……都……"是一组表示无条件关系的关联词语。"不管"用在前半句中表示排除一切条件,常带有疑问代词、副词或并列项;"都"用在后半句中的谓语前,表示在任何条件下结果或结论都相同。选项 D "即使……也……"表示假设关系,后一分句的结果不受前一分句假设的某种情况的影响。

The answer is A. "Bùguǎn... dōu..." is a relative phrase for unconditional relation. "Bùguǎn" is used in the first half of the sentence to show any condition can be eliminated. It can be followed by the interrogative pronoun or juxtaposed elements. "Dōu" is used before the predicate in the second half and indicates the result is the same under any condition. "Jíshǐ...yě..." in D shows supposed concession, the outcome in the second clause is not affected by the supposition in the first clause.

67. 选择 B。"即使……也……"是一组表示假设的让步关系的关联词语。"即使"表示的条件可以是还没有实现的事情,也可以是跟既成事实相反的事情;"也"表示的结果或结论不受前面情况的影响。

The answer is B. "Jíshǐ... yě..." is a relative phrase to show supposed concession. The condition shown by "jíshǐ" can be either something unrealized, or something contrary to the fact. The result or conclusion shown by "yě" is not affected by the condition or conclusion as mentioned.

68. 选择 D。"之所以……是因为……"是一组表示因果关系的关联词语。先用"之所以"引出结果或结论,再用"是因为"说明原因或理由。这一格式更加强调突出了原因或理由。

The answer is D. "Zhīsuǒyǐ... shìyīnwèi..." is a relative phrase for causative relation. A result or conclusion is made by using "zhīsuǒyǐ", then a reason is stated by "shì yīnwèi". This pattern emphasizes and highlights the reason.

69. 选择 B。"既……又……"是一组表示并列关系的关联词语。这一格式表示两种情况同时存在,可以连接动词或形容词,被连接的两部分的结构和音节数目常常相同。

The answer is B. "Jì... yòu..." is a relative phrase for coordinate relation. This pattern shows that two situations exist at the same time. It can connect verbs or adjectives. The structures and syllables of the two connected parts are usually the same.

70. 选择 C。"不仅……而且……"是一组表示递进关系的关联词语。"不仅"相当于"不但";"而且"承接上文,表示更进一层的意思。

The answer is C. "Bùjǐn... érqiě..." is a relative phrase for progressive relation. "Bùjǐn" is similar to "búdàn"; "érqiě" connects the former content to show a furthering meaning.

71. 选择 B。"如果……那么……"是一组表示假设关系的关联词语。"如果"引出一种事实或判断,"那么"引出相关的另一种事实或判断。前后对比,强调后者。

The answer is B. "Rúguǒ... nàme..." is a relative phrase for hypothetical relation. "Rúguǒ" introduces a fact or judgment, while "nàme" introduces another related fact or judgment. There is a comparison between the two, and the emphasis is on the latter.

72. 选择 B。"不是……而是……"是一组表示并列关系的关联词语。前半句用"不是"表示否定的一面,后半句用"而是"表示肯定的一面。前后正反相对,使肯定的意思更加突出。

The answer is B. "Búshì... érshì..." is a relative phrase for coordinate relation. The first half of the sentence shows negation by using "búshì", while the second half shows affirmation using "érshì". The contents are contrary, which highlights the affirmative meaning.

73. 选择 A。"只要……就……"是一组表示条件关系的关联词语。"只要"引出充分条件;"就"引出结果。这一格式表示在所说的充分条件下,肯定会产生某种结果。

The answer is A. "Zhǐyào... jiù..." is a relative phrase for condition. "Zhǐyào" introduces a full condition; "jiù" introduces a result. This phrase shows under condition as mentioned, there will be a certain result.

74. 选择 C。"不管……都……"是一组表示无条件关系的关联词语。"不管"用在前半句中表示排除一切条件,常带有疑问代词、副词或并列项;"都"用在后半句中的谓语前,表示在任何条件下,结果或结论都相同。

The answer is C. "Bùguǎn... dōu..." is a relative phrase for unconditional relation. "Bùguǎn" is used in the first half of the sentence to show any condition can be eliminated. It can be followed by the interrogative pronoun or juxtaposed elements. "Dōu" is used before the predicate and indicates the result is the same under any condition.

75. 选择 B。"与其……不如……"是一组表示选择关系的关联词语。用"与其"先指出舍弃的某事;"不如"后指出选择的某事。需要注意的是,在这一格式中,无论是选择的,还是舍弃的,都不是说话人特别愿意做的事。

The answer is B. "Yǔqí... bùrú..." is a relative phrase for alternative relation. The part with "yǔqí" points out the thing given up; the thing to be chosen is pointed out after "bùrú". Please note that in this pattern, either the thing given up nor the one chosen is what the speaker is willing to do.

76. 选择 B。"只有……才……"是一组表示条件关系的关联词语。"只有"引出唯一条件;"才"引出期望出现的结果或实现的目的。这一格式表示如果没有前面的唯一条件,就不会出现或实现后面的结果或目的。

The answer is B. "Zhǐyǒu... cái.." is a relative phrase for condition. "Zhǐyǒu" introduces condition; "cái" introduces an expected result or realized purpose. This pattern shows if the sole condition is not mentioned, there will be no result or purpose to be realized.

77. 选择 A。"之所以……是因为……"是一组表示因果关系的关联词语。先用"之所以"引出结果或结论,再用"是因为"说明原因或理由。这一格式更加强调突出了原因或理由。

The answer is A. "Zhīsuǒyǐ... shìyīnwèi..." is a relative phrase for causative relation. A result or conclusion is made by using "zhīsuǒyǐ", then a reason is stated by "shì yīnwèi". This pattern emphasizes and highlights the reason.

78. 选择 D。"没有……就没有……"是一组表示假设关系的关联词语。"没有"表示与事实相反的情况;"就没有"表示与实际结果相反的情况。

The answer is D. "Méiyǒu... jiù méiyǒu..." is a relative phrase for hypothetical relation. "Méiyǒu" shows a situation opposite to the fact; "jiùméiyǒu" shows a situation opposite to the result.

79. 选择 D。"就算……也……"是一组表示假设关系的关联词语。"就算"可以表示没有出现的事情,也可以是跟既成事实相反的事情;"也"表示结果不受上述情况的影响。

The answer is D. "jiùsuàn... yě..." is a relative phrase for hypothetical relation. "Jiùsuàn" can show either something unrealized or something contrary to the fact. The result or conclusion shown by "yě" is not influenced by the condition as mentioned.

80. 选择 B。"要不是……就……"是一组表示假设关系的关联词语。"要不是"表示与事实相反的情况;"就"表示与实际结果相反的情况。

The answer is B. "Yàobúshì... jiù..." is a relative phrase for hypothetical relation. "Yàobúshì" shows an opposite situation to the fact; "jiù" shows an opposite situation to the result.

81. 选择 B。"一边……一边……"是一组表示并列关系的关联词语。这一格式表示两个动作同时进行。

The answer is B. "Yìbiān... yìbiān..." is a relative phrase for coordinate relation. This pattern shows two actions take place at the same time.

82. 选择 C。"虽然……但是……"是一组表示转折关系的关联词语。"虽然"先做让步,承认前一分句的事实;后一小句由"但是"做转折,指出后一事实的成立不受前面一事的影响,两件事相反或不一致。

The answer is C. "Suīrán... dànshì..." is a relative phrase for transition. "Suīrán" makes a concession first and acknowledges one thing; "dànshì" makes a transition in the second half of the sentence, which points out the existence of another thing irrelevant to the first one. The two things are contrary or not unanimous.

83. 选择 B。"也……也……"是一组表示并列关系的关联词语。这一格式表示两个动作或两种状态同时存在。"也"的后面可以带动词,也可以带形容词。

The answer is B. "Yě... yě..." is a relative phrase for coordinate relation. This pattern shows that two actions or states exist at the same time. "Yě" can be followed by verbs or adjectives.

84. 选择 C。"无论……都……"是一组表示无条件关系的关联词语。"无论"用在前半句中表示排除一切条件,常带有疑问代词、副词或并列项;"都"用在后半句中的谓语前,表示在任何条件下结果或结论都相同。

The answer is C. "Wúlùn... dōu..." is a relative phrase for unconditional relation. "Wúlùn" in the first half of the sentence can be followed by interrogative pronouns or juxtaposed elements, which shows any condition can be eliminated. "Dōu" is used before the predicate in the second half and indicates the result is the same under any condition.

85. 选择 D。"又是……又是……"是一组表示并列关系的关联词语。这一格式表示两个动作或两种状态同时存在。复句只有一个主语。

The answer is D. "Yòushì... yòushì..." is a relative phrase for coordinate relation. This pattern shows that two actions or states exist at the same time. The complex sentence has only one subject.

86. 选择 B。"不是……而是……"是一组表示并列关系的关联词语。前半句用"不是"表示否定的一面,后半句用"而是"表示肯定的一面。前后正反相对,使肯定的意思更加突出。

The answer is B. "Búshì... érshì..." is a relative phrase for coordinate relation. The first half of the sentence shows negation by using "búshì", while the second half shows affirmation using "érshì". The contents are contrary, which highlights the affirmative meaning.

87. 选择 B。"不仅……也……"是一组表示递进关系的关联词语。"不仅"用来引出前边的内容,承认一层意思,但这并不是说话人的全部意思;"也"引出后面的内容,表示比前面的意思更进一层。特别需要注意的是,前后小句的主语不同。"不仅"应在第一个主语前,"也"应在第二个主语后。

The answer is B. "Bùjǐn... yě..." is a relative phrase for progressive relation. "Bùjǐn" introduces the former content and acknowledge one meaning, but it is not the full meaning of the speaker. "Yě" introduces the latter content to show a furthering meaning. Please note the subjects in the two halves of the sentence are different. "Bùjǐn" should be put before the first subject, "yě" after the second subject.

88. 选择 C。"先……然后……"是一组表示承接关系的关联词语。这一格式表示两件以上的事情按照先后顺序发生。

The answer is C. "Xiān... ránhòu..." is a relative phrase for successive relation. This phrase shows that two or more things happen according to the time sequence.

89. 选择 B。"只有……才……"是一组表示条件关系的关联词语。"只有"引出唯一条件；"才"引出期望出现的结果或实现的目的。这一格式表示如果没有前面的唯一条件，就不会出现或实现后面的结果或目的。

The answer is B. "Zhǐyǒu... cái..." is a relative phrase for condition. "Zhǐyǒu" introduces the sole condition; "cái" introduces an expected result or realized purpose. This pattern shows if the sole condition is not mentioned, there will be no result or purpose to be realized.

90. 选择 B。"不管……都……"是一组表示无条件关系的关联词语。"不管"用在前半句中表示排除一切条件，常带有疑问代词、副词或并列项；"都"用在后半句中的谓语前，表示在任何条件下结果或结论都相同。

The answer is B. "Bùguǎn... dōu..." is a relative phrase for unconditional relation. "Bùguǎn" is used in the first half of the sentence to show any condition can be eliminated. It can be followed by interrogative pronouns or juxtaposed elements, and "dōu" is used before the predicate in the second half of the sentence and indicates the result is the same under any condition.

91. 选择 C。"虽然……但是……"是一组表示转折关系的关联词语。"虽然"先做让步，承认前一分句的事实；后一小句由"但是"做转折，指出后一事实的成立不受前事的影响，甲乙两件事是相反或不一致的。

The answer is C. "Suīrán... dànshì..." is a relative phrase for transition. "Suīrán" makes a concession first and acknowledges one thing; "dànshì" makes a transition in the second half of the sentence, which points out the existence of another thing irrelevant to the first one. The two things are contrary or not unanimous.

92. 选择 D。"不管……都……"是一组表示无条件关系的关联词语。"不管"用在前半句中表示排除一切条件，常带有疑问代词、副词或并列项；"都"用在后半句中的谓语前，表示在任何条件下结果或结论都相同。

The answer is D. "Bùguǎn... dōu..." is a relative phrase for unconditional relation.

"Bùguǎn" is used in the first half of the sentence to show any condition can be eliminated. It can be followed by the interrogative pronouns or juxtaposed elements, "dōu" is used before the predicate in the second half of the sentence and indicates the result is the same under any condition.

93. 选择 D。"虽然……但是……"是一组表示转折关系的关联词语。"虽然"先做让步,承认前一分句的事实;后一小句由"但是"做转折,指出后一事的成立不受前事的影响,甲乙两件事相反或不一致。

The answer is D. "Suīrán... dànshì..." is a relative phrase for transition. "Suīrán" makes a concession first and acknowledges one thing; "dànshì" makes a transition in the second half of the sentence, which points out the existence of another thing irrelevant to the first one. The two things are contrary or not unanimous.

94. 选择 D。"虽然……但是……"组成表示转折关系的关联词语。

The answer is D. "Suīrán... dànshì..." is a relative phrase for transition.

95. 选择 B。"除非……才……"是一组表示唯一条件关系的关联词语。"除非"从反面指出唯一的先决条件;"才"表示只有在这一唯一的特定条件下才会产生的结果。

The answer is B. "Chúfēi... cái..." is a relative phrase for the sole condition. "Chúfēi" points out the unique condition from the opposite aspect; while "cái" refers to the result made only by this condition.

96. 选择 B。"只要……就……"是一组表示条件关系的关联词语。"只要"引出充分条件;"就"引出结果。这一格式表示在所说的充分条件下,肯定会产生某种结果。

The answer is B. "Zhǐyào... jiù..." is a relative phrase for condition. "Zhǐyào" introduces a full condition; "jiù" introduces a result. This pattern shows under the condition as mentioned, there will be a certain result.

97. 选择 A。"不仅……而且……"是一组表示递进关系的关联词语。"不仅"相当于"不但";"而且"承接上文,表示更进一层的意思。

The answer is A. "Bùjǐn... érqiě..." is a relative phrase for progressive relation. "Bùjǐn" is similar to "búdàn"; "érqiě" connects the former content to show a furthering meaning.

98. 选择 C。"不但……而且……"是最常见的一组表示递进关系的关联词语。"不但"用来引出前边的内容,承认一层意思,但这并不是说话人的全部意思;"而且"引出后面的内容,表示比前面的意思更进一层。

The answer is C. "Búdàn... érqiě..." is the most commonly seen relative phrase for progressive relation. "Búdàn" is to introduce the former content and acknowledge one meaning, but it is not the full meaning of the speaker. "Érqiě" is to introduce the latter content to show a furthering meaning.

99. 选择 B。"只有……才……"是一组表示条件关系的关联词语。"只有"引出唯一条件;"才"引出期望出现的结果或实现的目的。这一格式表示如果没有前面的唯一条件,就不会出现或实现后面的结果或目的。

The answer is B. "Zhǐyǒu... cái..." is a relative phrase for condition. "Zhǐyǒu" introduces the sole condition; "cái" introduces an expected result or realized purpose. This pattern shows if the sole condition is not mentioned, there will be no result or purpose to be realized.

100. 选择 D。"就是……也……"是一组表示让步的假设关系的关联词语。"就是"表示让步的假设;"也"表示无论前面的情况怎样,结果或结论都相同。

The answer is D. "Jiùshì... yě..." is a relative phrase for conceded hypothesis. "Jiùshì" shows conceded hypothesis; "yě" shows the result or conclusion is the same no matter what the condition mentioned is.

11 语序 Word Order

Examination Points

一、多项定语 Multiple attributes

1. 并列关系的定语 Attributes of juxtaposition

① 一般来说,并列关系的各项定语之间的顺序是自由的。

Generally speaking, the order of attributes of juxtaposition is flexible.

例:他会汉语、英语、日语和西班牙语等多种语言。 （√）

他会英语、日语、汉语和西班牙语等多种语言。 （√）

② 有时受到语用、习惯、认识规律等因素的影响,各项定语之间的顺序被固定下来。

Sometimes due to the influence of factors like pragmatics, customs or the law of cognition, the order of attributes is fixed.

例:父亲、母亲的话一直激励着我努力向前。(从男到女)

北京市朝阳区定福庄东街1号中国传媒大学的教学楼很漂亮。(从大到小)

任何人都无法改变生老病死的规律。(按照事物的发展规律)

2. 递加关系的定语 Attributes of progressive relation

按照距离中心语从远到近的顺序应该是：① 表示领属关系的名词/代词/名词性短语→②表示时间/处所的名词性短语→③指示代词/数量短语→④动词/动词性短语/介词短语→⑤形容词短语→⑥不用"的"的形容词/表示事物性质的名词

The order of attributes from far to near in terms of the word modified should be: ① noun/pronoun/nominal phrase of subordination→②nominal phrase of time/location→③demonstrative pronoun/quantity phrase → ④ verb/verbal phrase/preposition phrase → ⑤ adjective phrase→⑥adjective without "de"/noun indicating the nature of things

例:这是朋友。

①这是我的朋友。

②这是我大学时代的朋友。

③这是我大学时代的一位朋友。

④这是我大学时代的一位乐于助人的朋友。

⑤这是我大学时代的一位乐于助人的最要好的朋友。

⑥这是我大学时代的一位乐于助人的最要好的外国朋友。

在递加关系的定语中,数量短语或指示代词加量词的位置有时是灵活多变的,要根据具体情况来确定。

In the attributes of progressive relation, the position of the quantity phrases or demonstrative pronouns combined with quantifiers sometimes is flexible, depending on the specific situations.

例:这是我们学校一位最著名的教授。 (√)

这是我们学校最著名的一位教授。 (√)

二、多项状语 Multiple adverbials

1. 并列关系的状语 Adverbials of juxtaposition

① 一般来说,并列关系的各项状语之间的顺序是比较自由的,可以互换位置。

Generally speaking, the order of the adverbials of juxtaposition is fairly flexible, and their positions can be altered.

例:我对你、对她都一样。 (√)

我对她、对你都一样。 (√)

② 有时受逻辑关系或习惯等因素的影响,各项状语也会出现比较固定的排列顺序。

Sometimes under the influence of logic or customs, the order of the adverbials is fixed.

例:这样做对国家、对集体、对个人都有好处。(从大到小)

那个人上上下下、前前后后、左左右右地打量了一番。(按照先后顺序)

2. 递加关系的状语 Adverbials of progressive relation

递加关系的状语的排列顺序比较灵活,但也有一定的规律,顺序大体如下:① 表示时间的状语→②表示语气、关联、频率、范围等的状语(同时出现两个以上副词时的大致顺序)→③表示处所的状语→④表示动作者的状语→⑤表示空间、方向、路线的状语→⑥表示目的、依据、对象等的状语→⑦描写动作的状语。

The order of adverbials of furthering relation is fairly flexible, but there are some principles. The order is as follows: ①adverbials of time→②adverbials of mood, relation, frequency, range, etc. (when two or more adverbs appear at the same time)→③adverbials of location→④adverbials of agent→⑤adverbials of space, direction, route→⑥adverbials of purpose, basis, target→⑦adverbials of describing actions.

例:全班同学参加了比赛。

①全班同学昨天参加了比赛。

②全班同学昨天都参加了比赛。

③全班同学昨天都在运动场上参加了比赛。

　　④全班同学昨天都在运动场上积极地参加了比赛。

　　⑤全班同学昨天都在运动场上积极地为了班集体的荣誉参加了比赛。

　　⑥全班同学昨天都在运动场上积极地为了班集体的荣誉认真地参加了比赛。

　　表示处所、方向、路线、范围等的状语有时比较灵活，根据需要，位置可前后移动。

Sometimes the positions of adverbials of location, direction, route, range, etc. are fairly flexible and can be altered according to the specific situations.

　　　　例：请你给大家仔细介绍一下。　　（√）

　　　　　　请你仔细给大家介绍一下。　　（√）

强化练习 Exercises

■　1—5题，在每一个句子下面都有一个指定的词语，句中 ABCD 是供选择的四个不同位置，请判断这一词语放在句中哪个位置上恰当。

　　Please find the proper position out of the four choices of A, B, C, and D for the word below each sentence.

1. 她是 A 我们学院最 B 年轻 C 女 D 教师。
　　　　　　　　　杰出的

2. 安娜 A 把 B 毛衣 C 送给 D 我了。
　　　　　　　自己的

3. A 联欢会并不像 B 事先 C 那样 D 热闹。
　　　　　　　　所想象的

4. 我回忆起 A 跟同学 B 在北海 C 划船时 D 的情景。
　　　　　　　　中学时代

5. 我 A 把这张纪念邮票 B 从信封上 C 揭了 D 下来。
　　　　　　　小心翼翼地

■　6—20题，每个句子中有一个或两个空，请在 ABCD 四个答案中选择唯一恰当的一个。

　　Please choose the correct answer for each blank from the four choices of A, B, C, and D.

6. ＿＿＿＿＿＿ 你用上了吗?
　　A．我昨天抄的笔记给你　　B．我昨天抄的给你笔记
　　C．我昨天给你抄的笔记　　D．我昨天抄的笔记给你

7. 请同学们 _____。
   A. 明天早七点在北海公园前门等我
   B. 等我明天早七点在北海公园前门
   C. 明天在北海公园前门等我早七点
   D. 在北海公园前门等我明天早七点

8. 你这孩子是怎么带的？怎么喜欢让他 _____，这个习惯可不好。
   A. 在屋子里蹲着吃饭
   B. 吃饭跑着在屋子里
   C. 屋子里跑着在吃饭
   D. 吃饭在屋子里跑着

9. 这套衣服是 _____。
   A. 一位同学我妈妈的大学时代送给我的
   B. 一位我妈妈大学时代的同学给我送的
   C. 我妈妈大学时代的一位同学送给我的
   D. 我妈妈大学时代的同学一位送给我的

10. 在万里无云的天空中，三架飞机 _____。
    A. 从香山顶上快速地飞向远方
    B. 向远方从香山顶上快速地飞
    C. 向远方快速地从香山顶上飞
    D. 从香山顶上向远方快速地飞

11. 人人都知道，肯德基和麦当劳都是 _____。
    A. 进入中国的八十年代美国快餐连锁店
    B. 进入中国的美国八十年代快餐连锁店
    C. 八十年代的美国快餐连锁店进入中国
    D. 八十年代进入中国的美国快餐连锁店

12. _____，五十年没见过面的小学同学到我家来看望我。
    A. 夏天今年一个炎热的早晨
    B. 今年夏天一个炎热的早晨
    C. 一个炎热的早晨今年夏天
    D. 一个炎热的夏天今年早晨

13. 我们是 _____ 来学习汉语的。
    A. 去年八月一起坐飞机从英国到中国
    B. 一起去年八月从英国坐飞机到中国
    C. 一起去年八月从英国到中国坐飞机
    D. 去年八月坐飞机从英国到中国一起

14. 参加今晚京剧票友大奖赛年龄最小的是 _____。
    A. 一个小男孩儿刚刚四岁还有没换牙的
    B. 一个还没有换牙的刚刚四岁小男孩儿
    C. 一个刚刚四岁还没有换牙的小男孩儿
    D. 还没有换牙一个刚刚四岁的小男孩儿

15. ＿＿＿＿＿＿＿＿＿＿，今天吃午饭时，不小心让我弄脏了。
   A．昨天妈妈买的那件高档上衣给我
   B．昨天妈妈给我买的那件高档上衣
   C．妈妈给我买的昨天那件高档上衣
   D．那件高档上衣昨天买的给你妈妈

16. 西藏是一个神秘的地方，青藏铁路开通后为 ＿＿＿＿＿＿＿＿＿＿ 提供了方便条件。
   A．中外来到西藏旅游观光的客人
   B．中外来到西藏旅游观光的客人
   C．到西藏来旅游观光的中外客人
   D．来旅游观光到西藏的中外客人

17. 我们是从海南岛 ＿＿＿＿＿＿＿＿＿＿ 的。
   A．特意看冰雕展览来哈尔滨
   B．看冰雕展览特意来哈尔滨
   C．来哈尔滨特意看冰雕展览
   D．特意来哈尔滨看冰雕展览

18. 等我拿到车本，我就可以天天 ＿＿＿＿＿＿＿＿＿＿。
   A．接送妻子开着车上下班了
   B．开着车接送妻子上下班了
   C．开着车上下班接送妻子了
   D．接送妻子上下班开着车了

19. 两年不见，文静朴实的她怎么 ＿＿＿＿＿＿＿＿＿＿ ？
   A．变成了一个贵妇人珠光宝气的
   B．变成了一个珠光宝气的贵妇人
   C．一个贵妇人珠光宝气的变成了
   D．一个珠光宝气的贵妇人变成了

20. 中国是 ＿＿＿＿＿＿＿＿＿＿。
   A．具有一个悠久历史的文明古国
   B．一个具有悠久历史的文明古国
   C．文明古国具有一个悠久的历史
   D．具有悠久的历史一个文明古国

答疑解惑 Answers and Explanations

1. 选择 B。"杰出的"和"年轻"都修饰"教师"，按照汉语多项定语的排列顺序，用"的"的形容词要放在不用"的"的形容词的前面，因此只能说"杰出的年轻女教师"。

The answer is B. "Jiéchū de" and "niánqīng" both modify "jiàoshī". According to the sequence of several attributes, the adjective with "de" should be put before the adjective without "de". Therefore, we can only say "jiéchū de niánqīng nǚ jiàoshī".

2. 选择 B。"自己的"后面修饰的是名词,所以要选择 B。
The answer is B. The word after "zìjǐ de" is noun, so B should be chosen.

3. 选择 C。"所想象的"后面修饰的是名词性成分,"联欢会"和"那样"都符合这一要求,但根据句意,只有 C 是正确的答案。
The answer is C. The element after "suǒ xiǎngxiàng de" is nominal, both "liánhuān huì" and "nàyàng" match with the topic. But according to the context, C is the correct answer.

4. 选择 A。"划船"有三个状语,分别是"中学时代"、"跟同学"和"在北海",根据汉语多项状语的排列顺序,表示时间的短语应放在首位,所以 A 是正确答案。
The answer is A. There are three adverbials for "huáchuán": zhōngxué shídài, "gēn tóngxué", and "zài Běihǎi". According to the sequence of Chinese adverbials, the phrase about time should be put before the others. So A is the correct anwer.

5. 选择 A。"小心翼翼地"是修饰动作发出者"我"的,应该放在离动作发出者"我"最近的位置,所以 A 是正确答案。
The answer is A. "Xiǎoxīn–yìyì de" modifies the agent "wǒ", so it should be put nearest to "wǒ".

6. 选择 C。"你用上"的宾语是"笔记","我昨天给你抄的"是"笔记"的定语,因其结构较为复杂,所以提前到主语的前面。又因为时间词语要放在介词短语的前面,所以 C 是正确答案。
The answer is C. The object of "nǐ yòngshàng" is "bǐjì". "Wǒ zuótiān gěi nǐ chāo de" is the attribute of "bǐjì". As the structure is complicated, it is put before the subject. Furthermore, phrases for time should be put before prepositional phrases, thus C is the correct answer.

7. 选择 A。谓语动词"等"的前面有三个状语,分别是"明天"、"早七点"和"在北海公园前门",根据汉语多项状语的排列顺序,表示时间的短语应放在前面,介词短语放在后面。"明天"和"早七点"都是时间词语,但根据中国人对时间由大到小的表达习惯,"明天"在"早七点"的前面。
The answer is A. There are three adverbials for the predicate "děng": "míngtiān", "zǎo qī diǎn", and "zài Běihǎi gōngyuán qiánmén". According to the sequence of Chinese adverbials, phrases for time should be put in front and prepositional phrases after. "Míngtiān" and "zǎo qī diǎn" are both time phrases, but according to the habit of arranging time from big to small by Chinese people, "míngtiān" is put before "zào qī diǎn".

8. 选择 A。"在屋子里"是动作"吃饭"的处所,"蹲着"是动作"吃饭"的方式,按照汉语多项状语的排列顺序,A 是唯一正确的答案。

The answer is A. "Zài wūzi li" is the location for the action "chī fàn", and "dūnzhe" is the way of eating. According to the sequence of Chinese adverbials, A is the only correct answer.

9. 选择 C。这是一个比较复杂的强调句。首先应该知道,"同学"是谁的,"衣服"送给谁。我们很容易地知道"衣服"是"送给我的","同学"前有三个定语,分别是"一位"、"我妈妈"和"大学时代",根据汉语多项定语的排列顺序,只有 C 是正确答案。

The answer is C. This is a complex emphasis sentence. It should be clear that whose "tóngxué" the person is and to whom the "yīfu" is sent. We know without difficulty that "yīfu" is "sònggěi wǒde". There are three attributes before "tóngxué": "yí wèi", "wǒ māma", and "dàxué shídài". According to the sequence of Chinese attributes, C is the correct answer.

10. 选择 A。动词"飞"的前面有两个状语,一个是"从香山顶上";一个是"快速地",单音节动词"飞"的后面可以加上介词"向",补充说明动作的方向,所以正确答案应该是 A。

The answer is A. There are two adverbials before "fēi": "cóng Xiāng Shān dǐngshàng" and "kuàisù de". The monosyllabic verb "fēi" can be followed by the preposition "xiàng" to supplement the direction of the action, so A is the correct answer.

11. 选择 D。"进入中国"的时间是"八十年代",它们构成整体的动词性结构做"美国快餐连锁店"的定语,D 是最正确的选择。

The answer is D. The time of "jìnrù Zhōngguó" is "bāshí niándài", and the two together as the verbal structure is the attribute of "Měiguó kuàicān liánsuǒ diàn", so D is the correct answer.

12. 选择 B。汉语表示时间的习惯一般是从大的时间到小的时间,因此 B 是正确的答案。

The answer is B. In Chinese language, the habit of expressing time is from big to small, so B is the correct answer.

13. 选择 A。汉语多项状语的排列顺序是表示时间的状语→表示动作者的状语→表示方式的状语→表示路线的状语,所以选择 A 是正确的。

The answer is A. The sequence of Chinese adverbials is: time→agent→way→route.

14. 选择 C,"男孩儿"是中心语,按照汉语多项定语的排列顺序:数量短语→动词性短语→不用"的"的形容词,因此答案是 C。

The answer is C. "Nán háir" is the key word. The sequence of several attributes in Chinese is: numeral phrase→verbal phrase→adjective without "de", thus the answer is C.

15. 选择 B。"上衣"是中心语,按照汉语多项定语的排列顺序:表示时间的词语→主谓短语→指示代词/数量短语→不用"的"的形容词,所以正确答案是 B。
The answer is B. "Shàngyī" is the key word. The sequence of several attributes is: time phrase→subject-predicate→demonstrative pronoun / numeral phrase→adjective without "de". So B is the right answer.

16. 选择 C。"客人"是中心语,按照汉语多项定语的排列顺序:表示处所的短语→动词性短语→不用"的"的表示事物性质的名词,所以 C 是正确答案。
The answer is C. "Kèrén" is the key word. The sequence of several attributes is: phrase of location→verbal phrase→noun indicating the quality of a substance and without "de". So C is the right answer.

17. 选择 D。"来哈尔滨看冰雕展览"是一个连动式,副词"特意"应放在第一个动词前,所以 D 是正确答案。
The answer is D. "Lái Hā'ěrbīn kàn bīngdiāo zhǎnlǎn" is a continuous verbal structure. The adverb "tèyì" should be put before the first verb.

18. 选择 B。"开着车"是动词"接送"的方式,"接送"的宾语是"妻子",而"妻子"又是"上下班"的主语,所以 B 是正确答案。
The answer is B. "Kāizhe chē" is the way of the verb "jiē-sòng". The object of "jiē-sòng" is "qīzi", which is the subject of "shàng-xià bān".

19. 选择 B。"妇人"是中心语,按照汉语多项定语的排列顺序:数量短语→形容词短语→不用"的"的形容词,B 是正确答案。
The answer is B. "Fùrén" is the key word. The sequence of several Chinese attributes is: numeral phrase→adjective phrase→adjective without "de". So B is the right answer.

20. 选择 B。"国"是中心语,按照汉语多项定语的排列顺序:数量短语→动词性短语→需要用"的"的形容词→不用"的"的形容词,B 是正确答案。
The answer is B. "Guó" is the key word. The sequence of several attributes is: numeral phrase→verbal phrase→adjective with "de"→adjective without "de". So B is the right answer.

第一部分 (30 题, 20 分钟)

1—10 题, 在每个句子后面都有一个指定的词语, 句中 ABCD 是供选择的四个不同位置。请判断这一词语放在句中哪个位置上恰当。

Please find the proper position out of the four choices of A, B, C, and D for the word below each sentence.

1. 她 A 把写 B 的诗和信寄来 C 给我 D 看。

   经常

2. 老常现在 A 还不来, B 快要 C 把我们 D 急疯了。

   简直

3. A 前几分钟的 B 紧张之后, C 现在总算可以松一口气 D 了。

   经过

4. 曾广雄 A 像小学生 B 一样点点头, 感激地说, 听 C 老同学 D。

   的

5. A 一声炸雷响, 乌云 B 化做大雨 C 向干渴的农田 D 倾盆而下。

   随着

6. 那种感觉 A 是 B 因为我对 C 自己的做法产生了 D 怀疑的缘故。

   大概

7. 原来, A 吓跑她的 B 是路边墙壁上的一个 C 最近 D 刚出现的售楼广告。

   只不过

8. 他走进教室, A 惊喜地发现 B 前几次要的东西 C 竟然 D 躺在了课桌里。

   乖乖

9. 湖泊作为 A 降水和有效降水的历史记录, B 反映出气候的 C 空间 D 变化和区域特征。

   能

10. 语言上的障碍 A 能影响双方 B 的合作, 但认识上的矛盾则 C 必定会 D 造成合作的破裂。

    未必

第二部分

■ 11—30 题,每个句子中有一个或两个空儿,请在 ABCD 四个答案中选择唯一恰当的填上。

Please choose the correct answer for each blank from the four choices of A, B, C, and D.

11. 他希望能过 _____ 一种平淡安定的生活。
    A. 到   B. 上   C. 了   D. 回

12. 他们和朋友们一起吃了一 _____ 丰盛的晚餐。
    A. 场   B. 项   C. 盘   D. 顿

13. 他总能把遇到的事物 _____ 刚学过的课文与生字联系起来。
    A. 对   B. 给   C. 跟   D. 比

14. 一个 _____ 自己都照顾不好的大孩子,怎么能照管好一个一岁多的小孩子呢?
    A. 也   B. 就   C. 还   D. 连

15. 你就不要嘴硬了,_____ 我还不知道你?
    A. 反而   B. 难道   C. 居然   D. 竟然

16. 也正因为 _____ ,她才能够说出她心中的真实感觉。
    A. 这么   B. 那么   C. 怎样   D. 如此

17. 你不记得这个问题我们 _____ 在什么地方议论过吗?
    A. 果然   B. 始终   C. 曾经   D. 经常

18. 开展对外层空间的科学探索必须加大投资,_____ 很难达到预期目的。
    A. 否则   B. 尽管   C. 反而   D. 但是

19. 炎热的夏天,在马路上行走时,_____ 能撑上一把遮阳伞,人就会感觉有一丝凉意。
    A. 除了   B. 即使   C. 不管   D. 如果

20. _____ 是开放的国家,对于国家知识就了解得 _____ 多。
    A. 一……一   B. 也……也
    C. 越……越   D. 又……又

21. _____ 他的食堂顾客多了,_____ 效益却始终上不来。
    A. 因为……所以   B. 不但……而且
    C. 或者……或者   D. 虽然……但是

22. 小潘,今天 _____ 哪位来,_____ 说我不在,我要一个人安静一会儿。
    A. 固然……但   B. 即使……也
    C. 不但……还   D. 不管……都

23. 你 _____ 隔三差五地修理这辆旧车,_____ 买辆新车好。

A. 要么……要么   B. 与其……不如
C. 宁肯……也   D. 不但……反而

24. 武汉这个地方一直被人们称做"江城"。它 _____ 有着如此的称呼,自然
    _____ 它坐落在长江之滨的缘故。
    A. 之所以……是因为   B. 如果……那么
    C. 只要……就   D. 与其……不如

25. 容小立毕业后 _____ 睡过什么回笼觉。
    A. 从没几乎来   B. 从来几乎没
    C. 几乎从来没   D. 没来从几乎

26. 随着北京各大学 _____,其后勤的改革也势在必行。
    A. 实行扩招大规模   B. 规模大扩招实行
    C. 扩招实行大规模   D. 实行大规模扩招

27. 琴的手里捧了 _____ 围巾。
    A. 拉毛蓝色一条厚厚的
    B. 一条厚厚的蓝色拉毛
    C. 厚厚的拉毛一条蓝色
    D. 蓝色拉毛厚厚的一条

28. 黎向平在图书馆理员的多次催促下,挎着 _____ 绿书包走出了图书馆的大门。
    A. 那他发白的洗得
    B. 洗得他发白的那
    C. 他那洗得发白的
    D. 那洗得发白的他

29. 他 _____ 抢过那封信。
    A. 从兴奋地哥哥手里很快地
    B. 兴奋地从哥哥手里很快地
    C. 很快从哥哥地兴奋地手里
    D. 从哥哥兴奋地很快地手里

30. 天然气水合物的开发利用 _____。
    A. 目前的已经重视世界各国引起
    B. 引起的重视世界各国已经目前
    C. 目前已经引起世界各国的重视
    D. 世界各国的目前已经引起重视

参考答案

1. A	2. B	3. A	4. D	5. A
6. A	7. B	8. D	9. A	10. A
11. B	12. D	13. C	14. D	15. B
16. D	17. C	18. A	19. D	20. C
21. D	22. D	23. B	24. A	25. C
26. D	27. B	28. C	29. B	30. C

主要参考文献

1. 王还.《对外汉语教学语法大纲》.北京:北京语言学院出版社,1995年

2. 吕叔湘.《现代汉语八百词》.北京,北京:商务印书馆,1999年

3. 卢福波.《对外汉语教学实用语法》.北京:北京语言文化大学出版社,1996年

4. 北京语言文化大学汉语水平考试中心.《汉语8000词词典》.北京:北京语言文化大学出版社,2000年

5. 李晓琪.《现代汉语虚词手册》.北京:北京大学出版社,2003年

6. 赵菁.《HSK全攻略教程(初中等)》.北京:商务印书馆,2006年

7. 朱庆明.《HSK帮你顺利通8级之语法篇》.北京:清华大学出版社,2004年

8. 李增吉,冯增娥,钱丽玛.《教你关联词语100例》.天津:南开大学出版社,2004年

9. 李增吉.《HSK常用副词精讲精练(初中等)》.北京:北京大学出版社,2005年

10. 杨寄洲,贾永芬.《1700对近义词语用法对比》.北京:北京语言大学出版社,2005年

图书推荐
Highlights

HSK核心词汇天天学（上、中、下）
One Hour Per Day to a Powerful HSK Vocabulary
(3 volumes)
210 × 285 mm
▲ 汉英 Chinese-English edition
Vol Ⅰ: ISBN 9787802005945, 214pp, ￥49.00
Vol Ⅱ: ISBN 9787802005952, 214pp, ￥49.00
Vol Ⅲ: ISBN 9787802005969, 214pp, ￥49.00

● 帮助汉语学习者在一年内系统掌握3000个最常用、最有用的核心汉语词汇。
● Through the use of these textbooks, students will be able to master 3000 of the most common and useful vocabulary within one year.

HSK中国汉语水平考试(初中级)
（考试指南、模拟试题与词汇）
The Chinese Proficiency Test
(HSK Elementary-Intermediate)
(1 book, 1 MP3 and 1 CD-ROM)
▲ 汉英日韩 Chinese-English-Japanese-Korean edition
ISBN 9787802002043
175 × 255cm, ￥128.00

多种语言对照基础词汇
Multi-language Dictionary of Chinese
▲ ISBN 9787800528538
130 × 185mm, 720pp
￥55.00

● 本书收录汉语常用字词8000余条。
● 包括汉、英、法、日、俄五种文字注释，涵盖HSK考试大纲的各级词汇。
● 可作为HSK教学和学习的辅助工具书以及语言教学和语言学习的工具书。
● It contains 8000 commonly-used Chinese words with translation in English, French, Russian and Japanese, covering all the words included in the HSK test.
● It can be used as a reference book for Chinese language learning and teaching, or as a supplementary book for HSK test.

汉语分级阅读（1，2，3）（附MP3）
Graded Chinese Reader (I, II, III) (With MP3)
Selected Abridged Chinese Contemporary Short Stories
▲ 汉英 Chinese-English edition
145 × 210mm
Ⅰ: ISBN 9787802003743, 239pp
￥42.00
Ⅱ: ISBN 9787802003750, 257pp
￥42.00
Ⅲ: ISBN 9787802004153, 299pp
￥42.00

● 精选中国当代作家的中短篇小说，反映中国当代普通人的生活。
● 新出版的第三册为基础篇，汉语词汇量控制在1000个；第一册控制在2000个，第二册控制在3000个。
● Abridged versions of short stories and novellas written by contemporary Chinese writers reflecting everyday life of ordinary Chinese people.
● The newly published volume Ⅲ is for students of elementary level, containing about 1000 Chinese words; volume Ⅰ and Ⅱ contain around 2000 and 3000 Chinese words respectively based on the 1033 words of level A and some of level B listed in the HSK outline.

汉语快速阅读训练教程（上、下）
（附MP3）
A Course on Chinese Speed Reading
(I, II) (With MP3)
▲ 汉英 Chinese-English edition
285 × 210 mm
ISBN 9787802006294, 146pp, ￥65.00
ISBN 9787802006300, 156pp, ￥65.00

● 帮助中高级汉语水平学习者迅速提高HSK阅读能力。
● It helps to improve the HSK reading ability of intermediate and advanced learners.

汉语病句辨析九百例
Error Analysis of 900 Sample Sentences
▲ 汉英 Chinese-English edition
ISBN 9787800525155
140 × 200mm, 332pp, ￥35.00

汉语语法难点释疑
Difficult Points in Chinese Grammar
▲ 汉英 Chinese-English
ISBN 9787800522024
140 × 200mm, 245pp, ￥29.00

责任编辑：翟淑蓉

英文编辑：郭　辉

封面设计：梁　珍

印刷监制：佟汉冬

图书在版编辑（CIP）数据

HSK语法精讲精练 / 张婧编著. —北京：华语教学出版社，2008

ISBN 978-7-80200-451-1

Ⅰ．H…　Ⅱ．张…　Ⅲ．汉语—语法—对外汉语教学—水平考试—自学参考资料

Ⅳ．H195.4

中国版本图书馆CIP数据核字（2008）第052661号

HSK语法精讲精练

张　婧　编著

*

© 华语教学出版社

华语教学出版社出版

（中国北京百万庄大街24号 邮政编码100037）

电话: (86)10-68320585

传真: (86)10-68326333

网址: www.sinolingua.com.cn

电子信箱: hyjx@sinolingua.com.cn

北京外文印刷厂印刷

中国国际图书贸易总公司海外发行

(中国北京车公庄西路35号)

北京邮政信箱第399号 邮政编码100044

新华书店国内发行

2008年(16开)第一版

2010年1月第一版第二次印刷

（汉英）

ISBN 978-7-80200-451-1

定价: 58.00元